William A. Richards

Diaries of a
Frontier Surveyor

William A. Richards

DIARIES
of a
FRONTIER
SURVEYOR

in Nebraska and Wyoming

Lucia McCreery

Red Bank Press

William A. Richards Diaries of a Frontier Surveyor in Nebraska and Wyoming

Red Bank Press
Brooklyn, NY

ISBN: 979-8-9881016-0-4
Library of Congress Control Number: 2023906349

Front cover: Richards at age 25, about the time of the 1874 survey. Author's collection.

Map of the Sources of the Snake River…, 187?, Gustavus R. Bechler and F. V. Hayden, Library of Congress, https://lcnn.loc.gov/2009479469, accessed July 25, 2022.

Back cover photo: Allyn Collection, Riverton (Wyoming) Museum. From the 1904 survey of the Montana-Idaho boundary, whose terrain was similar to that of Wyoming's western boundary.

Please visit WilliamARichards.com for more about his life and legacy.

To Eleanor Alice Richards McCreery,
daughter and private secretary of
Governor W. A. Richards. These diaries and
other historical treasures were preserved
thanks to her efforts.

CONTENTS

ACKNOWLEDGMENTS

This work has been the journey of a lifetime, and there's no way I can adequately express my gratitude to those who made it possible.

There is W. A. Richards himself, who kept such engaging diaries. Then there are the surveyors who helped me understand his occasional use of terms ranging from chains and mounds to azimuths and other astronomical mysteries. Dr. Herbert W. Stoughton of Wyoming and Gene A. Thomsen of Nebraska greatly enriched this work with their detailed explanations, diagrams, and maps. They patiently dealt with my endless questions, as did others in their field: Stanton Abell, Dennis Bland, Glenn Borkenhagen, Earl Henderson, Steve Parrish, Edward Reading, Cody Schatz, Scott Scherbel, and Sonja Sparks and Timothy Quincy. The latter two are the chief cadastral surveyors, respectively, for the Wyoming and Idaho State offices of the Bureau of Land Management.

I found the knowledge and hardiness of surveyors to be truly awe-inspiring, and I think you will too, especially if you venture into the appendix.

This work owes its very existence to History Nebraska and to the State Archives and American Heritage Center of Wyoming, which preserved the diaries and so many other treasures. I am especially grateful to Carl Hallberg of the Archives for his help over so many years.

A heartfelt *Thank You!* goes out to those who made it possible for me to connect with Wyoming, where my great-grandfather W. A. Richards eventually put down roots. In his home territory are Worlanders George and Margaret McClellan and Stan and Linda Abell. The McClellans —related to "Bear George" McClellan, Richards's partner in Red Bank Ranch— arranged for me to visit the ranch and have offered their hospitality and friendship many times as I did research. Surveyor Stan Abell and his wife, Linda, provided a lot of valuable information and she also organized an exhibit about Richards and surveying. Terril Mills of Ten Sleep, a diligent historical researcher, identified people and places mentioned in the Bighorn Basin diaries, as did basin historian Lawrence M. Woods.

Richards himself owed a debt of gratitude to his elder brother, Alonzo V. Richards, and I owe one to his great-granddaughter Sally and her husband, James Mergener, for sending so many important papers and photos.

I am also greatly indebted to Wheatmark for editorial and design assistance and to Brandon Crowther of Affordable Editors.

Last, and far from least, in writing this book I've had the genuine joy of encountering many individuals who have a passion for precision, whether in the realms of surveying, history, or publishing.

PREFACE

Unsung Heroes of the Westward Expansion

WHEN WE THINK OF those who tamed the "Wild West," settlers and lawmen spring to mind. They are celebrated in stories, songs, and shows, along with explorers, mountain men, cowboys, and railroad workers. Unrecognized and unsung, though, are the surveyors. "Practically everything ahead of society was accomplished by surveyors," noted Denny DeMeyer, a member of the Surveyors Historical Society. "No government land was sold, no towns or cities platted, no railroads, canals, irrigation channels, or roads constructed or mines developed without them."[1] Land surveyors had to mark state boundaries, townships, and other subdivisions for settlement, and mark them precisely, to prevent future disputes.

This work began in colonial times. George Washington and Thomas Jefferson were surveyors before the Revolution. As President, Jefferson helped establish our system of dividing public land into rectangles. (The State of Wyoming is one example.) He sent Meriwether Lewis and the surveyor and mapmaker William Clark to scout out the vast Louisiana Purchase. Young Abraham Lincoln worked as a surveyor as he studied law. Those presidents were honored on Mount Rushmore, along with one who was not a surveyor. Theodore Roosevelt did, however, map a 933-mile-long river in Brazil. Daniel Boone surveyed frontier Kentucky. Henry David Thoreau's main source of support for his writing was surveying.[2] William A. Richards's experience in that line of work helped him deal with the vast remaining tracts of government lands when he attained state and national office.

Frontier surveyors had to do their job no matter how high the mountains, how wild the rivers, how dense the forest, how bad the weather, how relentless the mosquitoes—or how hostile the native people. Richards and his brother Alonzo Van Ness Richards turned down a contract in Nebraska because a surveying party had recently been massacred nearby, and Alonzo tried to obtain a cavalry escort for their survey of the south boundary of Wyoming Territory.

The work was difficult and risky. Accidents far from a doctor could be fatal. Contractors would forfeit their bonds on top of their other losses if they could not complete a survey because a river washed away their mules and supplies. Hunting and fishing helped vary the diet of beans and bread and occasional ham, but hunting could endanger the predator as well as the prey. If the main staples ran out and game was scarce, the crew lived on mush and molasses.

Books and articles have been written about frontier surveyors, but rarely for the general reader. Especially rare are diaries and first-person stories that vividly illustrate what surveyors went through. Writing in camp, perhaps by firelight, William A. Richards helps tell the surveyor's story, one day at a time.

ABOUT THIS WORK

These diaries were edited by Lucia Alice McCreery, great-granddaughter of William A. and Harriet Alice Hunt Richards and granddaughter of Eleanor Alice Richards McCreery, their daughter. Lucia has a B.A. in history and is a retired journalist.

Eleanor Alice transcribed the diary entries from 1873 and 1874, and Lucia transcribed the others, edited the complete collection, and wrote some supplementary essays. Editing of the diaries is minimal, with punctuation occasionally added, words capitalized for clarity, and potentially confusing abbreviations changed. No attempt has been made to make days and dates consistent. Words in brackets, with question marks, are guesses at hard-to-read words, and words in parentheses are written that way in the diaries and letters. Spelling and entries that seem questionable are left as is, with [sic] added only where it seemed appropriate. Underscored words in the diaries or letters are the writer's.

No attempt has been made to change the word "Indian" and related terms that are now considered derogatory. In her essays and footnotes, Lucia has gone along with wyohistory.org and other respectable entities in using "Indian" when the tribe's name is unknown.

In the text relating to the 1884 and 1885 diaries, "Bighorn" is employed per current usage for the basin, the river, and the mountains. "Big Horn" has not been changed in the diaries themselves. Likewise for today's No Wood River and Nowood Creek, originally the No Wood and No Water Creeks.

The 1873 and 1874 diaries were originally published in the *Annals of Wyoming*, and are republished with corrections and thanks. The 1869–71 diary is in History Nebraska and the others are in the Wyoming State Archives (WSA).[3]

This work also includes excerpts from letters that Richards saved. Unfortunately, few letters from him are known to survive.

Introduction

William A. Richards, Surveyor to Statesman

Dennis D. Bland

WILLIAM ALFORD RICHARDS was born March 9, 1849, in Hazel Green, Grant County, Wisconsin. In 1869 westward opportunities led Richards to Omaha, Nebraska. After various employment in the Omaha area, he joined a government surveying party working in southwestern Nebraska, which he called "the worst Indian country on the plains." Shortly thereafter, his elder brother, Alonzo Van Ness Richards, received a General Land Office contract for the original survey of the southern and western boundaries of Wyoming Territory. William was employed as a general assistant during the execution of these surveys in 1873 to 1874. General assistants were sworn employees of the contractor, usually responsible for such specific duties as cornerman or front or rear chainman. William was so capable that Alonzo left him in charge of most of the 1874 survey.

Richards's diaries, written while executing these surveys, described many trials and tribulations of daily activities and camp life.

After completing the surveys in late 1874, Richards moved to Oakland, California, and married Harriet Alice Hunt. They moved to nearby San Jose, where Richards was elected county surveyor of Santa Clara County. Unfortunately, health complications required Richards to move again, this time to an arid climate. In 1881 he and his family found their favorable climate in Colorado Springs, Colorado, where he served as city engi-

W. A. Richards, Commissioner of the U.S. General Land Office, 1905
Frison Collection, WSA[4]

1

neer and as El Paso County surveyor. With his health restored, Richards and his family homesteaded in the Bighorn Basin, Wyoming.

Richards soon began an active role in politics; he was elected a commissioner of Johnson County in 1886. In 1889 President Benjamin Harrison appointed Richards as General Land Office surveyor general of Wyoming to supervise all government surveying in the territory. Surveyors general were responsible for the acceptance and approval on behalf of the United States of the contract survey work returned by U.S. deputy surveyors. Appointments were for a particular region, usually by a state or states or territory. Because no land could be patented until these surveys were accepted and approved by the surveyors general, the influence of these positions rivaled that of the governors of their respective jurisdictions.

In 1890 Wyoming became a member of the Union. In 1894 Richards successfully ran for governor of the state of Wyoming and served in that capacity from 1895 to 1899; he declined nomination to a second term. In 1899 he was admitted to the bar by the Wyoming Supreme Court and appointed assistant commissioner of the General Land Office. While in this position, he gained national attention in 1901 as he conducted the opening of entry to Kiowa, Comanche, and Apache lands in Oklahoma (by a drawing for lots, which replaced the unfair land-rush system).

Richards assumed the duties of the commissioner of the General Land Office in 1903. He made these comments about his qualifications:

> Having lived in public land states and territories, and having been closely associated with public land business for 34 years, and being a surveyor, civil engineer, and lawyer, and having been a surveyor general and a governor, I am well-qualified for the position of commissioner of the General Land Office.

The effect of Richards' surveying background is evident in his comments; he chose to list his experience as a surveyor over those of governor, lawyer, or civil engineer. Richards, who was successful in all of his endeavors, never forgot the importance or value of an accurate and detailed land survey.

From Surveying and Land Information Systems,[5] *slightly revised. Mr. Bland was chief of the Office Operations and Review Section, Cadastral Survey Branch, Bureau of Land Management, Cheyenne, Wyoming.*

In State and National Office, Richards Promotes Irrigation and Conservation

"Were it not for [Commissioner] Richards's foresight and commitment,
we would most likely be archeologically much poorer today."
— John G. Douglas, preservation officer, Bureau of Land Management[6]

AS SURVEYOR GENERAL and then governor of Wyoming, Richards had the best possible mentor in the vital issue of land use in arid states. Elwood Mead, territorial and then state engineer of Wyoming, had devised water laws that were adopted by dry regions worldwide. The two would join forces to urge solutions to the region's other thorny problems.

The first law passed by Congress to promote irrigation in arid lands was sponsored by Wyoming Senator Joseph M. Carey. A million acres of federal land would be donated to states that caused those acres to be irrigated, and there were provisions to ensure the land went to settlers and not speculators. In early 1895, Governor Richards urged the Wyoming State Legislature to accept of the terms of the Act, quoting Mead at length. After some debate Wyoming became the first state to do so. Only a few projects succeeded, however, and in 1902 the National Reclamation Act authorized federal funding for the regional, large-scale works required to reclaim the arid West.

Farmers in the West needed pasture for their livestock. The open range was in trouble: overgrazing was destroying the rich grasslands, and there was strife between stockmen and settlers and cattlemen and sheepmen. To acquire their own turf, stock owners began leasing the lands Wyoming had been given by the federal government upon admission to the union. Those soon ran out, yet the government would not relinquish more acreage. Mead, Richards, and other Westerners tried to get all unappropriated federal lands ceded to their states, but were unsuccessful.

Another reason they wanted state control was the conviction that the West's remaining forests, like its open ranges, were not being properly managed by the faraway federal government. Some forests were set aside in reserves, unavailable to settlers for any use whatsoever but unprotected from their worst enemy, fire. In early 1897, twenty-two million acres of new reserves were created in the West after a scattershot investigation by a commission of Easterners, with no input from Westerners. Some settlements found themselves unable to cut timber or graze their livestock in the new reserves. Governor Richards was the most prominent western official who denounced these reserves in an influential national publication,

Forest and Stream. He charged that the commission's "blunders discredited and seriously imperiled a worthy cause." Richards, Mead, and others favored protection of the country's remaining forests, partly because they held snowpacks that would melt slowly for dry-season irrigation.

Early in 1898, he and Mead were among the principal speakers at the first convention of the National Live Stock Association. They both urged reform of land use to save the grasslands and forests, and maintained that states could do a better job of managing their lands. Richards's denunciation of the Land Office was so strong that he feared it would prevent his being appointed its assistant commissioner. It didn't.

The General Land Office (today's Bureau of Land Management, or BLM) was the largest bureau in the Department of the Interior. It had charge of one-third of the acreage of the United States, land that remained to be claimed by homesteaders and others. As noted previously, Assistant Commissioner Richards was praised for his fair and competent handling of the Oklahoma land openings. He also found a way for President Theodore Roosevelt to create the nation's largest forest reserve, and he took steps that resulted in the exposure of the massive Benson-Hyde land-fraud scheme. Roosevelt was so pleased with Richards's performance that he appointed him commissioner of the Land Office. Richards continued to fight the myriad forms of land fraud, was responsible for seeing that other land openings were conducted honestly, and made important contributions to Roosevelt's conservation agenda.

Prehistoric ruins and natural wonders of the vast West were wide open to looting or exploitation. By 1903 Congress had established six National Parks, but bills to protect numerous archeological and other important sites went nowhere until Commissioner Richards acted. In 1904, after New Mexico archeologist Edgar Lee Hewett sent him a long report about places needing protection, Richards published it in a circular with photos, maps, and related documents. This led to the Antiquities Act of 1906, which empowered presidents to create National Monuments. Among them would be Jewel Cave in South Dakota, Gila Cliff Dwellings in New Mexico, the African Burial Grounds in New York City, the Marianas Trench in the Pacific Ocean, and millions of acres in Alaska. The Grand Canyon, Bryce Canyon, Zion, and the Petrified Forest were National Monuments until Congress made them National Parks. Richards also helped Roosevelt create the world's first wildlife refuge, Pelican Island.

On top of the stresses of the position, Richards was accused of land fraud and illegal fencing by a special agent of the Interior Department in

1905 and 1906. Roosevelt, outraged by the agent's poor documentation and apparent witch-hunting, rejected the reports.

Was that the last straw? Richards had been in poor health for some time and no longer had the consolation of his family. His wife had died in November 1903, and by 1906 his daughters were married or away at school. He set his departure from office for March 1907, when his eight years in the Land Office would be completed. Contrary to some assumptions, he was not asked to resign. He returned to his Wyoming ranch.

Richards was soon recalled to public service. Appointed the state's first tax commissioner in February 1909, he resigned in December 1910 after Carey was elected governor on the Democratic ticket.

Tragedy soon drove Richards to leave his ranch forever: In the fall of 1911 his daughter Edna and her husband were found shot to death at their cabin there. He went to Australia in May 1912 with a group of land seekers at the invitation of Mead, who was in charge of the water supply and irrigation development in Victoria province. Richards decided to stay, but died of a heart attack in Melbourne on July 25, 1912. Mead accompanied the body back home. In Cheyenne, Richards lay in state at the Capitol, and after his funeral was given a military escort to Lakeview Cemetery.[7]

Strong Support From His Pioneer Family Helps Richards Succeed

WILLIAM A. RICHARDS came from a close-knit and loving family. In his younger days, he was encouraged—and often sternly prodded—by his elder brother, Alonzo. Their father, who had eked out a meager living in the lead mines, on farms, on the railroad, and as a barrel maker, offered William $150* out of his "pile" when his son wanted to homestead in Wyoming. William couldn't possibly accept; the old man was half blind and unemployed.

William (Will), Alonzo (Lon), and their younger brother, Austin (Aut), were the three surviving children of eight born to Truman Perry Richards and Eleanor Swinnerton Richards. Of colonial stock, they came from pioneer families and had met and married in Illinois.

Lon was born in Jacksonville, Illinois, on May 1, 1841, eight years before Will. He attended local schools and the Platteville Academy, working as janitor to cover tuition. During the Civil War, he saw action at

---

*About $4,620 in 2022, per measuringworth.com purchasing-power calculator

The Richards brothers about 1867, in Galena, Illinois.
Aut is at left, Lon at center. Will, at right, was
18 years of age in 1867.
A.V. Richards family photo[8]

Antietam and elsewhere in the Signal Corps of the Army of the Potomac. After contracting malaria he was stationed at Georgetown, near Washington, D.C., for the rest of the war. Will, age 14, joined him in 1863. Though too young to enlist, Will was a husky six-footer with teamster skills, so he drove ambulances. He returned home in 1864 and went back to school. Once graduated he became a teacher for several years.

In 1867, Lon married Flora Miner, a relative of General Ulysses S. Grant, and Grant tried to help them after becoming President. Will asked him for an appointment to West Point, but went west instead, to Omaha, Nebraska. After he took up surveying, he received from Grant a letter of recommendation to help him obtain contracts.

Will also worked as a newspaper reporter in Omaha. Lon was always looking for ways the brothers might get ahead, and running a newspaper was one idea. Other offers to edit or manage new publications later came Will's way, but he stuck with surveying.

Lon, a U.S. astronomer and surveyor, won the contracts for the southern and western boundaries of the new Territory of Wyoming—apparently without Grant's help, judging from his letters to Will. Lon kept urging Will to pursue opportunities in surveying, ranching, or other fields.

After the western boundary survey, Will traveled to Oakland, California, to marry Harriet Alice Hunt, whom he had met in Omaha. (Interestingly, she is not mentioned in his otherwise detailed diaries.) The daughter of a prosperous livery stable owner, she had attended private school and was a church soloist. Unlike her husband, she was a devoted Baptist, and her faith helped sustain her through their future trials. They lived in Omaha in 1875, with Will surveying, working for the Post Office, and reporting for the *Omaha Republican*.

When they returned to Oakland, Will continued surveying. He was away from home in December 1876 when Harriet gave birth to their first child, Eleanor Alice. The next year, the family moved to a farm outside San Jose owned by Harriet's relatives, and Will alternated routine farm chores with surveying. Aut followed them to Oakland, where he was employed off and on as a clerk in the tax collector's office and worked as a surveyor. Like so many in that country, Will developed lung trouble, forcing a move to the mountains of Colorado in 1881.

Lon had remained in Illinois, trying his hand at various enterprises including publishing and editing a newspaper. He continued to push a western ranch as the solution to the brothers' frustrations. Will was the only one of them who took the plunge. By 1884 he held secure county and city offices, but considered them inadequate support for his wife and two daughters. Despite being 35—middle-aged for the era—he set out for Wyoming. To finance his move and homestead, he surveyed settlers' claims and built the first major irrigation ditch off the Bighorn River for a company of Colorado investors.

Lon lobbied influential politicians to help his brother get appointed U.S. surveyor general for Wyoming in 1889, though his intercession might not have been necessary. As an actual surveyor and a resident of the underrepresented northern part of Wyoming, Will was the most qualified and most politically desirable candidate. While retaining his ranch, he and his family moved to Cheyenne, where he impressed state Republican party leaders. That led to his later nomination and election as governor. The Democrats painted the Big Horn Ditch tract as a land grab, to no avail.

Neither Lon nor their parents lived to see Will elected governor. Lon had died in 1891 after a brief illness, aged only 49. Aut stayed in Oakland, became a realtor, and died in 1930, long after his elder brothers.[9]

Surveying Terms, Tools, and Techniques Appearing in These Diaries

6	5	4	3	2	1
7	8	9	10	11	12
18	17	16	15	14	13
19	20	21	22	23	24
30	29	28	27	26	25
31	32	33	34	35	36

Township grid

IN 1869, W. A. Richards got his start in surveying in the new State of Nebraska, joining a party assigned to establish boundaries for future land claims by settlers. Starting at points determined by a previous survey, the men marked off grids known as townships, comprising six rows of six sections a mile square. The 640-acre sections would later be subdivided into quarters and lots.

Measurements were taken with a surveyor's chain, a kind of heavy-duty tape measure. Chains typically comprise 100 metal links that total 66 feet, like the ones in the photos on opposite page. Eighty such chains make a mile. Chainmen would hold each end, and one of them might act as compassman to establish the correct bearing at each chain placement. The townships and sections were marked off in rows, one after another, back and forth, mile after mile. Accuracy was essential to enable settlers to claim a specific plot of land and prevent future property disputes.

Richards soon became a U.S. deputy surveyor, which required greater skills and knowledge of advanced equipment such as transits.

A transit is mounted on a tripod, and its telescope is pointed at a tall

A transit from that era
National Museum of
American History[11]

pole with red and white markers on it, held by a "flagman." The pole can be either a flagstaff or a stadia rod depending on its attributes. (See p. 251.) The surveyor with the transit uses the fine cross-hairs in the telescope to focus on the markers on the pole, to determine direction (a process known as "sighting"). In those days cross-hairs were usually made of black widow spider silk, which is stronger than steel wire of the same diameter and of such uniform thickness that the line is well defined. But spider silk can be affected by temperature changes,[10] so Lon ordered a transit for the 1874 western

8

Surveyor's kit. Its door holds literature from the manufacturer,
Keuffel & Esser. A plumb bob, used to place the survey instrument
directly over the survey point, is on the upper left of the door.
On the upper right is a folding magnifying glass to help take
accurate readings of the instrument. On the lower left of the kit
is a Gunter's surveyor's chain bundled for transportation.[12]
Author photo, 2000

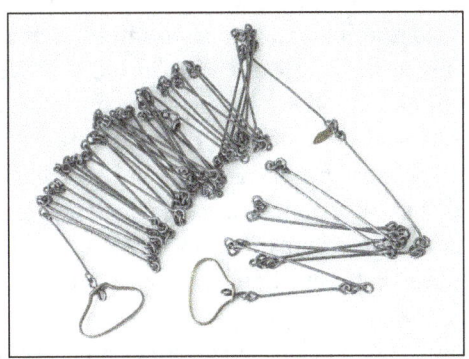

An unbundled Gunter's chain
National Museum of American History[13]

boundary survey that had the cross-hairs engraved on the glass. These lines were "very much finer, [making] errors of 'setting' much smaller," he wrote.[14] This would have been an improvement over the astronomical transit he acquired for the southern boundary survey. (Specifications for the second transit are on p. 250.)

Regular transits were used to traverse a line from a known position. In the case of boundary surveys, the known positions, such as a particular degree of latitude or longitude, were determined by astronomy. Surveys for latitude, such as the 1873 Wyoming boundary survey, required constant corrections and astronomical checks to the survey along an east-west curve. The crew would often have to retrace along the curve surveyed and correct points based on the latest astronomical readings. (See the essay on surveying for latitude, p. 259.) Surveys for longitude were less difficult because the surveyor just needed to sight Polaris (the North Star), then proceed along a straight line using that alignment. (This may be one reason Lon let Will do most of the western boundary survey.)

A standard transit has a compass in the base and a small window just left of the level bubble where horizontal angles were measured. The precision of a transit over a compass comes from the gradations etched on the circular plates, both horizontal and vertical, which are far more precise than compass readings. "So, for example," explains surveyor Earl Henderson, "you can set two points in the ground approximately East-West from each other and as far apart as is practicable for the telescope to see. Then at night you can set the transit up on one point and sight the other, then turn a horizontal angle to Polaris several times so you can mathematically determine the horizontal angle at the time Polaris (North Star) crosses the meridian (True North), which is called upper/lower culmination. At upper culmination, Polaris is at its highest position in the sky, and at lower culmination, Polaris is at its lowest elevation in the sky. When Polaris is at upper or lower culmination, the star appears to move horizontally. Knowing that angle you can add or subtract 90° to get to true East or West. This process is known as observing/determining the meridian (North).

"Once True North is determined and the rest of the field crew wakes up, you can set another point as far as you can see along that intended line and measure the distance between the instrument station and the next one. Today we use large nails in the ground and at each point we set the transit precisely plumb over the nail. Once the third point is set along True North and the distance measured you pick up the transit and set it on the third point, sight the second point (True South) and turn 180° to continue along

An astronomical station in a state boundary survey, 1902-03. This zenith telescope would have been about the same as those used in 1873.

True North. This leapfrog process is called traversing. In the old days it required that all trees and obstructions along the line be removed, and sometimes the terrain (hills, etc.) limited the line-of-sight distances more than the limitation of the telescope's optics."

In the case of the 41st parallel, the latitude they want to mark for the boundary is 90° from True North, he continued. But in order to determine that known latitude a zenith telescope was often used to sight directly, or nearly directly, overhead to known stars as they cross the meridian of longitude during the night. (They, of course, only seem to pass overhead as the Earth rotates.) Then the surveyors would switch to a standard transit, like in the photo, to survey the traverse.

The zenith telescope permits very accurate determination of astronomic latitude and longitude. (See p. 269 for more about these telescopes.)

And there's far more to surveying than the above. "It's a complex and confusing profession to most people," noted Garland Burnett, a New Mexico surveyor.[15] "Our work is somewhat esoteric unless you have some knowledge of math, computer science, geology, history, astronomy and real property law, to name a few."

Explanations and photo of astronomical station courtesy of Earl F. Henderson, president, Zenith Land Surveying, Boulder, Colorado,[16] with additions by Dr. Herbert W. Stoughton.

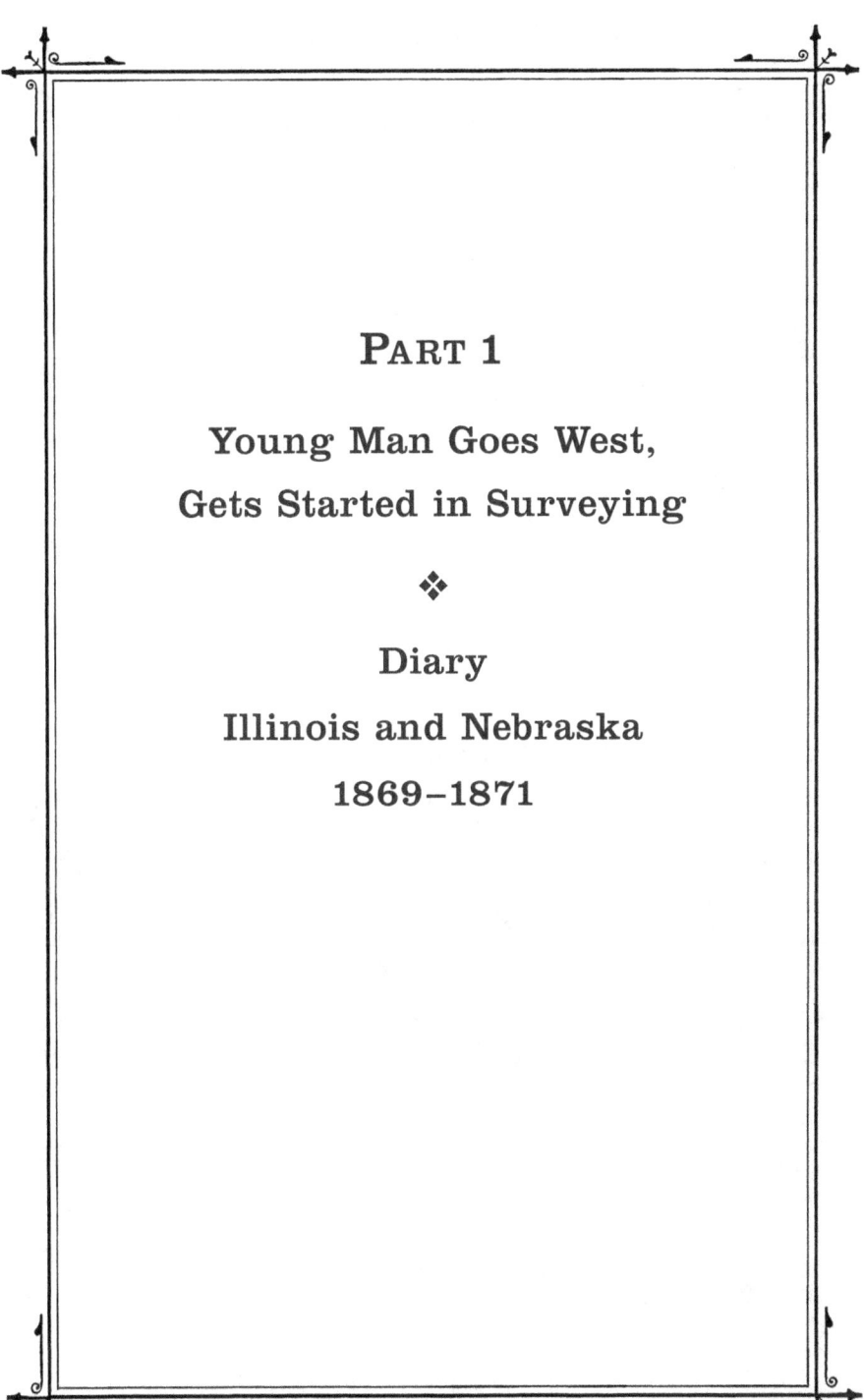

PART 1

Young Man Goes West, Gets Started in Surveying

❖

Diary

Illinois and Nebraska

1869–1871

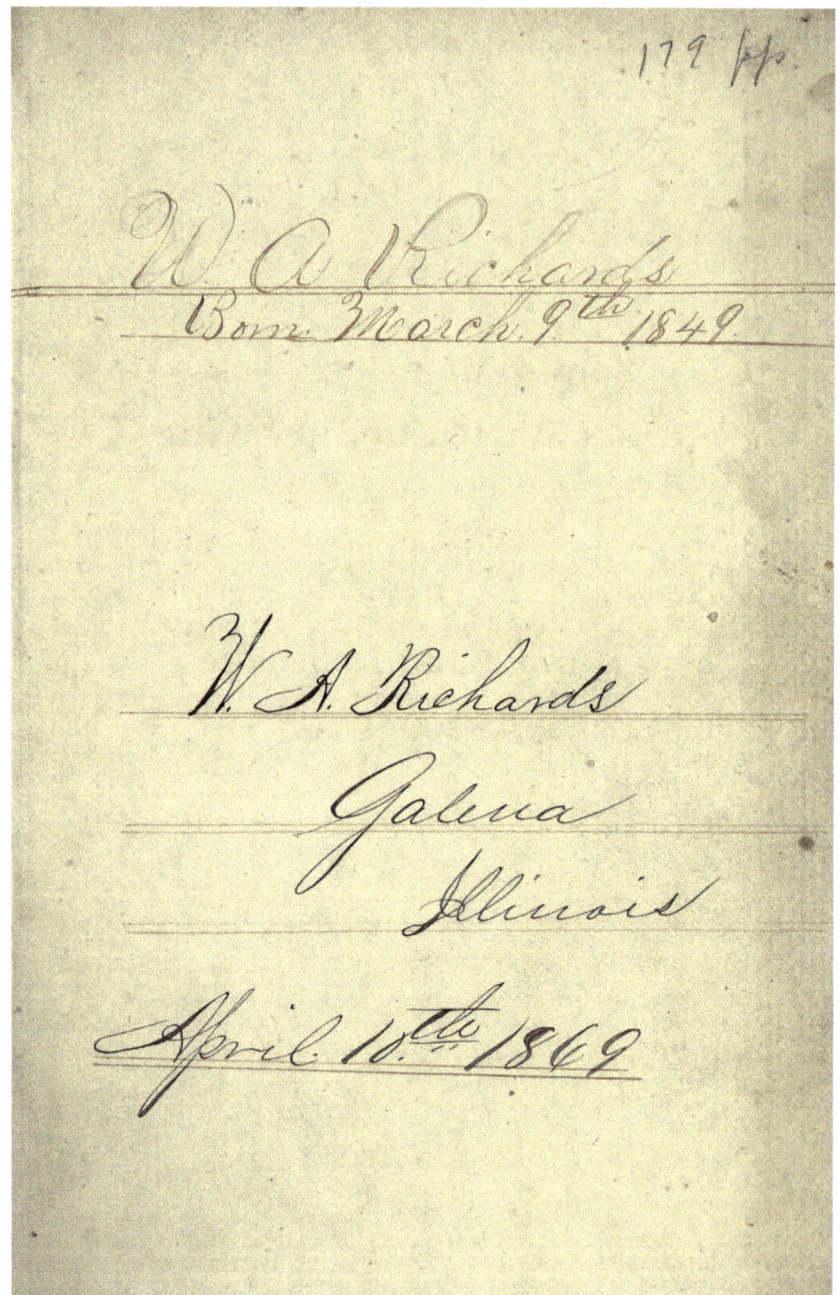

Title page of diary, actual size
History Nebraska[1]

Diary, Illinois and Nebraska
Background

RICHARDS WAS AMONG hundreds who flooded Omaha, Nebraska, after the Civil War. Though the Union Pacific was pushing to complete the transcontinental railroad, jobs in its shops (and elsewhere in town) were scarce. Finally, he obtained an entry-level position on a survey of land for future settlement west of Omaha, in today's Lincoln and Dawson counties. His summer as a surveyor, with its hardships, close encounters with *Bison bison*, and fears of close encounters with tribal warriors, forms the heart of the diary. Yet his sense of humor rarely deserted him.

The diary begins with a familiar resolution:

WITH THE NEW YEAR I begin anew to keep a record of my doings. Twice before have I began and after a short time thrown my book aside and thought no more of the matter, but now I am determined to persevere and commit to the keeping of this little book an account of the every day affairs of life, which though in themselves small go to make up a lifetime. It ought to be the rule of every man's life to take some notice of affairs as they occur so that in after years he can refer to them without having to trust to memory, which at that period of his existence is generally treacherous. I hope that I may tell all that I do to this little friend and have nothing written that I'll ever regret having done, though if long continued that would be a wonderful record indeed for few are they who can look back over a very lengthy period of their lives and see nothing that might have been done a little better. It may be that many beside myself may some time read these lines and it is my intention that, while I am truthful to my journal, they may find but little to condemn. With this programme I close my rather lengthy preface.

Dubuque, Jany. 1st 1869

I find myself this New Year's morning at a Hotel in Dubuque, Iowa, where I have been two days. My father who has been repairing bridges on the D.& S.C.R.R. [Dubuque & Sioux City Rail Road] this summer met with a severe accident the 29th ult. by being thrown from and run over by a handcar. A telegram was sent to Mother at Galena and she and myself came immediately to this place where he had been brought. Found him in rather a bad situation with no one to wait upon him but one of the men. He is now doing well and I hope in a few days to take him home.

Jan. 5th

Father has improved so fast that by carrying him to and from the cars we came to Galena today. Found Lon and Flora and Auttie* at the depot. Took him to Mrs. Maltby's where Mother is boarding, although Lon and his wife wanted him taken to their house but as they are occupying Gen. Grant's** house and all the people of Galena are waiting for something to complain about we thought best to not take him there. Mother and myself are about worn out with watching with him and with being compelled to eat the food at that Dutch Hotel where we stayed in D.

Moses Coit Tyler lectured here this evening but I preferred staying at home as I was too sleepy to enjoy a public lecture & I doubt if a private one would have kept me awake. His subject was "Caste" and he is master of it. His is the best of the course so far.

Sunday, 10th

This evening finds me again at Mr. Townsends away down in Rush township. I came out today in a two-horse cutter. Lost our way & did not reach here till night. Tomorrow I commence my school again, which I dismissed the night before Christmas. By the accident to Father I lost a week more than I had intended, which will make the close of the term rather late in the Spring. I have taught but one month & have [illegible] remaining.

Sunday, 17th

Nothing special occurred last week so I made no notes. A Mr. Jackson lately from England spoke twice today in our schoolhouse. He is a Universalist. Is not very much of a speaker though his sermon this morning on the Philosophy of Man was a good thing but it was written & may not be of his own composition. This evening took a team and a load of girls & went to the Center to church. Heard seven men and about seventeen old ladies speak. It is a Baptist church and they have a general "talking time" every evening. Well it's bed time so I'll turn in.

---

*Lon is William's elder brother, Alonzo, Flora is Lon's wife, and Auttie is Austin, the younger brother of Lon and William.

**General Ulysses S. Grant, who was about to be inaugurated as President. The townspeople of Galena had given him the house in gratitude for saving the Union in the Civil War, so perhaps that's why Will was worried about their possible objections. Grant didn't spend much time in Galena after the war, and that might be why he was letting Lon and his wife live there. Flora, whose maiden name was Miner, and Grant were seventh cousins, three times removed.[2]

Tuesday, 19th

Dr. Jackson spoke again on temperance. Done well. Guess he's "been there." Took up a collection, became disgusted, and left.

Sunday, 31st. 10 o'clock P.M.

Snowing a little. Good prospect for a storm.

Monday, Feby. 1st 1869

A very bad morning. Snow has fallen quite deep and as the wind is now blowing hard and the snow very dry it is very disagreeable outside. However I must away to school. Evening. Snow drifted bad. Roads all full. Contrary to my expectations I had a full school. Their parents brought them to school and came for them. No traveling on foot.

Friday morning 5th

Uncle George is going to Galena today and as his daughter Olive has agreed to teach for me I am going too.

Sunday, the 7th

Here I am again ready for the other half of my term. Found the people well at home. Father able to walk without crutches. Is doing finely. As an accident policy which he had on his life at the time he was hurt pays him ten dollars a week he will come out about even. John Richards was also in town. Folks at the Grove [presumably Elk Grove] all well. Pa went back with him and will stay awhile at the Grove. Roads are pretty good and weather very fine. Found a letter here from Schaeffer from Annapolis. He has graduated No. 2 in Mathematics. Sent me a photo of the highest seven. All fine looking fellows. His letter almost gave me the blues. As near as I ever come. When I get into the Military School, if I ever do, I'll show them how near I can come to No. 1.

Friday, 12th.

A very pleasant morning. Snow melting very fast. The nights are not cold enough to freeze any and the weather has the appearance of a break up. The going is very bad as the snow is all gone in the roads, and too muddy for a wagon. We have about concluded to have only three months of school as so much time was lost Christmas, that four months will bring the end of the term in April. I am willing as some of my larger scholars have left and it is not so interesting for me. Think I'll go in to the insurance business with Lon when I do finish up here, which if we have but three months will be about the first of March.

Saturday Morning 13th

Raining quite hard. The prospects are good for an early Spring, though if the ground opens now, there will be freezing weather before planting time. We could hear the ice breaking on the Miss. very plainly yesterday. Sounds like distant cannonading. Apple River is so high that the mails can't [get] through so we will be without our regular supply of Sunday reading matter.

Tuesday, 16th. 8:50 A.M.

Old Sol is out this morning in all his glory. The storm has passed, the weather has changed and the ground is frozen hard this morning. No snow.

Friday Evening, 19th

Another week is passed. Truly has it been said that time flies and it must have flown on eagle wings this week for it seems hardly possible that this week is gone. But it is and for good or for evil. I know that I have done my best and if I am censured it must be for lack of ability not of will. The people are not quite as impartial here as at Smelser, they take the report of their children instead of visiting the school. Nevertheless I think they are generally satisfied with the reports, at least very few complaints are made. It is snowing now very fast and fine. So we may expect good sleighing. The mails came through this week. I got two letters, one from Ella in Ohio and one from Cousin Dora. Murray McConnell was assassinated in his own house in Jacksonville on the 9th by a man who [illegible] him four hundred dollars. A small sum to sell out for.

Wednesday, Feb. 24th

Clear and cold, very much like winter. Nothing startling has transpired since my last report. I rec'd two letters last night one from Lon and one from Jake. Father is still visiting at the Grove, folks all well.

Friday, 26th 4:15 P.M.

This is the last schoolday of Feby 1869. It has been a very pleasant month and the weather is about the same now as at the first of the month, clear & quite cold. Next week will finish my school as per contract but I expect I will teach a week or so longer. As Lon don't want me yet I am satisfied to stay here. Spent last night with Mr. [Breed's?] family who live a mile from here and which is well represented in our little colony. Had a very good time & was cordially invited to come again. I intended to have visited around among the neighbors more than I have but some way I like to make one place my home and not rove around so much. In a few days the beloved Andy [Johnson] will have to vamos the ranche and make room for U.S. [Grant]. He has held the position about four years longer than he should have done.

Monday, March 1st 1869

Today another month is ushered in and if the old saying of "In like a lamb & out like a lion" holds good we may expect the closing scenes of this month to be very tragical, for a more pleasant day for the season of the year I never saw. I attended an exhibition last Saturday evening at the next school house north of here. It was very good for the time they were in preparing it. Rienzi's address was badly abused and Rienzi himself would hardly have owned it.

In their newspaper they had some local items that were rather too personal to suit my taste. A lady from New York, Miss Ella Evans, who is teaching near here and who went in company with our folks, felt really insulted at the mention made of her in connection with a young gentleman who had occasionally visited her. I was entirely neglected. Miss Evans and I became about as well acquainted as people usually do in two days. We talked laughed & played checkers together and the rest of the family left us to ourselves almost entirely. I escorted her from the exhibition and we had a fine chat & on Sunday I read poetry for her and we discussed matters in general some if not more. The rest of the people did not like her much and in some things treated her a little "shabby" but they should not expect a person who has always lived in town to be just like they are who have never lived off a farm.

One bad trait of character in the society here is too little charity. If a stranger is not just as they are they cry "Oh, he is terribly stuck up" and are not at all careful about hurting one's feelings. They are honest and straightforward but rather pride themselves too much on their rusticity and have too great a hostility for town people. I make no boast of being a city gent but dislike to hear quite so much said on the subject when I am near.

Thursday Eve. March 4th

One day more and my teaching in this vicinity is over. The people are in the habit of visiting the schools on the last day if on no other, a plan I do not like as I would much rather have the day to ourselves than have a crowded house all day. I would like to have taught a few weeks more but the District couldn't afford to pay so much.

Gen. Grant is inaugurated before this time, I presume, as this is the

4th of March. I have no fears of any riotous proceedings but would like to know how the affair passed off. A large number of people are there as the R.R. Co's carry passengers at half fare until the 12th inst. ["Instant" meant "of the current month."]

Friday, 4:30 P.M.

'Tis finished.' Everything passed off quietly and orderly. Not as many visitors as I had expected. Only two or three scholars from another district. I am afraid I have not given as good satisfaction as some teachers they have had but I know that I have done my "level best" and I want that if I am censured it may be on account of my ability and not my disposition to do better. If the parents had visited the school a little more frequently I think it would have had a good effect on the scholars. Upon the whole I have concluded that this shall be my last term of school. And it is my firm determination never to apply for another certificate as a teacher and never to take charge of a school again. If the Supt. knew my motives in teaching, that I teach merely because it pays better than anything else in the winter time, he would, or ought to, refuse me a certificate, and where a teacher teaches for nothing but money, he will never succeed, for his heart is not in his work

Galena, Monday, March 8th

Came home yesterday with Nell Townsend. Rode the entire distance in a lumber wagon & as a consequence feel a little sore now.

Found the folks all well. Stayed last night at Mrs. Maltby's. Pa is improving fast, thinks of commencing work this week. Commenced work this morning for Lon. Found that Washburne had been chosen Secretary of State, A. T. Stewart of the Treasury & [illegible] of the interior. Judge Hoar is chosen as Attorney Gen'l.

Friday, 21

Father went to Dubuque this morning to work if he can stand it. Snowing very fast.

Mr. Washburne has resigned and is going to France. Mr. Stewart is disqualified by an old law and has resigned and [George S. Boutwell] is to take his place. Fish takes Washburne's place and Gen. Rawlins is appointed Sec'y of War. So the cabinet is filled at last.*

---

*Elihu B. Washburne, Ebenezer R. Hoar, Hamilton Fish, and John A. Rawlins. Jacob D. Cox was secretary of the interior from 1869–70.

Monday, March 22nd, 1869

For ten days have I neglected my journal and the cause is scarcity of news or items. During last week Lon went to Elk Grove on Ins. [insurance] business but accomplished nothing. The people are all well out there and expect to always remain so I suppose. He insured John Richards' life for ten thousand dollars ($10,000)* some time ago & maybe Orson will do likewise but I doubt it a little. Today he has gone to Warren and will go from there to Darlington where he expects to do something in Ins. He will have [to] work carefully or the agents may make him trouble as it is rather out of his district.

Auttie went out there last Monday and will probably work for John Medcalf this summer.

I rec'd a letter from Uncle Henry last week. He is going into Nebraska to take up a claim under the homestead law and I think that I will go out there too in a few weeks. If I can make a good claim and get fixed so I can make it pay will have Auttie come out and live with me and spend the winter with. I don't want to have Father or Mother go into a new country like that but am afraid if we settle there they will come too. They are too old to go into a new country like that & rough it as they would have to do. I intend going though as soon as possible.

The weather is warm today and a good prospect for Spring. Streets quite muddy. Took dinner at Lon's and will board there while he is away.

Tuesday, 23rd

Lon returned tonight, did not do anything at D. Saw all the folks and all well. Auttie is coming home soon. Father also came home tonight. Work gave out and they discharged several. He will go to work again as soon as the frost is out of the ground.

Wednesday, 24th

Rather a dull day, but fine weather and thawing fast. Ice still closes the Miss. river. Last year boats were running by the 17th of March. The season is very backward. Wrote to Uncle Hank that I was ready to go with him at any time and if he has not gone will meet him in Omaha next week. Am getting ready now. Want to get a pair of heavy boots made and a pair of pants as I want to take clothing for a year and not very much at that.

Monday morning 7 o'clock

I have swept & cleaned up the office this morning and am now waiting for breakfast which we have at eight o'clock. I am getting tired of this way

---

*About $222,000 in 2022, per measuringworth.com purchasing-power calculator

of living and intend changing very soon. I may do worse in some respects but in some it would be impossible to do so.

Last Friday I spent the P.M. at the high school. It was the last day of the term and the closing exercises were very good though not very extensive. Several of our old scholars were there and it made me feel almost homesick, though the school is far from being what it was when I attended it. Saturday I spent in the office as Lon was out most of the day. He is likely to get the — Insurance Co. which would please him most wonderfully. I hope he will get it for it will be worth more than all the business he has in that line. His friend [Spensley?] also wants it bad and if he can get it away from him it will be good. Sunday we were all at Lon's to dinner and supper except Auttie. He is working for John Medcalf at Darlington and I hope will stay there all summer.

Yesterday we had a great discussion on Woman's Rights and Mother was the only disputant on the affirmative. [The text after that, about ten lines, has been erased, most likely by an older Richards who regretted his youthful views.] I am making my arrangements with all haste and hope to get off this week and if the claim business don't suit me I shall go on to the mines.

Thursday, April 8th

I am still in Galena though expecting to leave in a few days. Went up to Darlington last week & spent several days. Had a good visit. Auttie is going to stay there this summer and work for John Medcalf. Left there on the 5th, waited three hours in Warren for the train. Learned that Winfield Townsend who taught my school last winter had died of Typhoid fever very suddenly. Mrs. Prescott of this place died suddenly of paralysis today, leaves four children & a husband to mourn her loss.

Friday, 9th

Nothing special to write today. Intend leaving here for Omaha next Tuesday morning. Hope to meet Johnnie Skinner there, one of my old friends, and maybe we will go into some kind of business together. Col. Rowley promised to write to Gen'l Rawlins, Secy. of War, concerning appointment as Cadet at West Point which I hope to get next June. I will try what I can do out West and in case I fail to make a success of it will accept the appointment & go to school under U.S. appointment a year from next June & intend to do my level best this Spring & summer & if I fail will go for the highest mark on the list at W. P. Will come out a member of the engineers department if I can.

Have been taking quinine this P.M. for the "hiccups" which I have had for more than twenty four hours & which are beginning to make me feel used up.

Father rec'd a draft for his accident insurance of $102.86* today. He is still unable to work and ought to have held the claim a little longer.

Saturday, 10th

Stayed at Lon's last night. He & Flora want me to stay there till I go away. Will do so part of the time. Ten men from Elizabeth left here this morning for White Pine & the Silver Mines. Had I been ready would have gone with them. The quinine did the work for me but not till I had hiccuped 36 hours, nearly 48 hours. My head feels like a bee hive & am quite deaf from its effects.

Tuesday, 13th

Did not make a start this morning as I had expected. Lon was taken sick yesterday and I thought I would wait a day and attend to his business for him. He is better this morning & I will try and get off tomorrow. Snowed yesterday like fury but is all gone this morning. Two funerals yesterday & one appointed for today. Mrs. Fagan was buried and at the grave her son ten yrs old fell and began bleeding at the mouth and nose & has lain in a stupor ever since from which the physician says he will never rise.

Wednesday, 14

Stayed last night with Lon and Flora. Father and Mother were there also. Had an early breakfast & left Galena at 7 o'clock. At the depot met Mr. Rogers from Hanover with whom I am well acquainted, who is going to Omaha so we will go in company. Reached Dubuque at 8 and am now on board the train waiting for a start.

Left Dubuque at 10.30 & reached Farley at 12M. After waiting a couple of hours are again ready to be off. Go very slow on this.

Evening   Reached Cedar Rapids at 6 o'clock. Made out a good supper not so much in quality as quantity. Leave here at 1.20 tonight.

12 Midnight. Found [Jarvis?] McNulty here from Galena and in talking with him passed the evening pleasantly.

Thursday morning.

Left according to Programme. After a good deal of delay in getting freight car on the track, that had run off. Have heard of the fastest [writer?] & of the fastest walker &c but last night at Cedar Rapids we

---

*About $2,280 in 2022

Omaha about 1870
KMTV/Bostwick-Frohardt Photograph Collection at The Durham Museum, Omaha

found the slowest Ticket agent that there is the U.S., I'll warrant. He wouldn't make change at all although he had plenty and as there was a big crowd at the depot there was a good deal of swearing done.

Got our breakfasts at Boone. 75¢* for a poor breakfast is rather strong but we are getting into the country where everything is done strong.

Evening.   Reached Omaha at 4 P.M. Stopped at the Wyoming House and as we were somewhat hungry took in a pretty good supper. Before doing so I went out to find my friend Skinner who has a blacksmith shop here. Found the shop but he was out. On coming out from supper found him waiting for us. Went with him to his boarding house, where we are now. Pretty fair board at $1.00 per day. We were paying $2.00 at the hotel. Haven't tried to get anything to do yet but am going out his P.M. and will visit the machine shops. Wrote a letter home this morning.

Saturday Morning April 17th
    Well I have been in Omaha nearly two days and have done nothing yet. In fact have not tried very hard. Yesterday P.M. in company with Rogers and Skinner I visited the U.P.R.R. [Union Pacific Rail Road] shops and found them much more extensive than I had expected. Two thousand men are employed and they make nearly all their own stock. They get up some splendid cars. Skinner introduced us to several of his friends whom I found to be just like himself, good fellows.

---

*About $16.60 in 2022; $1 was about $22.20.

There are a good many of the noble red men loafing around here and if any one had any chivalrous notions concerning them and their mistreatment and alleged wrongs, they would relinquish them on a slight acquaintance with the originals as seen in the streets here. A more villan-[ous] dirty and degraded set of beings I never saw. Squaws with their papooses strapped to their backs like knapsacks and men with nothing but a blanket & pair of leggings to cover their nakedness. A few Pawnee scouts whom I saw at the depot were better looking men but I would not trust them out of my sight. Two companies of the 12th & 26th U.S.I. [Infantry?] left on the train last night for the west. These Regiments have lately been consolidated & John E. Smith of Galena who was Col. of the 12th was placed on the retired list. These two companies seemed to be composed almost entirely of young men and nearly all below the size of a common man. I never saw fewer fine looking or intelligent men in so large a company as this. Most of them were as modest looking men as ever cut a throat. Would prefer almost anything else to being a private in the Regular army.

In evening went to the Academy of Music and Saw Nobody's Daughter played. The principal part was acted by Miss Fanny B. Price, a young actress who is starring here. She performed her part well and brought down the house and was twice called before the curtain. She was well supported too. Had a much better performance than I had expected.

This place contains about twenty-two thousand inhabitants and is growing rapidly. There is a street railway & the town is lighted with gas. Gambling saloons are numerous and hurdy gurdy houses thick. And if a chap has plenty of cash he can find lots of amusement. I think this is destined to be one of the largest cities west of the Missouri if not the largest.

Weather this morning is fine. Vegetation is somewhat more advanced here than in Ills. but very much so. [sic]

Sunday, Morning.

This is a splendid morning clear and the sun shining as warm as one would want. Haven't anything special to do today. May go out to the Barracks about four miles from here where several companies of soldiers are stationed. A Regt. came in yesterday from Richmond and will remain at the Barracks about a month when they are going to Cal. Went to the car shops of the U.P. yesterday afternoon and applied for a job. If I were a mechanic of any kind could get work in an hour. As it is I may not get anything to do. Several of their men quit last night as they have not been paid off for more than two months & the Co. is owing more than two million dollars in this city. In the evening went around to see the town after dark. Visited the Academy of Fun which is a low theater & beer hall. Their performances were not very chaste surely. On our way home stopped at a keno bank to see how the thing was done. Found the house crowded and all playing. Don't think I'll ever invest anything in the business as a fellow is bound to lose by it if he continues it any time at all.

Wrote a letter to Auttie.

Morning of Monday.

Spent a very pleasant day yesterday. Went to the Presy. church in the morning and went with Mr. Dodds of Galena to dinner. After dinner we called for Skinner and went to Dodds' office (M.[S.?] Churchill) and had a good time telling stories, drinking soda &c. Would have gone to church in the evening but it rained. Has rained every day since I have been here.

Tuesday Morning.

Rogers and I have just returned from Council Bluffs. Went there yesterday morning. Found Messrs. S. S. & J. D. Bayliss formerly of Galena. They seemed glad to see us but were unable to assist us as they had just finished building a large hotel or rather repairing it (The Pacific House) and it had taken a great deal of money. Also went to the office of the Rock Island and Council Bluffs R.R. Could find nothing to do. Rogers telegraphed to Swift in Chicago applying for a position as operator on the road but rec'd no answer. Stayed at the Bryant House, a good place at two dollars a day. In the Reading room of the Y.M.C.A. met a man who is going to the D. & S.C.R.R. Think we will go up to Sioux City as we have worked this town up pretty well. Visited the Machine Shops where I had applied for a job and talked a few minutes with Mr. York. No chance there as every place is filled. Will get dinner here and there go over to the Bluffs and probably leave there this evening.

Tuesday, 20th

After writing up my diary this morning Dodds and I went to the U.P.R.R. shops again & as they talked very fair and seemed to think I might get into business there of some kind as soon as the road got straightened up about its money matters. So I concluded to wait a week or so longer but Rogers was bound to go somewhere. As he was about strapped I lent him five dollars though I have no money to spare, and he started for C. Bluffs. Spent a pleasant evening talking with Dodds. Like him the best kind. Skinner went to the Good Templars Lodge.* But came home before the close.

Wednesday, 21st.

Nothing new today. Skinner went out in the country to be gone a couple of days. Have heard of nothing to do yet. Met Mr. Aikin of [Mantana?] Iowa on the street and he came up to my boarding house to stay. Is here with some produce, but finds a very dull market.

Thursday, 22nd.

Have just had dinner & finished writing some letters. Wrote to Lon, Tom Bray, Uncle Hank and Mr. Yearnshaw. Talked insurance a while this morning with a man down town. He wants me to go to work but I don't like canvassing and he will give me nothing else. The U.P.R.R. effected a sale of bonds yesterday in Boston sufficient to finish the road, pay all the floating debt and put the road in good running order. I think my prospects are good now for a job. Shall make a bold strike for something any way.

Evening. The wind is really blowing big guns. It took a ferry boat three hours to cross the river today. Several steamers are laid between here and Plattsmouth unable to proceed on acct of the wind. It has blown this way for several days. Streets very dusty. Rec'd a letter from Rogers in Council Bluffs. He has engaged to work in a brick yard and has spoken for a place for me. Unless I can get something to do before next Monday will go to work. Wages $2.25.

Friday.

Still very windy & dusty. Went down the R.R. shops this P.M. but nothing has turned up there yet. Wrote to Rogers. Times are very dull here at present but I live in hope for I think I can get work before long. Am not going home because I can't make a living away from there I am very sure. This place is over stocked with men but my chance is as good as any ones and if I stick to it I know I can do well.

Rec'd a letter from Lon this morning. All well at home.

Saturday, 24th.

The principal excitement today is the report that the Steamer Ursilla struck a snag, burst her boiler & sank a short distance above Sioux City. Fifty passengers instantly killed. Wind still blowing hard. Rec'd a letter from home tonight, all well but a little blue. Father is at work though

---

*Founded in 1851, the Independent Order of Good Templars is still in existence, promoting abstinence from alcohol and drugs.[3]

hardly fit. I am undecided what to do. Would go to Lincoln and take up a piece of land but I can't hold it in my own name yet and more if I get the appointment to West Point next Spring I'll have to leave it any way. I would go to Fort Benton and the Silver Mines but I haven't the money. A hundred dollars with what I have would take me there, and the miners have so many of them left there for White Pine that work is plenty and wages good. If I can't go there though I'll try and make a living here. Mr. Aiken is still here, has left his produce with a Commission firm. And is now trying to buy some mules. He thinks the Mts. the finest place in the world, and he would have remained there but for his family. Mother said in her letter that she had heard from Uncle Hank and that he and his wife had both been sick, but that he would be in this place sometime the present week. As I expect to be in the Bluffs next week I'll leave a letter in the P.O. for him. This eve. we went to the Academy of Fun with Mr. Aiken that he could see what kind of an institution it was. I think the less a fellow is seen around such a place the better he will be off.

Monday morning

Put on my working clothes and am now on board the Big Muddy or rather the ferry boat crossing to the bluff where I hope to get something to do. Several boats at the landing bound for Fort Benton and the Gold Mines and each carries a howitzer. Would go up there if I had the money & see what I could do at mining.

Evening

After straying around all day put up at the Bryant House at $2.00 a day.

Matters look very dull. Too many men and more coming from both or rather every direction. Now that the U.P. road is about finished hundreds are in every day. Shall make one more dead set here tomorrow and if I don't succeed will try Omaha once more and if I can get nothing will go to Sioux City and go to work on the new rail road. When a fellow gets about out of money in a strange country he'll do almost anything.

Tuesday

After trying several places got a job of piling lumber for W. J. Young & Co. Made a half days work, the first for this country and the first of that kind for two years. The papers say the connecting rail will be laid today between [this?] and the Pacific.

Thursday Eve

Feel rather used up this evening as I have done no work for about a year it goes rather rough. Would much rather do it than loaf though. Guess I'll go to bed.

Friday evening

As it looked like rain this morning I went over to Omaha after our things and Rogers went with the team. Walked down to the river, about four miles, and on the other side from the ferry up town accidentally met Uncle Hank on the Street. He had been in town since Monday. Also met Mr. Yearnshaw on the ferry boat coming back. He is just from Lincoln going to Marion for his family. Managed to get dead headed across the river and on the train. Worked this P.M.

Saturday, May 1st

Worked hard today. But feel first rate tonight.

Sunday, May 2nd

This is a splendid day. The air is perfectly pure and when one draws a long breath he feels as though he could fly. The climate is very different here from that of Galena. I am gaining in weight all the time, now weigh one hundred & sixty five. Uncle Hank came over today and we had a pleasant visit. He is going to work in the car shops at Omaha & I think he can get me a job too. Wrote to Lon & wife, & Jake.

Monday, May 3rd 1869

Worked today piling lumber. Don't feel very well tonight. Expect I'll have nothing to do tomorrow. Col. Montgomery former editor of the Dem. paper here cowhided his old partner on the Street this evening. Cause slander. Result one man badly cowhided and the other paid $20.00 for the fun of giving him it.

Tuesday.

As I expected nothing to do today I went over to Omaha. Walked out & back. A very warm day too. Saw all the boys. Uncle Hank is at work in the paint shops of the U.P.R.R. and thinks he can get me a place.

A little excitement on the street again tonight. Judge [Larrimer?] fired five shots at a man named Miller. Missed every time, and although a crowd was standing around no one was hurt. No arrest made. Rather a loose way they have of doing business out here.

Several Co's. of the 21st Reg. U. S. A. left Omaha this P.M. for the plains. Quite a excitement was created at Columbus a hundred miles west of here this week by the Indians running off a lot of stock. It is thought that they are making arrangements for a general outbreak and that they will make a raid of the U.P.R.R.

Wednesday, 5th

Nothing to do this morning so I went back to Omaha to try once more for a place in the Shops. Uncle Hank has spoken to Mr. Hurd the time keeper for Stephens who is a friend of his & he will get me a position if possible. Is to let me know tomorrow. I fear I will be the least bit discouraged if I don't get into something pretty soon. I have been here nearly three weeks and have earned but ten dollars. Have written home for some more clothes and must wait for them or I would not stay in this vicinity another day.

Thursday, 6th

Went to the Shops today but can get no work for a week, if at all. Will go back to Council Bluffs tomorrow and try and make enough to pay my board until I can get away. Went to a reunion of the Good Templars this evening. Lots of fun pretty girls & good things to eat. Stayed till 11. o'clock but they were nearly all strangers & I didn't find much enjoyment. Rec'd a letter from Father. All well. Cary has declined the nomination as assessor of Utah [in Illinois] and Lon is making a dead set for it. If he succeeds can give me a Clerkship. But I think he will have hard work to do to get the appointment. Also had a letter from Schaeffer. They are going across the ocean again this summer on a cruise expect to go to France & England. Maybe I'll have a chance to see some of the world if I go to West Point. The future looks fair enough if all turns out as planned but the present is confoundedly mixed.

Friday

After calling on Uncle Hank this morning (whom I found unable to work on account of a bilious attack last night) and finding that Mr. Hurd could do nothing for me for a few days I came back to Council Bluffs. Nothing to do at the lumber yard and I could do nothing if there were for I have quite a severe attack of the piles, and must be a little careful or I'll be laid up. I guess it was the festival that caused it. Rogers is helping Col. Sealy to some papering.

Saturday, 8th

Am no better this morning. Have worked but one day this week. Am running behind fast. Must do better next week or I'll soon be out of money. I have lent Rogers ten dollars or I would not be so near out. Paid my board up square through tonight. Spent part of the P.M. in a veloci-pede* rink. Not riding though. This is quite a fast town. A faro & Keno Bank, two theaters, two Rinks &c.

Sunday Morning

A most beautiful day. Had a fine shower last night which laid the dust & cooled the air so that this is as pleasant a morning as I ever saw. From my window I can see Omaha on a gently rising slope just back from the river with a background of bluffs covered with green, on one of which stands the old capitol building, a large brick structure painted white which can be seen for miles. Between here and the river is an unbroken plain which looks like some fine lawn carpeted with soft grass. The dis-tance seems very short while in reality it is four miles. One peculiarity of this country is that the air is so pure that one can see much [more] than in the east where it is much more dense.

I have just written a letter to Auttie. He is at work and doing well. I yesterday recd my valise by express containing my black suit of clothes and a couple of white shirts. Also some Galena papers. They don't amount to anything when at home but when away from there are very acceptable. The river is very high there and rising. Father goes to work on the R.R. again tomorrow.

10 o'clock P.M. Have just returned from church where I heard a very good discourse upon the sin of worshiping worldly idols. The minister spoke without notes which is not often done by Presbyterians. Expect to go to work tomorrow.

Monday evening

Although this has been a very rainy day we have made a full day at work. Several little showers but none of long duration. My piles trouble me a good deal. The great railroad across the continent was finished today. The last rail was laid one thousand and eight[y] six miles from Omaha & (690) six hundred and ninety miles from San Francisco. Omaha celebrated the event yesterday but this town will wait a few days until the completion of the Rock Island road and then celebrate both at once. Amused myself a [short?] this evening at 1423.1.14.14.1.11.142.111.143** at another fellows expense. Rec'd a letter from Lon. No chance of his getting the office of Assessor of Utah. Thinks it has been sold out to poli-ticians. All well at home.

---

*Bicycle with a large front wheel, a small back one, iron tires, and no chains
**Signal code for B Tootards

Tuesday

Nothing of interest to write today. Weather very cold and windy mixed with rain. Worked all day piling flooring. Went to see Plunketts troupe play "The Wild Irish Girl," Mrs. Selden Irwin taking that part. She played her part well but was poorly supported. They have not improved very much since they played in Galena. The C.R.I.&P. [Chicago, Rock Island and Pacific Railroad] was completed to the point yesterday so that the celebration will come off tomorrow. I can't afford to lay off a day on account of it for must earn enough to pay my board this week.

Wednesday, May 12th

Very cold indeed. The coldest weather I ever saw this time of the year. Rained this P.M. too. As the grand celebration came off today, we did not work this afternoon. The celebration was good and would have been very fine but for the rain. There was a long procession, cannon fired, speeches &c. in the evening an illumination & more speeches. Rec'd a letter from Auttie. He likes his place well.

Thursday

It was so very disagreeable that we did not work this forenoon. Made a good half day this afternoon though piling flooring. My piles are about well so that I can work with a little more comfort. Weather a little milder this evening.

Friday evening

Worked all day piling flooring. Weather much warmer. Last night a couple of fellows from the U.P. got into a little difficulty in a saloon near here and stepped into the street and exchanged several shots by way of argument. No one hurt. Either the people out here are very poor shots or they are afraid of hurting some one as no body get hurt their encounters [*sic*].

Saturday, 15

Another week finished. Worked five days this week. Made ten dollars. Paid six for my board & one fifty for incidentals leaving a balance of two & a half. Not making money very fast at that rate but a good deal faster than a great many who are here without anything to do.

Sunday, May 16th

Went over to Omaha today. Saw all the boys and had a good time. Took dinner with Uncle Hank at the Jones House. Had the best dinner I have eaten since I have been away from home. Walked down to the river and back and feel a little tired. Must go to bed as I must go to work in the morning. Wrote a letter to Father this evening.

Monday 10 o'clock A.M.

As there was nothing in the yard for us to do this forenoon we went down to see the new bridge or what will eventually be a bridge for there is nothing like one visible now.* It is quite a novel affair. The piers or abutments are to consist of an iron tube ten feet in diameter and an inch & a quarter thick. When this has reached a solid foundation it will be filled with stone and thus make a solid column. It is lowered in sections twelve feet long by atmospheric pressure. In commencing, one section was sunk to the level of the ground then another was placed on that and a cap placed on the top of it and the air extracted by means of an air pump when the tube sinks by the pressure from above. One tube is down seventy-five feet and six inches. Each of the sections weighs nine and a half tons.

I have been out here now a month and have done very little. Still I have done better than many who have not made a cent, and though I have no chance of getting into anything very good here. Still I think I had better stay where I can make my board than to go further west where report says matters are much worse than here. As soon as I think it safe to do so I will leave this part of the country <u>very</u> <u>sudden</u>. So many men are coming in from the U.P. that everything is full here, and those who know say it is worse if possible out further.

Evening. Worked this P.M. After supper went up town and then "our room" had a game of old Sledge and any amount of fun. "Our room" travels on its muscle and can afford to do so. There are four of us in it and I am the lightest and I can bring down a hundred and sixty five. Our aggregate weight is seven hundred and the average a hundred & seventy five apiece. We are all young, too, though I am the youngest, two of the others are not twenty-two yet. One of them under twenty one. We challenge any room in town to turn out the same weight to the number of occupants. Retired at 10 o'clock.

Tuesday Evening

Have been loafing all day. Called on Mr. Davenport an insurance agent this P.M. and spent an hour very pleasantly. It almost seemed like seeing an old friend to meet some one who knew anything about the business. He represents several Co's that we used to have in Galena. Even that business is so overrun that he does not want even a canvasser. Must stir up

*The railroad bridge connecting Omaha and Council Bluffs

something tomorrow to make my board at this week. I think I'll have to go over to Omaha where I can board without having to pay every week.

A great number of emigrant wagons pass through here every day notwithstanding the Railroads and reports of hard times out west. Mr. Wadleigh was intending to discharge one of his old hands this morning on account of his being drunk all the time, but the fellow promised so strong to do better and being a very good man he concluded to give him a trial once more. If he had discharged him I would have taken his place. As it is I am out of employment all together and this is a hard country to do nothing in.

Wednesday Evening

Loafed this forenoon, and after dinner went down to the office to get my pay when Mr. Wadleigh told us to go to work. Piled 20 ft boards, very wide, rather heavy work. It is now raining hard. Have played two games of cribbage this evening. Guess I'll turn in.

Monday, Afternoon 24th

Raining like [illegible]. Have done no work since my last entry. Worked only one day last week and had hard work to pay my board. We could have worked today but for the rain and will probably have work the rest of this week. Wrote to Uncle Hank and received a letter from Flora last week. Also rec'd one from Jake. Lon's house was entered by a burglar last week who stole several hundred dollars worth of jewelry &c. The thief has been arrested & is now in jail. Something seems to be happening all the time to keep some of our family before the public. Lon has changed his residence again. Moved from Gen. Grant's house into a house on the hill near Wm Miner's [probably a relative of Flora's]. Will write a letter to Jake and one to Dodds this afternoon.

Tuesday Evening [late May].

Worked today piling [dimension?] stuff and feel a little tired. Nothing new under the sun.

Wednesday

There being no work again this morning I called for my time got my pay and left Council Bluffs in search of something by which I could make a living. Came to Omaha but expect to stay here but one day & will then strike down the river.

[Finds work with a surveying party]

Thursday

I heard today of a surveying party which will leave here next week. If I can get a place in the [word missing] I will go. Went to Castello's circus with Dodds this evening. Nothing very interesting about it. I lost my taste for circuses about ten years ago and have been to but one since.

Friday Evening

Saw Mr. [Chauncey] Wiltse the leader of the surveying party today and although he did not engage me he said he would let me know by Monday night. I however don't propose to wait so long for an answer but will find out tomorrow.

Saturday

Have made an engagement with Mr. Wiltse. He is going out on the U.P. about 250 miles and will work there all summer. The pay is not very large but a man will have it all as there is no expenses to pay and no chance to spend money. Expect to leave here Tuesday evening.

Sunday

A Beautiful day. Read most of the day. In the afternoon went out to Sherman Barracks about four miles up the Miss. with friend Jimmie to see dress parade but a little shower came up and compelled us to come back. In the evening attended the first Pres. church.

Monday

Went to the Bluffs this morning after my baggage. Found four letters and a paper awaiting me. One was from home, all well there. One from Schaffer, one from cousin Ella & one from Lida. Cousin Nettie is at last married and to an awful homely man. That's the way handsome girls always choose opposites. Paid my board up & took passage on the stage for Omaha. Reached just in time for dinner. Spent part of the P.M. with Uncle Hank. He met with quite a severe accident last Saturday by getting burned with some spirits of Turpentine. His left hand is badly burned and he will not be able to work for two or three weeks. His pay will go on the same, though.

Tuesday, June 1st 1869

Today ushers in another month. And who can say what it may bring forth. It is Election day here and there is considerable excitement. The Reps. made their nomination & some of them split off and got out a new ticket. The working men got out another so that four tickets are out. As the

Dems. have a straight ticket they will probably elect their men. We did not go as we expected on account of not hearing from our teams. They left Columbus last week and we must wait until they pass Ft. Kearney before we start from here. We'll probably leave tomorrow.

Wednesday, June 2nd

Did not start today but will surely leave tomorrow. Spent part of the day with Uncle Hank and in the evening wrote a letter to Pa at Cedar Falls. Mr. McIntosh was hurt last Thursday in the same manner that Father rec'd his injuries last Winter. Also wrote to Lon to send me his Henry rifle to Willow Island. Also wrote to Lida. Carson Scott of Galena came in on the P.M. train. Reports all well from that place.

Thursday, June 3rd 1 o'c

Have just had dinner at which we raised the old nick generally. Am all ready to start and will be off at 4.20 P.M. Left Omaha at 4.20 in company with Carson Scott of Galena, Mr. Wiltse and two other men belonging to our party. Took supper at 6.30 at Fremont. A good meal for which Mr. Wiltse paid one dollar. Left there at 7 o'clock and are now riding over an apparently endless prairie. Reached Columbus about 9 o'clock. Not much of a place to be sure.

12 o'clock Have had a good sleep. Went into the baggage room, got my blankets and spread them down on the car floor. Slept splendidly. Mr. Wiltse now has the floor. Are now stopping at Grand Island the men are [rounding?] and oiling the car wheels & making preparations for a long run. Friday morning June 4th 4.30 o'clock Have just landed at Willow Island. Only a station house, a grocery and two sod houses or adobe houses as they are called here, to be seen. Six soldiers are stationed here under a corporal. They live in a log house weather boarded with sod. The Indians are much worse out here than I expected. They had a fight last week with a Co. of Cavalry at or near Plum Creek twenty miles from here and on the opposite side of the [Platte] river. Six white men were killed and about fifty Indians. They also attacked a party of emigrants near the same place but were defeated. I expect we will have to go onto the South side of the Platte next week and then we will need to be on our guard & look out for the red skins.

We were out surveying today. Each man carried a revolver & knife at his side. I expect we will have to keep this up all summer. We saw a drove of antelope and any number of Jack Rabbits but could not get a shot. Quit work at two o'clock. Walked Eleven miles.

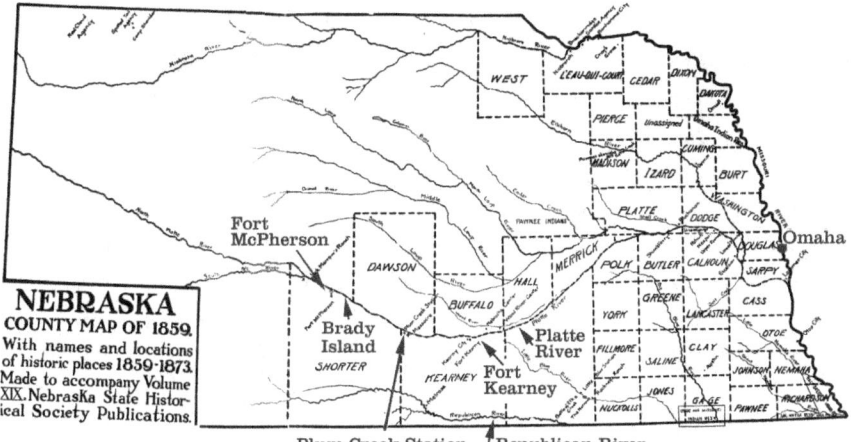

Map annotated in brown. See pp. 241–48 for detailed maps of the surveys.
History Nebraska[4]

Saturday, June 5th

Have had a very hard days work. After an early breakfast, packed up and marched to Brady Island 18 miles & stopped for dinner. After dinner we crossed the Platte or a large branch of it three hundred yards wide to Brady Island. We stripped to the buff & with a long rope helped to pull the wagons across. We crossed the river three times. Then marched up the Island several miles to the Ford. This place is over half a mile wide now as the river is high and is from one to four feet deep with a swift current. Again we played canal horse. Pulled one team across & all took a drink of whiskey. I took about three times as much as I intended and by the time I had got halfway back on the third trip I was about wilted. I couldn't keep up against the current & had to stop on a little Island. I rode to shore on a Govt. team & when I reached our tent I fell insensible or dead drunk I don't know which. The men changed my shirts & put on my pants & left me till morning.

Sunday, June 6

Feel all right this morning. A little sore after my spree. We walked 25 miles yesterday and forded the Platte six times. We do nothing today but repair damages. Nearly all the men need a little repairing & we broke a wagon tongue in crossing. We are stopping near what used to be Cottonwood Springs but which is now called Fort McPherson. 11 Co's of Cav-[alry] are camped here and are going down on the Republican* [river] in

---

*Named after a band of Pawnee.—Kansas Historical Society Kansapedia, other sources

the same direction we are going. [Illegible sentence, perhaps about trains needing the cavalry.] Pawnee Scouts came up today and are going down there too.

Monday, June 7th

Broke camp at 5 o'clock and took up our line of march down the Platte River. Nothing of interest happened on the route except that our feet got pretty sore. Went into camp at 1 o'clock and as we expect to leave the river tomorrow to be gone several weeks we will lay here till tomorrow morning. We all washed our clothes this P.M. As we are now in the Indian country we must keep a guard out at night. I go on from 12 M till 2 o'clock. So I'll turn in.

Tuesday, 8th

Had a very rough night of it. It commenced raining about 9 o'clock and continued several hours & a more terrific rain storm I never witnessed. The lightning was very vivid & the thunder deafening. Our tent was soon afloat and we had to pile up our blankets & stand up. Toward morning it abated somewhat and we got a little sleep. Broke camp at 6 o'clock. Marched south across a dead level to a range of bluffs across which we must go. We hitched three teams to one wagon and [with] all the men pulling on a long rope we managed to reach the top, two hundred feet above the river level. On reaching the top we beheld a sight which astonished us. The country seemed like a drift of snow blown by the wind. Deep cannons running through the bluffs seam & cut it up so that it is almost impassable. We tried to go around on the bluffs with the wagons but found that it could not be did. We can only get down by following down one of these cannons. So we will camp here tonight near a little pond of water as we expect to get none except what we take with us for several weeks. Water is a precious article out here.

Wednesday, 9th

Rained again last night but we have learned to be more careful and was prepared for it so we did not get wet. Broke camp at 5.30 and by taking the mules off the wagons and letting them over the bluffs by means of ropes we reached the valley below. We followed this up four miles and went into camp at noon, in a little valley running into the main one. It is a good location being protected from the wind on all sides & cannot be seen till one is nearly to it. We expect to stay here several days as we are now on our work. In the P.M. we went out on the lines, after helping Mr. Allison up the bluff which we did by hitching all our teams and men to his wagon. He leaves us here & strikes west. We will also work west with one line of Townships and then work back and that will take off the worst of our work. We walked to-day fifteen or eighteen miles besides our pulling and consequently all feel pretty tired tonight. Got lost coming into camp which made us more walking. Mr. Wiltse shot at three elk in a drove today with his revolver but missed. We are now 30 miles from any civilized town & 12 miles from water. If the Indians should surround us and keep us here a few days without water we would have pretty hard times. We have seen no traces of them yet but stand prepared for a fight at any time. I & several others carry a Carbine & revolver on the lines in addition to our other tools.

Thursday, 10th

As my feet are very sore & I feel generally used up I stay[ed] in camp today. We have fourteen men & but ten can work so that leaves one man in camp besides the two teamsters & the cook. The teamsters are now out looking for a pass to get to the river by as they must go for water tomorrow. The cook is boiling beans & Pork & I am writing. I would like to go to Willow Island as my mail will come there & I am expecting a Henry rifle from home. It would be a nice thing out here. Evening. The men came in at noon entirely tired not so much from fatigue as from thirst. Two were left on the way and I went out after them with a canteen of water. Found them under a tree and more grateful fellows I never saw.

Friday, 11th.

I went out on the lines today and as I did not feel very well to start with I gave out entirely before reaching camp. Stopped under a tree till a man could be sent from camp with some water. This made me feel like a new man & I came into camp all right. I would not work another day like this for fifty dollars.* Our work runs over high bluffs and down through deep canons and the lines must be run direct if it goes over a mountain. If the work was going to be as hard all the summer I would leave in two days. As it is I will stick to it till I get used to it or it uses me up.

We are encamped in a deep ravine about ten miles from the river, which is the nearest water we know of. The teams went to the river today and brought up a supply of water which will last three days. If the Indians were to surround us here & cut us off from the river our only show would be to try and cut through them. We have not seen any signs of them yet but are very watchful. Keep a guard over the camp every night and all sleep on our arms.

---

*About $1,110 in 2022

(12th) Saturday.

Didn't feel very well this morning and stayed in camp, or rather did not go onto the lines for we broke camp at sunrise and moved three miles west into another township. Hoisted a flag that the others might see us & put up the tents &c. The men came in at noon. One party had found water about three miles south of camp & were feeling jolly. The other party missed their count in chaining and will have to go over their work again tomorrow, which is rough as the rest of us will stay in camp it being Sunday. Just as dinner was ready the cook spied an antelope & we started after it. I could not get nearer than a hundred yards so I fired. Made a good shot but struck it in the fore shoulder. It dropped like dead & I felt mighty big but it got away after all. The cook killed a young one and an hour or two after one of the boys brought in another. As we have had nothing but pork since leaving Omaha it will go very nice. One of the boys went to Willow Island and we all wrote letters to send home. I hope I will get a letter on his return but hardly dare expect one as I only wrote home last Sunday telling them where to direct.

5 Sunday, 13th. 10 o'clock A.M. [Numbers before the date indicate miles walked that day.]

Have had breakfast, washed, combed & fixed up as well as we can afford and am now sitting in our old tent which the wind is shaking around terribly. Writing a few lines in my little diary that in after years I may look back & see how I felt & what I was doing on this Sunday on the plains. Though am far from civilization & with nothing to do but think & write there is no card playing or anything else going on that is not seen every Sunday in town. The men are all so tired that they are willing to lay aside all else & devote their whole time to resting. I would like to go to church today & to have a home paper to read but those are luxuries denied us wanderers.

We are all going out to the ponds near here to take a good swim after dinner and will then probably go to sleep. Our young antelope was splendid. Never ate any kind of meat which tasted half so good. I expect we will not lack for game from this [day] on.

Evening   I was elected to go off with the team after some timber to make stakes of. Saw a drove of antelope. Was unable to get a shot. Did not get my swim. Tom* who went after the mail has not returned yet and we

---

*This may be the Tom [Ratchford?] mentioned on July 11. The only names in Wiltse's field notes are George T. Kendall and Albert G. Kendall, chainmen; W. A. Richards and C. P. Moore, axemen & moundmen.[5]

are feeling a little uneasy about him as he will have to cross the Platte twice and it is very high. It may be that he is on a little spree and will turn up tomorrow.

Monday, June 14th
15 Did not have a very hard day's work. Walked fifteen miles. Tom did not come today. Something has surely happened to him or he would have been here before this. He is a very plucky fellow and it is hardly to be supposed that he is drowned or has been killed by the Indians. The belief is that he has vamosed. Moved camp two miles west.

Tuesday, 15th
25 Had the hardest day's work today I have ever done. We left camp at 5 o'clock in the morning and did not get in until 6 in the evening. Had nothing to eat and not much water in the afternoon. I was about played out when I reached camp and ate the largest meal I ever did. Bean soup must suffer when us fellows come in hungry. No mail when we came to camp. But after I had gone to bed I heard some one shout Hurrah for Tom. We were out of bed in a twinkly. He swam the river at Willow Island but came near getting drowned. Was carried down stream two miles. After getting the mail he went up above Brady Island to cross the river and yesterday traveled over fifty miles. Swam the river with the letters tied on his head. I got a letter from Lon and one from Ella. Also a bundle of papers from Lon. Such a jolly crowd of fellows is seldom seen as we were when we had got our mail.

Wednesday, 16th
15 Got into camp at 2 o'c. Ate dinner and lay down & read the papers. Something we can't do every day. Washed up my clothes & myself as we may not be near water soon again.

Thursday, 17th
15 Rained very hard last night. I sure did not sleep very good. Got a little wet and felt pretty stiff this morning. Made our regular days work though. Surveyed six sections and walked fifteen miles. Found no water in any quantity on the road and came into camp a 2 o'clock pretty dry. Ate our dinner of bean soup with a good relish.

Friday, 18th
20 Went south from camp this morning three miles & west two miles and started from the township corner & ran north six miles over a very rough country. Came back three miles and got into camp at three o'clock. Walked nineteen miles before dinner. After walked about six miles more

after an elk but could not get him though we got close to him. Ran our line through a village of prairie dogs who seemed very much surprised to see their village surveyed. Came across an elk horn five feet long with seven prongs from twelve to fifteen inches in length. It must have been an enormous animal to carry such horns.

Carried my carbine today which I have not done for several days but the Indians are getting so near that we think it best to be very careful.

Saturday, 19th 1869
15 Had a hard days work. Ran through canons and over bluffs. Besides one of our chainmen gave out and four of us did the work of five. Got into camp at 2 o'clock. An elk came right up to camp after dinner and one of the men who thought himself a crack shot went out after him, fired three times and missed each time. Walked fifteen miles and very long ones too being over the bluffs. Got up at daylight this morning and wrote a letter to Uncle Hank and one to Dodds before breakfast. Am going to send them in to the Fort by one of the men who is going to leave tomorrow on account of a fuss with Mr. Wiltse.

Sunday, 20th
Resting today with a vengeance. Blessings on the man who invented Sunday. Truly it is the poor man's day. Had rice for dinner instead of beans. Don't like the change. Mailed a letter to Auttie and wrote one to Lon but did not get it done in time to send up by our deserter. We will all feel like working tomorrow much more than if we had worked today. If we had found no water to camp on would have been compelled to work. The country here is terribly rough and hard to travel over. I will be glad when we get onto the level once more.

Monday, 21st 1869
4 As one of our chainmen was sick I went with the chain. We ran ten and a half miles with the chain and walked fourteen miles from the time we left camp till we came in. Ate a big dinner of bean soup. Saw seven elk on a bluff near and went out with my rifle to get a shot but another fellow came up and spoiled the whole business. They were a fine looking drove. As I must go on guard after twelve o'clock I'll turn in.

Tuesday, 22nd 3 o'c
14 Have finished our days work, had our dinner, pitched our tent and now we lie in the shade enjoying ourselves. Had an easy day. But the teams did not get up till after we were through, consequently had to wait for dinner. We have crossed no water in two days and expect we will have

to haul water for a few days. We were very fortunate in coming south of the Platte first, as if we had waited till mid-summer we would have been out of water all the time. Now we are working toward the river and hope in a few days to be on the level. Finished up another township today making the fourth one we have worked twenty four miles west. Mr. Wiltse gets five dollars a mile or three hundred and sixty dollars* a township, so he is making a good thing of it. He is going to run the township lines of a town on the west of us tomorrow for which he gets six dollars per mile.

Wednesday, 23rd
10 Have finished our days labor and now at three o'clock are [laying or lazing] off in the shade. Five men and Mr. Wiltse left camp at sunrise to run a township line six miles west then six miles south then they will come back on the line six miles to the corner where one man will be left with the provisions. Each man carried a blanket as they will have to lay out. The running will not be very hard but it comes hard to walk six miles af[ter] running a line twelve. I was left out of the detail as my foot was sore but I did not ask it and was ready to go. We moved the camp five miles & ran three miles of line over a very rough country & then postponed the rest till tomorrow.

Would give a V [a V-like symbol; $5?] for a newspaper, expect one when the team goes to Cottonwood which will be in a day or two. Our line crossed a road yesterday and one would hardly think we could be so interested in a naked road but it was a sign of civilization and anything that looks human is very acceptable to us. I think the road runs from Cottonwood to the Republican. We heard the evening gun from McPherson last night so we can not be more than twelve miles from there, as it is but a six pounder.

Wednesday 24th Thursday
10 Had a hard run today. Left camp at 5 o'clock, ran ten miles of line and got into camp on the north side of the township. The party that went out west yesterday came in this P.M. pretty well tired out. Didn't sleep any while out on acct of the mosquitos. Found water on the route.

Friday, 25th
8 Raining today by spells, so agreed to keep it for a Sunday and work on that day. Have a good time lying around generally, playing cards, checkers &c. Went out this P.M. and connected the line which we ran yesterday.

---

*In 2022 dollars, $360 equaled about $8,000 and $5 about $111

The teams came in at 5 o'clock. Brought me two letters from Lon written on the twelfth and twentieth. He is likely to be appointed City Clerk of Galena & will give me a job when I am through here. Sent me an application in the International Life Insurance Co. but I can't get the Surgeon's Certificate filled. The teams brought a supply of beans & sugar, which we need very much. They paid $5.70 for the beans. Turned in at sundown.

Saturday, 7 o'clock
26 Have had the hardest run today we have yet made. Walked six miles to our S. W. corner, ran six miles N. over a very rough country then three miles east when we met the other party who had traveled only 9 miles while we had gone 16. We were then ten miles from camp which we reached at 6 o'clock. Ate a very big supper of bean soup &c.

Several men have been to camp today. Wood choppers working the canons near here. The papers report a fight on the Republican, but of no moment. They also report that Spotted Tail has left his reservation with two hundred lodges & is coming south with what intentions it is not known. The team has gone to the Fort again to cross to Brady Island and get some shoes & other articles which we need. As it is near sundown I'll turn in.

Sunday, July [sic] 27th [June 1869]
12 For the first time in my life I have done a day's work on Sunday and I don't like the operation. I felt about as near used up today as I have for two weeks, partly on account of such a hard day yesterday and partly because the country was very rough. We traveled twelve miles and got into camp at 3 o'clock. Have spent the remainder of the afternoon reading the newspapers as one of the men has some from home. Am in hopes that the team, which we are expecting every minute, will bring me some papers & maybe a letter. I suppose the home folks are quietly eating their supper about this time. I would like to be there until morning but would want to be back here in time to work tomorrow as I am bound to go through with this job if possible.

Monday, 28th
14 Made our usual run today. Nothing out of the usual routine except that we saw a couple of deer. They were close to us and the old buck's horns were just in the velvet. Got into camp at 1 o'clock, had an easier run than usual as our boss played out the first time since we have been out. It is nearly dark and neither of our teams are here. One has not returned from Cottonwood and the other has gone to the river for water. We would be in a bad fix if they did not come tonight. We are on top of a hill ten miles

from water and not a gallon of water and no tents. We have confidence though that they will come in all right. Found the remains of an old camp near here today with two broken wagons & things looking as though the Indians had broken it up.

Sundown. The teams came in together and all right. Brought us a supply of shoes and stockings & some additional provisions & a stock of water for three days. I had the good fortune to get three letters, one from Lida, one from Cos. Dora and one from Rogers. I will have to drop some of my numerous correspondents as it is too much trouble to write letters in camp. I don't care much for letters from anywhere but home now either.

The Indians charged into North Platte about twenty miles from here one day last week and fired several shots. Gave the people a good scare, but no one was hurt. We are a little too far east for them. Allison's party was attacked about twenty miles from here a few days ago but came off victorious and no one hurt. Thirty Indians came on them very suddenly at nine o'clock in the morning but were routed. It may be that we'll get a dash from them yet but I hope they'll come when we are ready for them. If they do we will give them a good reception.

Tuesday, 29th
13 Nothing new today. Had a green hand on the lines which made us out a little longer. Made our usual run and had dinner. I wrote a letter to Mother & will now wind up my day's business by eating a lunch & going to bed.

Wednesday, 30th
10 Warm & clear. Got into camp at twelve o'clock. Wrote a letter to Lida. All serene.

Thursday, July 1st
Today ushers in another month. How varied and numerous will be the changes which will occur before its close. Nations may rise & fall. Empires be built up & kingdoms torn down, & we away out on the Plains of Nebraska know nothing of it. We too may some or all of us lose our scalps but that is a subject upon which we think little & say less. The reality will be bad enough if it ever comes without our imagining the performance every day. Some of the party seem to live in mortal terror but I can say that I seldom think of Indians especially when in camp. Often when going into a deep canon covered with small trees & underbrush & a half mile away from any of the party I keep my hand on my revolver and a sharp look out ahead. I expect I would be scared out of my wits if they ever attacked me, but I know my instinct would make me shoot & probably my fear would

make me run. We haven't seen a fresh trail since we came out & have nothing to scare us very bad. Done our usual amount of work & got into camp at noon.

Friday, July 2nd
20   Ran north today saw the river & a train of cars which was truly refreshing. Camped at twelve o'clock. The teams & some of the boys have gone to the river for water. I preferred remaining in camp and resting. Had a little spat with the boss this morning but he was wrong & knew it and apologized when he got cooled off a little. Wrote to Jake.

Saturday, July 3rd
20 Left camp at the usual time & ran a line five miles east across the worst bluffs we have had yet. Closed* on the bluffs where we went in four weeks ago. It's a hard looking place. We might have gone up a canon if we had only looked around a little but instead climbed over the highest cliff in sight. Our camp had been moved on to the river & when we got to the bottom we could not see half a mile for the smoke which had made it bad sighting all day. Wandered around looking for the trail, till we traveled ten miles at least. Struck it at last though & have now had dinner, done my washing, had a good swim and feel much refreshed. This is the first living water we have seen for four weeks, the longest I ever was away from a stream and the old river looks mighty good <u>sure</u>. It is very high too, so high that we can not get across to get our mail or anything to celebrate with. I guess our 4th will go off rather dull. It's some fun to lie still & have plenty of water. I wounded a buck antelope this P.M. with my revolver. Made a long shot but could not get him.

Sunday, July 4th
   The sun is almost set and the ninety third anniversary of the declaration of Independence is almost passed. We thought we could celebrate on Sunday as well as any other. Have done nothing outside our usual manner of spending Sunday. It is a great treat though to be near so much water and we have made good use of it. I think the Platte river water is the best I ever drank & it should be coming from the mountains & mountain streams & running over a sandy bottom. It is not navigable so that all it is good for is water to drink. I suppose Father & Auttie are both at home today & having a good visit. Well, I'll get around there by Christmas & take a chat with them too. Tomorrow will be the day they celebrate &

---

*This means that the survey line he was running met a previously surveyed line at the expected location.[6]

while they are having a good time I'll be roaming over these Nebraska prairies, earning my bread by the sweat of my brow, but I would not give up the job for I am bound to go through with it. Amused myself this P.M. mending my pants & reading the Bible and they go first rate together. No sacrilege in that, I hope.

Monday, 5th 5 o'clock

19 Another days work finished. Have traveled twenty eight miles today had the team to carry us nine of it. Weather smoky but clearing up a little. Are still camped on the river. I suppose the home folks are having a high time today. I hope they'll enjoy themselves. I spent a very pleasant day. Yesterday was tired enough to rest well.

Tuesday, 6th

15 Ran about fifteen miles today. Had a terrific storm of rain, hail & thunder this P.M. The largest hail stones I ever saw. On the road near our camp stands an old deserted ranche or Dobie which is a house built of sods. Near it is a solitary grave surrounded by a neat white paling. The ranche was formerly kept by one Dan Smith, a notorious character, and the grave is that of his wife whom he shot. He was afterward hung in Cheyenne by a Vigilance Committee.

Wednesday, 7th

15 Walked fifteen miles. Rainy this morning clear & pleasant this P.M. Can see the trains on the other side of the river on the U.P. Reminds one strongly of home. Wrote to Lon.

Thursday, 8th

18 Weather fair and mosquitos thick. Are camped on the river twelve miles from Cottonwood. The teams are going up tomorrow & will get our mail and some provisions. Have a good bath in the river every day.

Friday, July 9th

18 The warmest day of the season. Thermometer stood 95° above zero in the shade at Cottonwood. Walked twenty miles part of the way in the bluffs where not a breath of air is stirring. The wind on the bottom is very hot. Much like the si-moon of Asia. It is a wind peculiar to the state and where it comes from no one knows. We started on three pints of water each & I gave part of mine to some of the other boys, consequently I was nearly famished when I reached camp. The teams came in at sundown & then there was joy in camp. I got six letters, three from home, one from Schaeffer, one from [illegible] & one from the dead letter office with a paper. I read my letters & went to bed but not to sleep for the mosquitos

vetoed that recreation. We tried every experiment & finally gave up in despair & agreed to grin & bear it. It is hard to work like we do & not sleep much. I hope the wind won't blow tomorrow as a still day is preferable to the wind.

Saturday, July 10th
18 Nothing out of the regular routine today. Except that we shot a couple of nice fat coons on the line this morning but couldn't afford to carry them fifteen miles & had to leave them. Also saw another surveying party going west to be [fooled?] on this miserable country. Walked eighteen miles & got into camp at 2 o'clock. After disposing of our bean soup & taking a nap, went down to have a bath but the mosquitos drove me out. I washed a couple of shirts & [illegible]. Weather not so warm. Mailed letters yesterday to Mother, Lon, Skinner, Lida. This makes twenty four days I have worked without losing a day & excepting Sunday & I have walked in that time three hundred & seventy-five miles.

Sunday, July 11th 4 o'clock P.M.
8 Have been enjoying myself today resting myself. Had a corn meal pudding for dinner which is the first delicacy we have had since we have been on the trip. It was mighty good, surely, and still at home I would not consider it so fine. On acct of a misunderstanding yesterday we were obliged to go out and run a few miles of line this P.M. Although it was not my fault I went as five of the boys crossed the river this morning to Brady Island Station where our provisions are stored & have not yet returned. Weather fine. Slept well last night by having a smoke on all sides of us. Sundown. We have had a sad accident happen [to one of] our boys who crossed the river. In crossing the North Platte one of them, Thomas [Ratchford?] lost his confidence in himself & was carried down by the current & drowned. He was a young man and one would have thought him the most able in the party to cross the river. He crossed it four weeks ago with two large revolvers in his belt & his clothes on with the river much higher than at present. He was very loth to go this morning & some of us tried to persuade him to stay in camp but he started & crossed the S. Platte and when they came to the N. Branch at the same place we crossed coming up, he hesitated and waited till three of the others had crossed. The one who stayed on this side urged him to stay with him but he said "I will cross it swim or drown." They were his last words. He plunged in & in three minutes sank. The current is very strong & it will be difficult to recover his body. A young man was drowned here last Sunday & his body found several miles below. Tom's death has cast a general gloom over the party. He

was a genial companion & ever ready to do his share or a little more at anything in the line of duty. He was from [Penn.?] & we hired him near Willow Island. Peace to his ashes.

Monday, 12th

Contrary to the expectations of nearly all the boys we went to work as usual this morning. After Wiltse saying last night that he would do all he could toward recovering Tom's body & that he did not want to act like a heathen. He let <u>one man</u>, a great friend of Tom's, go off this morning afoot & alone & without money to go up the river [ten?] miles, cross & come down on the other side & get some of the citizens at the Station to help him search the river. It is very comforting to us here to think that if we were to meet a like fate we would be left to feed the fishes or be recovered by strangers. The fidelity of the boys to their boss has been considerably damaged by this affair.

It looks like the Almighty dollar was all he cared for & I think that is just the state of the case. Sometime he may be in a tight place & then I fear he may find that he has damaged himself more than he thinks in the eyes of his men.

We walked eighteen miles today and ran twelve miles of line (a big days work on level ground) through the worst kind of bluffs. Went from six A.M. until 4 P.M. without eating and working all the time. If we don't get tough out here it won't be the fault of the boss. Weather very hot. Had a heavy rain last night which left water standing in little pools on the dells.

Mailed a letter to Lon yesterday on biz.

Thursday, July 13th

Had a very hot sun today & the Buffalo gnats were very bad. I never saw anything to compare with the mosquitos that were on duty last night. We took the precaution of smoking & whipping them out of the tent before turning in & stretching a mosquito bar across the mouth & when we lay down & could hear them outside like a swarm of bees and all quiet within, we thought we would have a good nights rest. I dreamed that I had been captured by Indians, tied to a tree and they were dancing around me and every time one went around he'd flip a porcupine quill into me, generally in some tender spot. Finally they charged simultaneously & I awoke to find the tent filled with our American Platte river Cousins & every one as he passed was spiking into me. Then there was hurrying to and fro. We built a fire inside the tent although it was a very warm night and as it was almost impossible to breathe for them outside there we sat and sweat & swore vengeance. Again I resigned myself to nature's sweet restorer balmy sleep and again after a horrible dream awoke to find myself lying [in] about three inches of water. A sudden rain had flooded our tent & now sleep was out of the question. Another kind of swearing was now indulged in somewhat resembling the Episcopal litany and we passed the remainder [illegible] standing up. From my experience so far I have drawn the following conclusion to wit that this part of Nebraska is chiefly to raising cactus, sage brush, mosquitos and Buffalo gnats, all & each of which seem to thrive & enjoy good health. We are now within four miles of the garrison & can hear the band. Can get our mail every day for a little while. The team went up today & for the first time on the trip failed to bring me a letter. Feel somewhat disappointed but was well favored the last time.

Wednesday, 14th

Have had an easy time today lying around camp. The most of the party crossed the river this morning to Brady Island to hunt for a line, but as I can't swim & some one must stay behind I was the lucky one. The others had a hard day of it. Heat intense and mosquitos numerous. They were also bad last night, rained too, the third night it has routed us. Am getting used to it and think I can sleep outside tonight though the prospect is good for rain again. Got a bundle of papers today. The second I have rec'd. They are very acceptable in this country.

Thursday, 15th

We ran the township line on the northwest corner of our work & though we ran but six miles & had the team to take us to & from the line it was a hard day. Ground the roughest we have had yet. Was at the Fort. The boys were paid yesterday & [illegible] having high times. Rained again last night and between that & the Ms. I didn't sleep an hour. Oh the beauties of Surveying & of the Platte Valley.

Gen Carr* had fight with the Indians on the Republican opposite Julesburg on the 11th inst. Killed fifty two and captured seventeen besides three hundred & fifty head of stock. It is rumored that he and Custer got together afterward & followed the trail & killed a hundred & fifty more.

Friday, 16th

Did not do a very large days work today. Closed on the reservation corner. The Govt. reserves a tract four miles square for the Fort. Rained again last night and I found myself lying in a half foot of water. Left the tent and spent the remainder of the night in a wagon. The man who went to search for Tom returned today. Found nothing of him. Brought us another man

---

*Major General Eugene A. Carr, captain of 1st U.S. Cavalry[7]

in his place. The teams crossed the river to get some more "chuck."

Saturday, 17th

Had a pretty hard time today as we had nothing for breakfast but fried mush,* bread & coffee without sugar. Wiltse gave out and I hoped he would have to lie down beside the road that I could have a chance to leave him as he did me the first week. The team returned bringing a supply of beans, meat, molasses, sugar & dried apples. I got a bundle of comic papers from Jake. A good thing to pass off time and raise a laugh. Rained again last night. This raining at night and being fair in the daytime is telling on us fellows. My legs feel like the rheumatism today.

Sunday, 18th

This seems the most like Sunday of any one since I left home. Nothing unusual. Rec'd a letter from Lon and three papers. All well at home. Mailed a letter to Mother.

Monday, 19th

Went out with one man & connected a line we ran last week. Reached camp at 3 P.M. Went to the Fort after supper and swore to a lot of notes Wiltse had taken of the work we have been over.

Tuesday, 20th

Have a large boil on my shin right on the bone which disables me from working. Stayed in camp. Slept nearly all day. The men are surveying Bradys Island & it's the worst job we have had & I expect the boss will pass some of his slurring remarks on my staying in camp. If he does & I hear of it he'll have one man less mighty sudden. Moved back to our old camping ground which we left last Friday. Weather very warm.

Wednesday, 21st

Stayed in camp today. Nothing new. Weather fair.

Thursday, 22nd

Finished our work on the south side the Platte yesterday & today moved to Brady Island via McPherson Post & Station. Weather fair. Ford good.

Friday, 23rd

Surveyed on Brady Island today. Forded the stream waist deep besides minor channels. Wet all day. Finished the Island. Came to camp pretty well used up. Mosquitos terrible.

---

*A thick porridge usually made of cornmeal

Saturday, 24th

Moved three miles east. No mosquitos. A fair prospect for a good nights rest.

Sunday, 25th

Rainy today. The first rain we have had in the daytime yet. It is reported the Indians attacked & burned the station house & Big Springs one hundred miles west of this. Killed seven men. Rather doubt the story. Weather hot.

Saturday, 31st

Reached Willow Island last night having been gone eight weeks. Found no mail but an express package containing Henry rifle &c. Have been confined to camp for the last week with boils and am laid up yet. Two more days will finish the work on this job.

Wrote today to Flora.

Tuesday, 3rd [August 1869]

Concluded today to go with the party to the Republican. I have been hesitating about it because of the uneasiness it will give the home folks, but the reports from there are favorable & it will be worth more than a hundred dollars to me. If I quit now it will take all my wages to get home with. We will be gone but six weeks when we will strike for Omaha.

Thursday, 5th

Left Willow Island for Ft. Kearney this morning. Passed Plum Creek at noon & made thirty miles.

Friday, 6th

Broke camp at 6 o'clock. Passed Elm Creek at noon. Reached Kearney Station at 6 o'clock. Made thirty miles today.

Saturday, 7th 7 o'clock. A.M.

Have had breakfast & in an hour or two will start across the River. The ford at this place is nearly five miles wide. On Monday we start for the Republican, and will not be inside civilization again for six weeks. Will write home today. Will leave our baggage here till we return.

Saturday, Aug 7th Eve.

Crossed the river this morning by putting four mules on a wagon and hiring a ranche man to take the other wagon over with oxen. The crossing is very bad, caused by quicksand. Got into camp at noon. In the afternoon had a pretty fair view of the eclipse which was almost total.

Sunday, Eighth of Aug.

Spent today in cleaning our arms, mending our clothes and getting ready for a start tomorrow. Reports here from the Republican are discouraging. Indians said to be bad &c but I have started and am going through.

Monday, Aug. 9th

Broke camp at sunrise and bidding farewell to civilization for a time. Struck out across the sand hills for the Kansas line which will be our starting point. Traveled over sand hills for four miles when we struck a high rolling prairie. But no water. Traveled twenty-eight miles and made a dry camp for which we were prepared. Saw a few stray buffalo but as we didn't understand hunting them didn't kill any.

Hempstead and the Rogers Brothers amused the camp with an exhibition of the manly art of self defence in earnest. I guess they'll get some of the fight taken out of them before we travel this road again.

Thursday, 10th

Broke camp at sunrise. Four of us being ahead came upon some buffalo. Had the good luck to kill an old bull too old to eat. I was just in at the death.

As we neared the river they became more plenty and about five o'clock we were compelled to halt to allow a herd to pass. We fired into them and killed two. A cow which I shot which we left untouched and a heifer which was fine eating. Was so much delayed that we made a dry camp within three miles of the river.

Wednesday, 11th

Broke camp at sunrise and started for the south side of the Republican. Crossed at 10 [illegible] Quicksand very bad. [Hunnison?] who is with us now came down here last summer to work [up?] this contract but was attacked by Indians and driven out of the Country. One man was killed. He was flaging on a mule when the Indians rode out of a clump of trees and surrounded him, killing & scalping him in plain view of the rest of the party who could render no assistance having no arms. The Indians then attacked the main party (only six) who made their way toward Fort Kearney which they reached in fifteen hours. Sixty miles. They lost everything. We visited his old camp today and found the remains of some things which they could not burn. Hunted for the bones of the poor fellow who was killed but could find nothing but his coat with seven ball holes through the back and one or two other little articles. The wolves had destroyed all other traces of him.

This is the best hunting ground in the west. Buffalo. Elk, antelope, deer and smaller game are abundant. Consequently the Indians will fight for it to the last. I anticipate trouble with them but I shall always be prepared if possible. [*sic*]

Thursday, 12

Moved camp two miles west, country very broken. Water in nearly every ravine. We are now one mile from the river and far from the Kansas line. There are three of us in camp Kendall, Glenn, Gay* and myself. We have plenty of arms and keep a sharp lookout all the time. One of the men, Good, had a little fuss with Wiltse yesterday and this morning after the others had gone out to work gathered his "traps" together and taking one of Wiltse's carbines was going away. We told him that we were left to guard camp and must do it & would do it against white men as well as Indians. He became exceedingly hostile and tried to scare us, talking of shooting &c but finding he couldn't get away with the gun he very quietly concluded to remain with us. Weather fine but rather warm.

Since writing the above the men have come in. Bad luck certainly attends us. Geo. Kendall in attempting to swim Prairie Dog creek which was swollen by recent rains, with the tripod, became confused and in trying to swim against the rapid current lost the instrument. After trying all day to get it have decided to start for Kearney tomorrow where Wiltse will take the cars [railroad] for Omaha and get a new tripod. He will have about seventy-five miles to go by land and then two hundred on the cars to procure an instrument worth twenty dollars.

Friday, 13

Started for Kearney at daylight. Wiltse, Moore & myself with Scott's team, a hundred rounds of ammunition apiece and a weeks rations. Have nothing to guide us but the trail we made coming down. Lost it at ten o'clock by giving our attention more to a herd of buffalo than to our business. Crossed Turkey Creek at noon and camped for dinner. Fortunately found a good crossing in an old buffalo trail. I secreted myself behind a big tree and waited for a herd of buffalo that were quietly grazing near to come down to drink. I had not long to wait when they came down with a rush and the creek was literally full of them in front above and below me. I was watching for a chance to shoot a fine fat calf but which kept dodging around among the others so that I had no chance for an aim, when a

---

*In 1871, a U.S. surveying contract was awarded to Richards and Joseph W. Gay, probably the same man. See p. 244 for map and particulars.

young bull urged by a thrust in the rear from a patriarch of the tribe rushed forward and through the underbrush almost touching me as he darted past. The others followed suit and I was compelled in self protection to open fire on the whole herd and thus I lost my calf. I killed a fat young male though at the first fire. The finest eating we have had this summer. About 5 o'clock we were overtaken by the heaviest storm of rain & wind it was ever my fortune to be exposed to. We have an open wagon and no means of shelter so we got the full benefit of it. The mules could make but little headway against it. We have been running since we lost the trail by a pocket compass which I chanced to have but during the storm we must have got some distance off our course. For two hours this afternoon we were followed by a body of some kind of troops which made a great dust. They kept in a large ravine and we on the divide. They were probably Indians as no kind of wild animals would have kept so close to us for so great a distance. Since the rain we have seen nothing of them. Should a very large body of them attack we would probably fare badly but with a small party we could hold our own pretty well.

Camped at sundown on open prairie with not a tree nor a shrub in sight. After eating our supper of buffalo steak, bread, and tea, we lay under the wagon and talked and watched the stars. It is a beautiful evening after the storm. This is the first rain we have had in the daytime since I have been on the plains, although we had frequent rains in the night. We divide the guard tonight between us. Wiltse standing first, Moore next and me the last shift.

Saturday, 14th

Was on our way at daylight and reached Fort Kearney, without anything of very great interest taking place. Crossed the river at noon. Although we ran fifty miles by a pocket compass we came to the river within half a mile of the Ft. Made camp near the Station. Bought some milk and had a splendid dinner of steak, bread & milk.

Sunday, 15th

Wiltse started for Omaha at 5 o'clock. Got telegram from Lon yesterday. Wants me to come home and work for him. Told Wiltse I thought of going but he said he couldn't get along without me. Offered me an advance on my wages so I concluded to stay. Wrote home to that effect. We amused ourselves by reading the papers and after dinner went down to the river, took a swim and hunted for moss agates. Found one with red moss, very fine. Shall have a set made of it.

Monday, 16th

Rec'd letters from Lon, Nettie and Henry Schaffer. Wrote several letters. Severe thunder storm. Every telegraph as far as we can see st[r]uck by lightning.

Tuesday, 17th

Wiltse got back at 10 o'clock. Brought a supply of potatoes, corn and onions sufficient for a few days. These were sent out by Mr. Hitchcock [Nebraska Senator Phineas W.[7]], and come very nice. We started immediately for camp. Made twenty five miles before dark and camped on the open prairie. In the whole tract of country between Kearney & Turkey Creek—nearly fifty miles—there is no water, and we carry water with us.

Wednesday, 18

Broke camp at daylight. Lost the trail soon after. Kept our course however by my pocket compass and st[r]uck Turkey creek at 12 M within a few rods of our former crossing. Reached camp at dark. Camp had been twice moved and we would have laid out again had not some of the boys come out several miles to meet us & pilot us in. It really seemed like getting back home to come in sight of our two old tents, the wagons & mules and the familiar old kettle of beans. And although we had been gone but a week we had a great many things to talk about. Our first subject however was supper as we had almost exhausted our supply of provisions and had not stopped to make a full meal since leaving Kearney. I think we were very fortunate in going seventy five miles through the worst Indian country on the plains and back without being attacked. I would not care to repeat the trip unless absolutely necessary. The other boys have been working hard since we left and all are anxious to finish.

Thursday, 19th

Had a big scare last night but of short duration. Bill Rogers who was sleeping out doors, as we say when he stands guard, probably dreamed of Indians or imagined he saw them. At any rate he fired his gun at he, she or it and alarmed the camp. It showed what the state of affairs would be in case of an attack. Of the thirteen men two were ready for the game. I happened to be one and Scott the other. We lay flat down and by looking against the sky could see two objects coming which we took to be ponies and we [were] just going to fire when we discovered that they were our dogs. The boys tried to laugh at us but I think we had the best of them as they were not ready to fire if they had been Indians.

Moved camp to the north side of the river. Although I selected the best place to cross I could find I got stuck with the first team when almost across. Came near losing the leaders in the quicksand. Carried the load out by hand and drew the wagon out by tying a long rope to the tongue and leaving the mules on shore. Crossed the other team safely. It is not the least pleasant working in the water to one's waist and sand over your ankles and not know how many noble red men may be watching you from the woods on either side [of] the stream. Owing to the delay we camped on the bank of the stream contrary to our practice and had barely got our tents pitched when a terrific storm of wind and rain came up which blew the old one off its legs in no time. By dint of hard work in the rain we kept the other up. Wiltse & party came in at three, hungry as wolves & wet through. [Hunnyson?] & party got lost in the storm and found camp by mere accident just before dark. Kendall & Scott on guard tonight. Rough on them as the rain still comes. The boys found the remains of an old Indian camp half a mile above us. Among other things found a ball about the size of a base ball but harder which we will send to the Smithsonian. The Indians have a game similar to the Irish game of [shiumy?] which they play and at which they show great activity and skill.

Friday, 20th
Moved camp two miles north & west a mile and camped on small stream. Weather cloudy.

Saturday, 21st
Weather foggy. Stayed in camp. Saw a huge old Buffalo on the prairie about a mile distant. Walked around till I got right behind him (he was lying down) and then walked up to within range and shot him. I don't [think] another species of animal on the plains would allow a hunter to fool them that way. The meat came very good as we had been without some for days.

Sunday, 22nd
Moved camp seven miles east. Camped on small stream inhabited by beavers. The men worked by their own wish. Killed three half grown Turkeys at four shots.

Monday, 23rd
Moved camp three miles east & camped on Turkey creek. Weather fine but very hot. Geo Kendall & I went east several miles & killed a fine fat cow. Carried some of the meat into camp on our backs using strings cut out of her hide and cooked the meat over a fire made of buffalo chips. That is living off the country, I guess.

Tuesday, 24th

Moved two miles east. Killed a buffalo.

Wednesday, 25

Moved two miles east. Seeing three buffalo near went out to get one. Succeeding in doing so after shooting him nineteen times and following him a mile. When on the top of a ridge coming to camp I [saw] six young bulls coming at the other side. Lying down I waited till they were within thirty yards of me when I opened fire. Brought one down at each of the two first shots and with the remaining thirteen shots I killed the other four, the last one falling about a half mile away. We are trying to fill a jar with tongues for Senator Hitchcock to pay him for his vegetables sent to us or we would not kill so many buffalo. Nothing is wasted however as the coyotes and buzzards clear away all but the bones in a very short time.

The boys have been wanting some meat to dry and will now have a good opportunity as the game is not more than half a mile from camp.

Thursday, 26th

Moved north to Town line & east one mile. Camped on Turkey creek. Weather fair but very hot.

Friday, 27th

Moved three miles north. Camped a mile from a small stream, preferring to haul wood & water to having our American cousins continually drawing on us. Just as Gay and I were starting down to the creek an old bull came over the hill & stood very calmly looking at us. Being within easy range I gave him a settler from the wagon and he retired a short distance over the hill and then retired from active life or any other kind. Upon a careful examination I came to the conclusion that he had determined upon leaving the cares and sorrows of this world and had come into our camp for the purpose of the necessary medicine with which to commit suicide, for I never saw so poor a specimen of four footed nature in my travels in the west, and I think his equal can not be found except in some Chicago butcher shop. [All underscores are writer's.] We left him to the wolves & crows and I don't think they will get fat out of his carcass.

Upon going to the stream for water we were obliged to follow it some distance before finding any and it was standing in a pond, the main stream being dry.

Saturday, 28th

Moved camp west four miles to Town line. Killed a fine young bull. No relation to the old chap I shot yesterday. Dried a little of the meat. The men are now doing a township in two days, which is very fast working. But as the season advances the Indians will come in here to hunt and trap and we will have to vamoose and we want to finish the contract.

Sunday, 29th

Did not move camp today nor did the men work. This will be the last resting day we will have before reaching Omaha unless the red men corral us where we can't get out. Just as we were eating breakfast this morning an old Bull came across the stream and up within a few hundred yards of camp and took a quiet survey of the whole arrangement. We thought we would fire a salute in his honor so we formed in line and at the word all fired together. He seemed much surprised but very little hurt. After crossing the stream again I tried him at four hundred yards with my rifle & struck him fair. But the wound was not mortal, as he ran off with his [word missing] up as though he had not been the observed of all observers & the target for our eyes & guns for five minutes.

Monday, 30th

Moved camp four miles west. Hauled wood & water from last camp & made a dry camp. Weather cool & pleasant.

Tuesday, 31st

Moved camp two miles west. Cloudy and cool.

Wednesday, Sept. 1st

Moved three miles west. Made dry camp. Weather fine.

Thursday, 2nd

Moved one mile west, took dinner there. Moved six miles north and two west. While going North the men saw what they supposed to be an elk and waited till I came up with them to go after it. It proved to be a fine claybank mare with an Indian lariat on. Was not able to approach near enough to catch her. Stood guard last night and killed a young bull before breakfast. Heavy rain last night. Saw fresh signs of Indians today. Camps & ashes and plenty of tracks.

We are now in the north tier of Townships and have five more to do. Only ten days work—and Good Bye Republican.

Friday, 3rd

Moved camp west three miles and camped on small streams with perpendicular banks from ten to twenty feet high. Gay and I spent the afternoon in hunting for a ford. Found a place a mile up stream which will answer with a few hours shoveling.

Saturday, 4th

Another heavy rain last night. And our small stream is this morning a roaring torrent. The banks are full and in many places overflown. It would be an utter impossibility to cross with our teams at its present stage. The men felled a tree across the narrowest point we could find and by wading a little got across, did a days work and walked back to camp. A large grey wolf came down to the creek and took possession of a small patch of brush where he made a business of howling for a couple of hours. They certainly make the most dismal noise of any living animal.

Sunday, 5th

There is only two days work west of the creek, which is still impassable, and the men went over to do [illegible] this morning taking their blankets with them. Glenn and I transformed ourselves into packmules and acted the part of supply train. Carried two days rations for the men on our backs five miles, also a kettle full of water with which we made the men some soup. Waited until they came in when started back to camp where Gay had been left alone. Saw him pacing in front of the tents evidently anxious for our return long before we reached camp. Although a heavy wind was blowing which had capsized one of our tents we built a fire in the old stove, put it in the tent and made a good supper of fried mush and molasses. Nothing like a good appetite to make a fellow contented with short rations. We had the first frost of the season last night. We divide the guard between us tonight as there are but three of us.

Monday, 6th

It was with difficulty we could keep warm last night, even in the tent. The dogs seemed to feel the absence of the men and were very uneasy. The men came in about noon and after dinner we moved three miles east. Before breaking camp had a chance at some antelope running past camp. Knocked two down but both escaped. They are very tenacious of life and unless struck in some spot which causes instant death they will run till they drop dead.

Tuesday, 7th

As Jack left his coat at old camp I chained in his place while he went back after it. The horse I saw last week came around and Glenn & Gay succeeded in catching it. She is quite gentle but has evidently broken away from the Indians in some fight as they could have followed her had she only strayed.

When I reached camp the boys told me they had seen three buffalo about half a mile up the ravine. Although tired and hungry I took my old rifle and went for them. Found them lying down but could not get nearer than three hundred yards. Succeeded in getting two of them. The men came out with a team after dinner and took in the hind quarters. The boys are drying some of the meat to take home. Weather very fine.

Wednesday, 8th

Moved four miles east over a very rough country. The men saw Indians three miles north of us. Quite a large party. Three more days we'll [or will] finish this job and if nothing unknown occurs next Sunday we will dine at Fort Kearney. Kendall and I each killed an old bull this morning. Took only the scalp. Our boys had just seen the Indians when we opened fire on the buffalo and when they heard the rapid firing they mounted their ponies and struck down a canon at full speed doubtless thinking a large party of soldiers were near. Weather beautiful. Stood guard last night.

Thursday, 9th

Moved camp three miles east across Turkey Creek. Found a good crossing. At the crossing came upon two buffalo. Killed them both before they could get out of range. One was inclined to fight but was too slow entirely.

Friday, 10th

Moved camp three miles east & struck level plain. For the last month we have been in a very badly broken country, sometimes having to travel miles to get around a canon which we could not cross but from here to the Platte we [word(s) missing] nothing worse than a few low sand hills. Killed a bull who fell exactly at a section corner. After dinner went back to Turkey creek & got a supply of water to last us to the river. That sounds like we [were almost?] through.

Saturday, 11th

Moved camp three miles east & camped for dinner. Wiltse's party came in at eleven o'clock and Geo. Kendall and I went out to have a last shot at the buffalo. Came upon a herd lying down about three miles from camp. Killed one and wounded another at the first fire or before they had time to get out of range. We then started after the other one which had one of his hind legs broken. He could keep ahead of us though and we could only get a shot occasionally at long range. At last he laid down after leading us a chase of more than a mile, but after he was down we could not get near enough to finish him with a knife and we did not care to waste any more ammunition on him as we were now some distance from camp & might need it all before getting back. Finally we [came?] a little strategy on him. George came up as near as he dared in front and while the old fellow was trying his utmost to reach him with his horns I came on the blind side and finished him with a stroke of my knife. I took his scalp as a trophy. He was the largest one I ever saw and I think his weight was not less than a ton. He was struck by twenty six balls from rifle and revolver before he fell, several in the immediate vicinity of the heart. When we came in sight of camp the men were on the march for Kearney, running the last line as they went along. The wagons were loaded and they were only awaiting our return to start also.

We were pretty well used up with running and going without our dinners when we reached the teams but a cup of tea and another of bean soup made that all right. We went twelve miles north after dinner and made our last camp south of the Platte on a high and level prairie with not a tree or shrub as far as the eye could reach, a heavy wind from the S. E. which threatened to capsize our tents while raising them. It being our Canadian friends turn for guard duty and they shamming illness to avoid it we slept without a guard for the first night on the trip.

Sunday, 12th

At daylight started for the river. Reached the Fort without anything worthy of note taking place at 10 A.M. Stopped a[t] [Dobey?] Town, bought some milk & had it & mush for dinner. Gay & Glenn sold their pony for eighty dollars, a big price for an Indian pony.

Commenced raining at Noon. After dinner went down to the ford supposing we could find wood but not finding much it was put to vote whether we should cross or camp there and all except one voted to cross. That one was Gay & he "vowed" he had gone as far on Sunday as he was [going to] and declared he would not drive the team across. Wiltse told him he could do as he d—-d please and might go to the d—-l for all he cared & I started in with my [word(s) missing]. The crossing at this point is fully [two?] miles wide including the sand bars which divide the channels. Gay and I were the only ones who rode, the boys tying their clothes on their backs and plodding through. It was raining hard and very cold and altogether quite "onpleasant." At one point I had forgotten just where the channel ran and got a little too low down and into deep water. I called to Gay who was behind to keep further up the stream but he misunderstood me and tried to cross below (not using his judgment at all which would have shown which way to go) and the first he knew his team was swimming and his wagon going down stream. They soon touched bottom and jumped off into water up to his armpits and of course could do nothing toward driving and old "Jinnie" true to her nature (very lazy) laid down. As soon as I struck a sand bar I went back to help start his team along and a hard time we had to get a wagon and two tired mules out of quicksand which would imprison a man so fast that he never could release himself. Gay was completely overcome and not worth anything. We finally reached the shore having been in the water an hour & a half with the rain pouring down. We were now two miles from the Station for which place we immediately started with J. W. using Presbyterian cuss words all the way and wish-[ing] we had stayed on the other side. Upon reaching the station Wiltse got permission from a store keeper to cook supper on his big stove & we were soon sitting around a roaring fire. Those who had a change of clothing put on dry ones and those who did not stood up before the fire till they were dry. We soon had supper of bread & molasses, cold ham and coffee and spreading our blankets in an empty box car on the U.P.R.R. we retired thanking our lucky stars that we had such good protection from the rain which was still coming down with unabated fury, accompanied by wind which almost overturned our bedroom.

Monday, 13th

Still raining hard. Wrote to Pa and Lon who were doubtless surprised to hear from me as I told them I would be gone on the Republican about two weeks longer than we expected to be out, that they would not be uneasy. Heard that Secretary Rawlins and Senator Fessenden were dead.* All the world might have died and we not known of it. Heard also that [Douglontry?] of Dubuque had a fight near Julesburg with a hundred and seventy five Indians. Held them all day with ten men and five guns and escaped under cover of the night losing all his supplies, mules and compass however.

Retired at dark to our sleeping apartments.

Tuesday, 14

Not rainy though cloudy. We were very fortunate in getting into such good quarters while enjoying the equinoctial. Scott took his team and started for Omaha. Taking the Rogers boys, George, Tom & Charlie. The latter two have been drunk ever since we reached the Station. Our party consisting of Wiltse, Glenn & George Kendall, Hempstead, Moore, Gay

---

*Gen. John A. Rawlins and W. P. Fessenden of Maine

and myself started for Willow Island. Camped at Elm Creek twenty miles from Kearney. Feel greatly relieved to get the mean men out of the party but pity Scott on his trip down the road. At the Section house where we took dinner the lady sent us out a loaf of light bread and some butter, the first we have had on the trip.

Wednesday, 15

Broke camp at daylight. Took dinner at Plum creek. The country we have passed over this morning is the worst for Indians on the line of the R.R. Several attacks have been made on section hands and two trains have been thrown from the track and burned between here and Elm Creek. Their trail to the South runs through the same country and large parties often pass. We were very fortunate in escaping without an attack but I would like to try my Henry on them once.

Made thirty miles today and camped ten miles from Willow Island. Weather fair.

Thursday, 16th

Reached Willow Island at 10 A.M. Did not find supplies as we had expected. Borrowed some flour, loaded up and started for our work which is six miles north of the Station. Have two Townships to run and then we will strike for home.

Friday, 17th

Was ready for a start at day light and made a big days work. Ran two tiers of Sections making 17-1/2 miles of chaining and 27 miles walk. The largest day's work ever made on the plains to the knowledge of Wiltse who worked in the Surveyor General's Office and says he knows.

Geo. Kendall & I chain, Moore and Hempstead mound* and Gay & Glenn Kendall stay in camp, of course Wiltse runs the compass.

Saturday, 18th

Ran the same amount of line as yesterday. Weather fine but a very heavy wind blowing.

Sunday, 19th

Laid in camp today mending my clothes, washing a little &c. The team went to the Station and got our supplies shipped from Omaha. We now

---

*Placing mounds of stone (when available) around the cornerstone or corner post where practical, for support and additional witness. Richards was hired as a mound-man and axeman, according to Wiltse's field notes.[5] More about the history and problems of mound building is on p. 258.

have potatoes and we'll have them all the way home. Weather fine.

Monday, 20th

Ran a double tier to Northern boundary and finished the Township. We made the fastest chaining yet done and got into camp at two P.M. We are now doing in one day what formerly took two to do but everything is favorable[:] level country, cool weather, and we occasionally find ponds of water which we never did on the South part of the contract.

Tuesday, 21st

Ran two tiers today. Weather fine.

Wednesday, 22nd

Ran two tiers today and struck the sand hills on the North and West. Tomorrow however we'll finish the job and we will do it if it was through mountains instead of sandhills. Glenn killed a very large buck antelope and carried him two miles on his back. Quite a feat for a slim boy.

Thursday, 23rd

Was at work by daylight. Ran a double tier of sections through sand hills for three miles, the rest on level plain and stuck our last pin before Eleven A.M. The idea that we were on the last day enabled us to fairly o[u]tstrip ourselves. After putting in our last stake and firing a parting volley over it from our revolvers we took a bee line for camp distant seven miles. We had a regular walking race on the way and the chainmen kept up their reputation for pedestrian[ism?]. We did ample justice to a fine venison stew and then started for Willow Island. Found a letter from Lon mailed the 20th. Five years ago & it would have been a month coming here instead of two days. Also received a letter from Auttie. This is the first word I have received from home for six weeks.

Friday, 24th

Broke camp at daylight and bade adieu to Willow Island and our friends the Agent and telegraph operators, who have treated us with marked kindness all Summer.

Took dinner at Plum Creek Station. The coal depot here burned yesterday from a spark thrown out by an engine. Loss heavy.

Camped for night at two section houses yesterday between Plum & Elm creeks built for mutual protection as this is such a bad Indian country. At all the section houses, which are generally six miles apart, a guard is stationed every night. So when we can camp near them we need no guard of our own. Passed a very large herd of Texas cattle going to North

Platte. These cattle are very wild and require constant watching & will stampede at anything which frightens them a little. Yesterday the Sioux came down on the Pawnees at their Reservation in retaliation for their helping Gen. Carr in his campaign against the Sioux on the Republican last Spring. They killed two Pawnees and ran off seventy five ponies. They left a note in the officers quarters, written by some half breed probably, saying that they did not want to harm any of the whites but came down after the Pawnees and d—-d if they were not going to get some of them.

Saturday, 25th [September 1869]

Reached Kearney at 5 P.M. Rather rainy this afternoon so we sat in the wagon a[nd] played eucher all the time after dinner. We have had very little card playing this summer. Had but one pack in the party and for weeks at a time they were not used.

Passed a large drove of sheep going out the Forts. Some of the natives stole the horses last night of that party and they and their sheep are now camped on the roadside and the men are scouring the canons hoping to find them secreted somewhere.

Omaha, Nebraska, October 15th 1870.

After a neglect of more than a year I again open my little book which has been with me so many weary and so many pleasant days. My last entry being made at Ft. Kearney on our homeward bound trip last fall, I will now add from memory a synopsis of the principal events transpiring within the limited field of my experience, giving general items but being compelled to omit the little particular occurrences of every day which go to fill up our record and which make the chief attraction of a Journal. We can all remember the more momentous events which take place without committing them to the keeper of an assistant like this but it is the trifles and little incidents which in after years, when we in an idle moment, refer to our journal first to see what we were doing ten years ago today that so vividly portray to our minds those scenes of olden times which bring back the recollections of dear friends then with us now laid beneath the sod, which show us what were then our fond hopes and expectations and in reading over those old pages we live again the scenes of other days. We feel the influences we felt then. We forget the present and think only of the dear old past.

And still we felt no such admiration and enthusiasm over the events which now so fill our souls with pleasant recollections at the time they transpired; this distance lends enchantment, and in after years we will look back upon the transactions of today with the same feeling of affection and regret that the good old times are gone.

Feeling then that these small items are the precious ones we will after bringing up our story in a general review of the main points, turn over a new leaf and hereafter be more attentive to this my only confidant.

After a very pleasant trip down the road from Kearney through a farming country where we were enabled to procure vegetables and butter and milk in abundance which were great treats to us, we reached Omaha on Saturday, Oct. 2nd, 1869. To say we were glad to be again within the bounds of civilization but feebly expresses the truth.

I remained here a week, then in company with Skinner started for Galena. Arrived there safely. Found Father at home. On Oct. 1st began clerking for Lon, he being city clerk, boarded at home with Mother and Auttie, he attending school. Living in Whittam Row Mrs. Madison and [illegible] next door neighbors. About Dec. Lon was compelled to resign his position by reason of the collection being ordered of a heavy tax to pay off a portion of the bonded indebtedness of the city, which tax he could not collect without engendering much hard feeling and ruining his business for the future. In my restlessness at being out of employment I took charge of a billiard hall on the 23 of Dec. I did this against my inclination but on the advice of friends older and more experienced but I shall never allow myself to be influenced again to do anything contrary to my own convictions. Although I retained it but one month and conducted myself honestly and it being a temperance hall not very bad I felt ashamed of my business, felt out of place and disgraced by having anything to do with it. I gave it up on Jany. 23rd. Soon after took a trip up into Wisconsin, had a very pleasant visit. Spent a few days at Orson's, at Uncle's, at John Medcalfs and made a general visit. Getting the Western fever I started for Omaha about the first of April. Began working for Mr. Wiltse the next day after my arrival. After having been here two weeks went up on the Elk Horn River with Mr. W. and Judge [Judson R.?] Hyde to select Forty thousand acres of land for the O. & S.W. and O. & N.W.R.R.'s.* Went with the old team of mules. Had a fine trip, was gone ten days. In May applied for and rec'd a letter of recommendation from Gen. [President] Grant to [U.S. Surveyor] Gen'l. Livingstone [Robert R. Livingston] of this State and on the strength of it was promised a contract of surveying of six thousand dollars on the Elk Horn River. Remained here making preparations and

---

*The Omaha and South Western Railroad was a subsidiary of the Chicago, Burlington and Quincy Railroad. He must have meant Chicago & North Western Railway.

occasionally doing some surveying until the middle of July when Livingstone sent me a letter offering me four thousand dollars worth of work in company with another man, said work lying on the Republican River. Telegraphed for Lon, he came out immediately, and we declined the whole matter.* On the 10th of August I came into Judge [Eleazer] Wakeley's office and began the study of law. This I intend to follow till I am admitted [to the Bar], and be guided thereafter by circumstances.

This is Saturday, cloudy cold, inclined to rain and a dreary day generally. Nothing to do but study. Have been expecting a letter from home for two weeks. Rec'd a package left this week containing some shirts, my dressing gown, scarf, and this little book. Mother and Auttie keeping house, Auttie attending school. Lon, wife and baby all right. Pa still in Iowa on the Rail Road. Really, our family are badly scattered.

Attended a reception last night at the church. Very pleasant time. New minister Mr. Stewart in whose honor the reception was given.

Before closing my general history of past events I must mention the elections. Great excitement prevailed. A state ticket was elected and the legislative ticket was governed by their choice for Senator, it being for or against [John M.] Thayer, the present incumbent. In this county he carried the day outside he has not succeeded so well. The regular Republican state ticket is elected according to the reports so far. It will be greatly to my interest to have Mr. T. defeated but the matter will not be settled until December.

Sunday, 16th [October, 1870]

Clear and rather cold. After a late breakfast cleaned up my room and myself and went to church. An excellent discourse. After church attended Sunday school. Enrolled my self as a pupil in the Minister's Bible Class. Took a walk in the P.M. and attended church in the evening.

Monday, 17

Cold and disagreeable. Office very uncomfortable there being no stove in it. However, I studied nearly all day. Finished the third book of Blackstone. This is my first reading of it though and I expect to read it all over again.

---

*Grant's letter had helped Will get accepted as a U.S. deputy surveyor. Richards wrote Grant again to complain that Livingston reneged on his original agreement. (This letter is on p. 218.) Lon and Nebraska Senator Hitchcock lobbied against Livingston in Washington, D.C., and the surveyor general was replaced.[8]

*Richards (right), Judge Eleazer Wakeley (left), and George Hunt,
Richards's brother-in-law (standing). Photo may have been taken
on a visit to Omaha when Richards was governor of Wyoming.*
Frison Collection, WSA[9]

Thursday, 18th
Spent the day in the office reading. Reviewed the three first chapters of Blk. third book. Spent part of the evening with Glenn Kendall. Attended Lodge. Wrote a letter to Auttie. Retired at 10 P.M.

Wednesday, 19th
Rec'd three letters this morning. One from Father who is at Parkersburg, Iowa. One from Lon and one from Mother. All well at home.

Thursday, 20
Spent the day in the office, the eve in my room. Weather cool.

Friday, 21st
Ditto

Saturday, 22
Nothing new

Sunday, 23rd
Arose at eight. After breakfast and a change of my clothing &c went to

church. After church attended Sunday School. Room smoked and we had rather a dull time. Dodds and I took dinner with Mr. Skinner and wife. Took a walk around town. Went to church in the evening.

Monday, 24th

Cloudy and cold. No stove in the office, consequently very uncomfortable. Studied all day however.

Tuesday, 25th

Ditto. Attended Lodge in the evening. Was nominated for W.C.T. but declined. Was elected W.R.S.* After Lodge had a degree meeting and a very pleasant evening taken altogether. Retired at 12 M.

Wednesday, 26th

Judge Wakeley went to Fremont. Nothing new to record. Rain in the evening.

Thursday, 27th

Mr. Wiltse & Dr. Warren went to Plattsmouth today hunting. I should have gone also but for the Judge being absent. Have a terrible pain in my head today. Study too hard I guess.

Friday, 28th

Yesterday P.M. promised to sit up with a young man at the hospital who has Typhoid fever. Forgot about our having arranged for a party at the Lodge room the same evening. Went up there however and stayed till 9:30. Very pleasant affair. The remainder of the night was rather tedious. Alone with a delirious man who imagined he wanted everything. Feel a little sleepy today. Mr. W. returned. Received a letter from Ella. Weather fine.

Saturday, 29th

Wrote last night until nine o'clock getting up an answer to a petition. Rather hard work after being up all the night before. Did a good deal of writing today. Began my first suit in the Probate Court. Had summons issued on a note for two hundred dollars.

Sunday, 30th

Rained last night. Pleasant today. Went to church, after dinner took a walk. Church in Evening.

---

*Good Templars Lodge. W.C.T. was Worthy Chief Templar. Author is unable to find W.R.S. Will was active in Good Templars at least through January 1874.[10]

Diary, May 18, actual size
History Nebraska[1]

Female Suffrage

Points.

Protest of [cour.?] of Ladies. Expression of Lady as regards mental capacity. [Susais's?] lecture. No change in marriage relation. But ladies to propose. What women will vote. Can't legislate themselves rich nor choose the good places to the exclusion of the bad ones. Female influence now. What will it be then. Vinnie Ream* & Johnson's impeachment. Woodhull and Claffin.* Constitutional amendments. Construction of Statutes. Citizen. (Shaks. A townsman's a man of trade: not a gentleman: Webster. The native of a city, or an inhabitant who enjoys the freedom and privileges of the city in which he resides: the freeman of a city as distinguished from a foreigner or one not entitled to its franchise.)

Webster says. In the United States a person, native or naturalized, who has the privilege of exercising the elective franchise or the qualifications which enable him to vote for rulers and to purchase and hold real estate.

[Handwriting changes slightly; the following may have been added later.]

Change of fashion may result when ladies are compelled to pay for her own dress.

Dr. [sic] W. A. Richards in acct. with Mrs. Wyman
To board from Dec. 29 '70 at Five Dollars per week
May 18, 1871 Twenty weeks board $100
Paid balance due and quit Mrs. Wyman's establishment. I'm Afloat! Afloat!

---

*Lavinia "Vinnie" Ream was the first female artist to receive a commission from the U.S. government. In 1866, at age 18, she was chosen to sculpt a memorial portrait of Abraham Lincoln.[11] *Woodhull and Claflin's Weekly* was published by Victoria Woodhull Claflin, a leader of the women's suffrage movement. She was the first woman to own a brokerage firm on Wall Street, the first woman to start a weekly newspaper, and she would run for President in 1872.[12]

THE MONTH AFTER Richards became "Afloat!" he signed a joint surveying contract with Joseph W. Gay, likely an associate on the 1869 Wiltse surveys. (Map and details are on p. 244). This was the first of a number of joint contracts Will fulfilled in Nebraska. When not surveying, he sometimes worked as a reporter, for the *Omaha Tribune* in 1871, the *Omaha Republican* in 1875, and possibly others.[13]

Chauncey Wiltse had become a firm friend and advisor to the Richardses, even posting half of the bond in 1872 for one of Will's contracts (see pp. 246–47). Will and his bride lived in Omaha before moving to California in the fall of 1875. Wiltse tried to lure Will back to become business manager of the *Republican*, but Will's brother Aut, who lived in Omaha, advised against it because of local political turmoil.[14] Will and Wiltse remained friends for years.[15]

Early in 1871, Lon had proposed a newspaper venture:[16]

> You and I both seem to have a kind of natural gift with a quill. Can we not worm into some good newspaper either at Omaha or some other favorable point, and make a good thing. Now I think we would make a full team and plenty of rocks if we could. I can get some money from sale of my business and borrow a little more, and I believe by interesting some of the politicians out there we could make a riffle. I would rather however go in independent than be trammeled by any politician, if we could. Think this over—talk with Wiltse, and look the ground all over thoroughly. It pays well enough once you get a good paper in circulation.

The idea was premature, but after Lon became editor and publisher of the *Freeport (Illinois) Journal* in the fall of 1875, he urged Will to join him.[17]

> Don't do anything rash, and don't conclude to come here just to help me. If you come, come because it's business. If you were here, I would go ahead and start a daily. ...My paper is better now than it ever was before and the people like it.

Will did go to Freeport to run the paper in 1878 when Lon went to Washington, D.C. That year Will also received an offer to run a new paper in Evanston, Wyoming. By then, Lon's bitter experience in journalism led him to warn his brother of its pitfalls.[18]

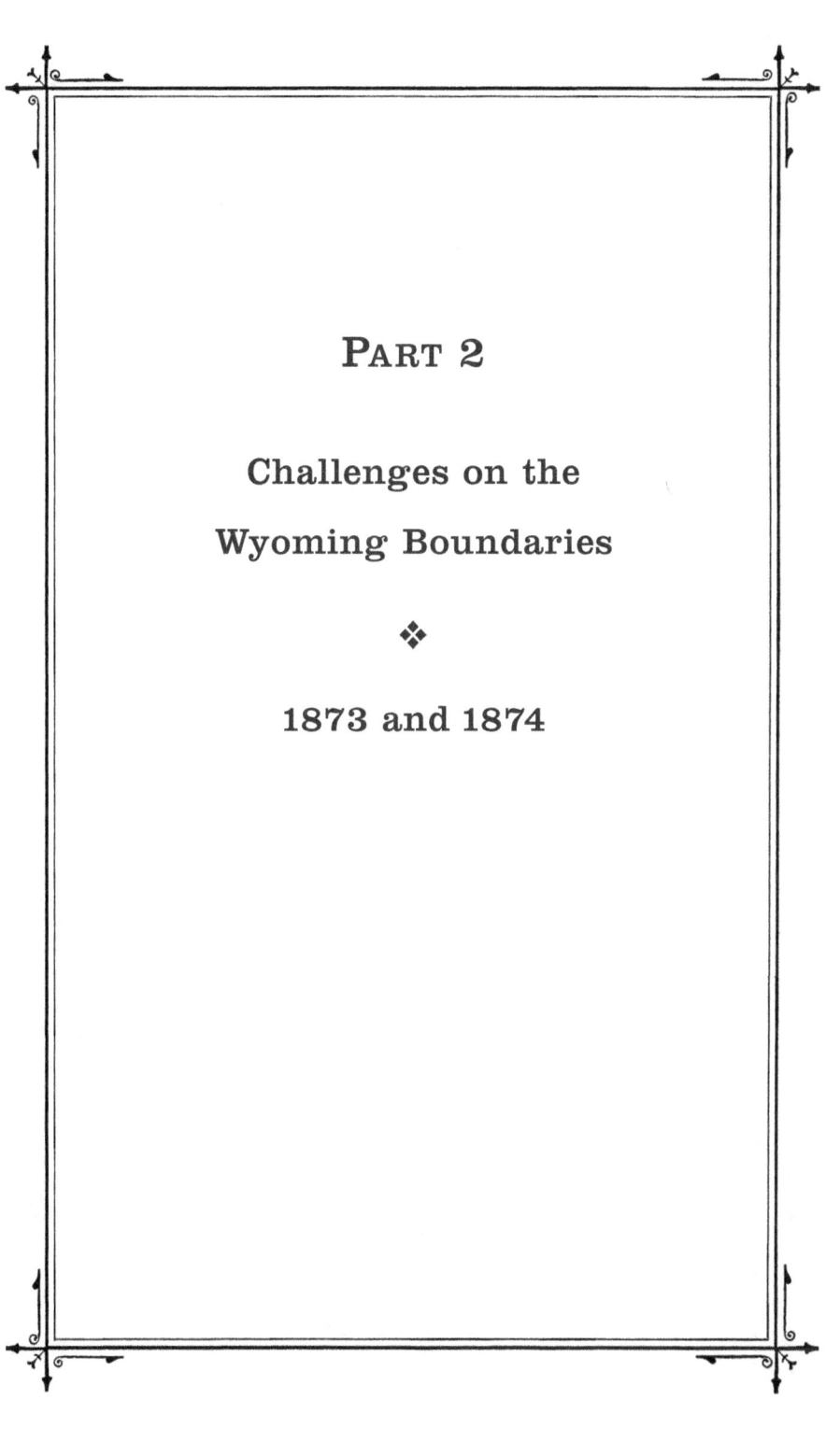

PART 2

Challenges on the
Wyoming Boundaries

❖

1873 and 1874

Survey of the South Boundary of Wyoming Territory, 1873

Background

WHEN LON RECEIVED the contract to survey the south boundary of Wyoming Territory, Will signed on as general assistant. He would be introduced to the rugged country of Wyoming—and to advanced surveying instruments and techniques. Boundary surveys required astronomical observations to locate the point on the ground that corresponded to the designated latitude or longitude.

Wyoming Territory was created in 1868, having been carved out of the Dakota, Idaho, and Utah territories. Like Colorado, it was a simple rectangle defined by particular latitudes and longitudes. Its eastern boundary had been surveyed by Oliver N. Chaffee in 1869, and the Richardses would complete the southern and western edges of the box. The northern boundary was done in segments, had to be resurveyed, and was not completed until 1882.[1] The southern survey would place Evanston and the immense coal deposits at Almy firmly inside Wyoming.

Federal statutes required land to be divided into rectangles except in a few cases when natural boundaries such as rivers and mountain ranges were employed as territorial boundaries. It was far from easy to mark straight lines on the high mountains and irregular valleys of the West, and surveyors had to mark the grid on the landscape no matter how irregular it was.[2]

Surveyors were also instructed to describe the landscape as they went along: mountains, rivers, visible minerals, soil type, and vegetation,[3] so the government would know more about what was in those millions of acres acquired in the Louisiana Purchase of 1803.

The south boundary of Wyoming was to run along the 41st parallel of latitude, starting at the monument Chaffee had set where the 41st parallel intersects the 27th meridian; it was to end at the 34th meridian.* The

---

*It might have started at the 34th meridian: The superintendent of the Union Pacific Rail Road and the surveyor general of Wyoming Territory had expressed interest in establishing the Southwest Corner first, but nothing came of it. (Diary, June 4, p. 80.)

The point of reference for these meridians was the dome of the old Naval Observatory at Washington, D.C.[4] (In degrees from Greenwich, the system adopted later, Wyoming's south boundary line runs from 104°3′ W to 111°3′ W longitude.)

The original white limestone monument set by Chaffee still marks the spot. It was fenced and given a new base in 1990.[5]

75

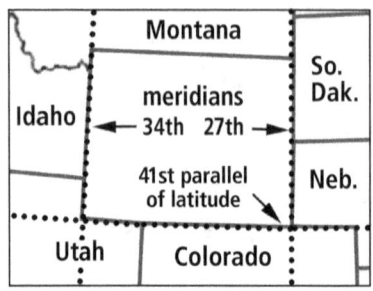

Dotted lines show the meridians and the 41st parallel.

south boundary of the Nebraska panhandle was on the 41st parallel as well, but beyond it, that parallel had not been surveyed.

Determined to succeed, Lon wrote Will, "Am getting all the astronomical arrangements made, so as to do the best boundary work that has been done yet in the great West." Surveyors in remote, difficult country often let precision slide on the assumption that nobody would notice or care, but the Richardses took pains to set precise boundary posts and monuments no matter how rough the terrain. Lon was a U.S. astronomer himself, yet he engaged "the best observer in the U.S.," Augustus MacConnel. [Underscores throughout are the writer's.] An alumnus of Harvard University, MacConnel had worked at its astronomical observatory and at other observatories teaching astronomy and collecting volumes of astronomic data. He had been recommended by Truman H. Safford, professor of astronomy at the University of Chicago and director of the Dearborn Observatory. As for instruments, "I have not yet secured an astronomical transit," Lon wrote Will, "but have one or two in view. I now need someone who can put in the Topography. I think it would pay us to get a Professional draftsman in order to have this work O.K. in every particular."[6] Artists who could accurately depict three-dimensional terrain on two-dimensional paper were in demand, but Lon was willing to incur the expense for one.[7] (Astronomical transits are described on pp. 10–11.)

During the survey, observations would be taken nightly, weather permitting, to ensure the line was correct. Five astronomical stations were set up along the line between Chaffee's monument and the western terminal monument. At each, five stars were observed, then the instrument was reversed, and five more observed. Signals were then sent to others in the party, and the process repeated.[8] The monuments at the astronomical stations were all of stone, since good wood was hard to come by, but wood had to be used for the mile posts. To obtain it, they sometimes traveled 50 miles afield.[9]

The miles could be measured off with chains, but transits and flagstaffs served that purpose better in mountainous country.[10]

The two boundary contracts were executed during the tenure of Wyoming Surveyor General Silas Reed.* The 1873 contract paid sixty dollars per mile and the 1874 fifty, since surveying for latitude is more complex than surveying for longitude.

The survey of the south boundary of Wyoming used the identical procedure employed by Mason and Dixon for the Pennsylvania-Maryland parallel of latitude (1763–67) and by Chaffee (1869), Dr. Stoughton noted. The procedure is an application of classical spherical trigonometry.

Dr. Stoughton's article on spherical trigonometry continues on p. 256.

Crew Members Mentioned in the 1873 Diary

Their full names are taken from field notes or letters and matched up with names from diary where possible (in brackets).[11]

ARTIST AND TOPOGRAPHER Robert Swaim [Bob]

CHAINMEN A. B. Campbell, M. J. Lorraine [Matt], Benj. F. Morgan [Ben], M. H. Tobin [Mack, Max?]. Morgan also served as cook, as he did in the 1874 survey.

FLAGMEN Richard L. Rossiter [Dick], Arthur C. Wakeley (Judge Wakeley's son)

AXEMEN & MOUNDMEN W. H. Bordway [Billie], J. L. Getner, Frederick Huth, James L. Pattison [Pat]

TEAMSTERS Neill Cartwright, A. C. Harwood, G. A. Scott [George]; W. S. Byers (discharged on July 3)

Byers, Lorraine, Morgan, Pattison, Rossiter, and Wakeley worked on the Richardses' Nebraska surveys on the way to the Wyoming boundary survey. See p. 246 for a map and other information about those surveys.

---

*Dr. Silas Reed, of Illinois, served as that state's surveyor general from April 17, 1841–September 12, 1841, and from March 17, 1842–May 11, 1845. During the Civil War, Reed served under General Ulysses S. Grant as a medical doctor, and when Grant was President he nominated Reed for surveyor general of the new Territory of Wyoming. Reed was appointed on March 2, 1870. Reed had no oversight authority of the Richardses' parties, and only casually mentioned their presence in his annual reports to the commissioner of the General Land Office.[12]

Did Reed help Lon obtain the 1873 contract? "If there is anything in Wyoming worth having, I can get it through old man Houghton who is a particular friend of the Sur-Gen. (Reed) ....," Lon wrote Will on April 5, 1872. He probably means Horace H. Houghton, a retired Galena newspaper publisher.[13] Whether either man helped Lon win the contract is unknown.

A veteran of the Army's 1865 Powder River campaign against the Lakota Sioux and other tribes, Lon was undaunted by his impending return to Wyoming. He had applied for a cavalry escort, but by August he had come to think they would be a "terrible nuisance."[14]

Alonzo V. Richards
American Heritage
Center[15]

The country itself was more hostile. The line would run through mountainous terrain, with ascents difficult even for the mules. Altitudes were often 8,000 feet above sea level and temperatures below freezing. They sometimes camped without tents in snow, hail, or rain—but wild strawberries reminded them it was summer. Hacking through dense timber could limit their progress to two miles or less per day. Replacing lost or damaged instruments was expensive and time-consuming. Crossing deep canyons or locating water or wood could require traveling miles out of their way. Rations ran short and game was scarce. Settlers were scarce as well, but they did lend supplies. The crew received mail only at Cheyenne, Laramie, and Green River.

Lon praised his brother in his field notes:

Mr. W. A. Richards as general assistant had charge of the camp and commissariat, and it is only justice to him to say that the successful termination of the expedition is largely due to his indefatigable energy and perseverance.[16]

Will's surveying skills must also have advanced enough for Lon to put him in charge of most of the western boundary survey the following year.

His diary begins on May 26, Sunday—1873
Left Omaha and home at 11:30 a.m. to rejoin the boys at North Platte. Took dinner at Fremont; supper with Mr. Fox at Grand Island. At Elm Creek received orders to lay the train up till morning, on account of washouts on the road. Spent the night in the mail car with Johnson and O'Sullivan. A good bed and sound sleep. Breakfast at section house. Reached Brady Island about 1 o'clock. Country through we had passed all overflowed, and a bridge out between B. Is. and N. Platte. Waited two hours; no dinner. Got into my trunk in baggage car and set up the bread-doughnuts and cake, for the trainmen and mail agents. Reached camp O.K. at 4:00 p.m. Glad to get back. All well.

Tuesday, May 27

Called on Col. Park to have boys sign notes. Found him insensible from paralysis. Signed notes to P. R. Bdry [Pacific Railroad boundary] & subdivision before Goodale N. P. [Notary Public.] Had dinner. Made arrangements with Foley & Seuter to ship corn and flour at .60 and 4.45 per cwt. [100 lbs.] the last in seamless sacks and corn sacks to be returned. Lon waited in North Platte to take train for Cheyenne. The boys and I made west and camped for night at O'Fallon station. A dozen emigrant teams camped here too. Voted after supper for the "handsomest man" to receive Mrs. Wakeley's present— Pattison was elected. Voted that Swaim make a picture for Mrs. W. of the recipient of her gift—a cake of soap. Moved by Schneider that "Dot bicture was tooken pefore he could use dot soap." Heap of fun. Weather fair. Roads good.

Wednesday, 28

Just at breakfast passenger [train] came up; Lon aboard. Took his overcoat— Left camp 6:30— made Alkali—14 miles—for dinner— took twenty minutes for same— reached Roscoe siding at 3:00 p.m. and camped as I telegraphed Judge Wakeley we would camp here tonight. Big Springs tomorrow and Julesburg Friday night. Took a bath in Platte. Had axes and tools ground. Cooking done and all preparations for a big drive tomorrow, as it is 29 miles to Big Springs. Came 24 today. Weather fine. Roads hard and dry; sometimes sandy. Surface Sand Hills last ten miles—

Thursday, 29

Left Roscoe at 6:30 a.m. Camped for dinner near Brule 17 miles. Now camped for night at Big Springs— No Judge last night. Wind is now high and a good prospect of rain.

Friday, 30

Reached Julesburg at 1:30. Found Campbell waiting with gun etc. from Omaha. Laid up for night as some corn we had ordered did not come in and I had telegraphed Judge W. that we would camp here. Prospect good for rain. At 3:00 p.m. received dispatch from the Judge at Columbus saying that he got left by the train at that place. Telegraphed him at Grand Island that we would leave Julesburg tomorrow morning.

Saturday, May 31

Raining at daylight. Did not start until 8:00 a.m. Camped for dinner at Chappel, a flag station. Found an American as Sec. master [foreman or master of that section of the U.P.R.R.]. Used their stove. Learned that there were buffalo just south of Lodge Pole Creek (along which we have traveled today) in the bluffs. After dinner Campbell and I with the pony left the road and teams and went into the bluffs hunting—taking the pony. Sighted buffalo within mile from the road— Campbell gave chase and had a heap of sport but killed nothing; while he was gone I killed a fine doe antelope—the first game for my new gun. Struck another herd of buffalo on our way to camp, but very wild. Reached camp at Lodge Pole Station at dark.

Sunday, June 1st

Just as we were ready to start this morning learned that the Judge was almost here on a freight train. Waited for him. Gave him a warm (cold) breakfast and moved on. Teams all stuck crossing a slough just out of the station. Delayed an hour. Camped for dinner on Lodge Pole. Had a good meal with cakes and bread furnished by Mrs. W. and antelope steak. Reached Sidney at 5:00 p.m. A three Co. [U.S. Army] post is here, an eating house and quite a little town. Water runs through the street brought from Lodge Pole two miles west. The Judge left for home. At depot saw Meachem, Captain Jack's intended victim, on his way East. A tall fine looking man. Saw Laughton, Sith Cole and Johnny Warner on train. Sixty-three miles to Pine Bluff[s], must make it in two days—

Monday, 2nd

Left camp at 6:00 a.m. Camped for dinner at Potter. 19 miles. Found Waters our pilgrim "put off here again." Moved on west. Overtook Waters "Put-Off" again. Will go with us to Pine Bluffs. Camped at 5:00 p.m. on Lodge Pole. Just north of Bennett station. A fine camp ground— Four emigrant wagons in camp here too. Regulated sights on my gun with target practice. Campbell and I on guard—

Tuesday, 3rd

Dinner a mile east of Bushnell— Reached Pine Bluffs at 5:30— Found Lon and MacConnel in waiting. Got in ten minutes ahead of us. Camped a mile north on Lodge Pole— Put up the new tent. Lon and Mac—Bob & I occupy it. [Mac or MacC mean MacConnel.]

Wednesday, 4th

Spent the a.m. in reloading & regulating wagons and camp, writing letters and taking leave of civilization. Supt. [W. T.] Sickles of the U.P.R.R. and Dr. [Hiram C.] Latham, Sur. Genl. Wyo. are anxious to have us establish the S. W. corner of Wyo. first, and Mr. Sickles offers through Latham to furnish us transportation and passes while out here to do it at once. We are open for such propositions. Left the Sta. at 1:00 p.m. Lon, Mac and four men going down the line; I and the teams going around the bluffs S. W. We met at the cor. of Wyo. Colo. and Neb.—at dark. No water in the country, and timber two miles. Boys tired and hungry— Tried to get a station rigged for astronomical observations, but failed. Went to bed of course. Lon and Mac working until 12:00 M. [midnight] —

Thursday—5—73

Took three men and a team and cut a load of posts on the bluff, took them 6 miles west and left them. Dug a well on Muddy Creek three miles west of camp. Good cold water. Weather hot— Reached camp at 7:00 p.m. tired and hungry. Killed an antelope coming in— Campbell did do [ditto]— Reorganized guard duty, putting three men on each night. Bob, Arthur and I on first night. Lon and Mac worked until 1:30 a.m. taking observations to test this initial point. So Lon took my "chance" and part of Bob's. Weather fine and warm— Lon rode the pony to Pine Bluffs for mail but got none

Friday, 6th

Went to the station on a mule— Sent the old Winchester in to be repaired, ordered axes and grindstone from Edgar, to Cheyenne. Got dinner at a section house— Bought a pick. Reached camp at 6:00 p.m. Lon ran four miles of line. Dick killed an antelope, and Pattison do [ditto]— Cloudy— No observations tonight. Wrote to Miss H., Judge W. and Aut.

Saturday, June 7

Can't move today— Took four men and went post hunting— Picked up the load of posts and took them to a point 8 miles west of camp at a spring. Killed a very large antelope coming in. Prospects good for rain.

Sunday, June 8th, '73

Raining nearly all night. Slept 'till 7 this morning. No stars last night, consequently must lie in camp all day. Finished Martin Chuzzlewit and was well pleased with the sequel. Tom's vindication, the happiness of Martin-Jim-Mary-John and Tom's sister Ruth brought about by their well being and well doing forms a strong and striking contrast to the downfall and utter ruin of Pecksniff and Jonas. The moral is good and impressed at every step of the narrative. Be generous, good and wise; truthful, honest and kind and prosper and be happy; fail in these essential qualifications and misery, ruin and death must follow— Before dinner (at 3:00 p.m.) Campbell and I took a stroll of three hours for our health. After dinner read Harper's and mended up some. The Prof. discovered that the Level on the Astronomical Transit was broken—how no one knows. This is an aggravating and expensive accident as it will necessitate the ordering of a new one to be forwarded to Cheyenne and cause further vexatious delays. It is now impossible to test this point, so we will start west with the line tomorrow. Lon going to the station. Had a camp fire roast of antelope and retired— 7 antelope brought into this camp.

Monday, June 9, 1873

Breakfast at 5:00 a.m. Lon started on the pony for Pine Bluffs to open communication with Chicago and Washington about a level. The team started west for a new camp 8 miles west, and I took the line. At the edge of the bluff 1 mile 65 chs. [chains] from corner [1.8 miles total] in setting the 2nd M.P. [mile post] found the west end of the line incorrect. Ran on to 4th M.P. and found the line as previously run too far south. Returned to edge of bluff and reran it; but made it a random line to camp. In going over it west the first time, Matt accidentally shot Mack through the outside edge of his right foot with his revolver, while both were firing at a large rattlesnake. Campbell ran 5-1/2 miles to camp and brought back a team in a little over an hour. The team took a load of wood from the bluff and taking Mack, went to camp. We proceeded with the work. Reached camp at 5:00 p.m., 12 hrs. btwn. meals. After supper, dressed Mack's foot; not a bad wound—only through the flesh. 10:00 p.m. Have been working with MacC —taking observations. Sky full of light clouds, making it slow work, Lon not yet arrived. Think he must have stayed all night at the station as he knew where we would camp—and had been nearly here. Hope he is not out on the prairie. Am not much anxious as he knows how to come home. List of attractions tonight—Mosquitoes—first and nearest— Lon out of camp—whereabouts unknown—level broken—line crooked this soon—Mack wounded and weather cloudy—and all hands tired— rather bad but jolly still. see Tapley*

Tuesday, June 10, '73, 7:00 a.m.

Worked last night until day was breaking. Got some observations for Lat. [Latitude] and a few for time [necessary for determining Longitude**]. Got the transit on the North Star [Polaris] at its Eastern Elonga-

---

*Mark Tapley, a character in Dickens's *Martin Chuzzlewit*, remained jolly through any adversity.

**Surveyors measure the time it takes for a specific star to cross two meridians. A timing mistake of one second would cause a surveying error of 1,167 feet on the ground.[17]

tion, and found the true Meridian [longitude], turned a right angle after deducting the distance from Polaris when taken to the true Meridian and found my line of yesterday correct. Am waiting now at 8:00 a.m. for Prof. to make some calculations for Lat. from last night's work, when we will go to work again. Lon not in yet. Kept a red light out all night. Team has gone west with Al and Pattison to take a load of posts on west. The weather is beautiful this morning. Air clear and pure. Good weather for running. We are camped on a small spring near the line about eight miles from the initial point. Soil strongly impregnated with Alkali but good water to be had by digging a few feet— 6:00 p.m. Went to work at 11:00 a.m. At the same time started Neal for the station on a mule bareback—to see why Lon didn't come. Got into camp at 4:15 p.m. At same time Lon and Neal hove in sight. Lon was waiting for an answer to his telegrams. Failed to hear from Safford, but got word through from Washington. Can get a new one in a week.

Wednesday, June 11, 1873

Started from camp at 5:20 a.m. with the line. Reached the Crow Creek and had dinner at 12:00 M. [noon]

8 miles. This is a stream 25 lks.* Swift running and good water. A few scattering cottonwood and willow trees in the bottom. Country rolling. Soil gravelly, 2nd rate. Large herds of cattle grazing near. Antelope plenty. Lon killed one coming over this morning. After dinner ran two miles west without building the mounds [see footnote on p. 64, and short essay on p. 258] as we will take Latitude and Azimuth** tonight and start anew tomorrow. The line seems to be a little to the north of the Parallel now. Got caught in a heavy rain coming to camp. A herder passed through camp with a wagon going east to his ranche during the storm. Followed him on pony to inquire as to water west on line. Found that there was water at 4, 7 and 15 miles. Will make one of those places tomorrow. Also found Shorty's umbrella in his wagon. He asked if we had lost one. I told him I thought we were liable to lose one.

Thursday, June 12, 1873, 7:00 a.m.

MacC— and Lon got a few observations last night and are now working them up. Morning opens clear and pleasant. Mosquitoes plenty on

---

*Links. A chain has 100 links 0.66' long (or 6.92" long), so 25 links = 13.75', 20 = 11', 10 = 5.5', etc.

**The azimuth is the "direction" of a line with respect to the meridian (or true north). —Dr. Stoughton. See his article, p. 265.

Crow Creek but no Crows— Evening— Moved west at 11 o'clock. Built up 17 and 18 miles and ran 7 miles farther through very rough country. High rocky bluffs putting into the bottom south of us. Camped 25th mile post on edge of bottom near E. end of Big Simson Canon. Iliff* of Cheyenne has a ranche in this canon and 1,200 head of cattle in all on the plains. Lon and Mac taking observs. nearly all night.

Friday, 13th

Started with the team to distribute stakes along the line while the obsers. were being figured up. Found the country too rough. Sent team back and Campbell and I scouted about 6 miles ahead. Back by 12:00 M. Mac had found our Lat. unchanged. So we moved on. Ran four miles west. Very rough. Lon brought posts in on a pony. Camped in Simson Canon— 29 mile— Thirteen miles to the U.P.R.R. so reported. Will try to make it tomorrow.

Saturday, 14th

Left camp at 5:20 a.m. Reached the R.R. at 1:30 p.m. 41st mile post on R.R. track. Camp E. of R.R. line and near it. I killed an antelope with a needle gun at 300 yards. Same very good steak for dinner. Broil for supper. Snow capped Mts. very plain from here. We could see a snow storm there this p.m. though they are 75 miles away. Indications of rain—

Sunday, 15th

Ran line three miles west. Camped at a beautiful spring just east of Lone Tree Creek. Summit Siding is just south of us and Terry Bros. cattle ranche near us on the west. [Henry G.] Hay and [John B.] Thomas, surveyors under Reed.** Now cattle and sheepherders are two miles N. of us. The herds of this Co. start a Round-up tomorrow. Each ranch sends a man, they scout the country, get up all the cattle. Then each man picks out his stock and drives them in— 35 men start this time and they expect to pick up 50,000 head of cattle. Did some washing. Read Kenelm Chillingly [a novel by Bulwer-Lytton] and Harper's for June. Slept some and wrote to Alice and the home folks. Now at sundown, will close— Tomorrow,

---

*John W. Iliff in 1875 was said to be the largest range-cattle operator in Colorado and Wyoming, with an estimated 26,000 head.[18]

**Hay was also a director of the First National Bank of Cheyenne,[19] along with Reed. Hay would be elected state treasurer in 1894, when Richards was elected governor. Reed, U.S. surveyor general for Wyoming from March 2, 1870 to March 26, 1873, lost his position as a result of Republican factional feuding, and was replaced by Dr. Hiram C. Latham, also a physician. After an appeal to President Grant, Reed was reinstated on July 18, 1873.[20]

Surveyors line up for a meal.
Allyn Collection, 1904, Riverton (Wyoming) Museum

Lon and I go to Cheyenne to get supplies, and send out and get mail— No rain last night— Weather beautiful. Thermometer 90 degrees at noon. Bar[ometer]. indicates 6,275 feet—

Monday, 16th

Went on guard this morning at 2 o'clock. Breakfast at five. Campbell and four men with a team started west to the Black Hills* for wood. Lon, Billie and I with a team and the pony started for Cheyenne nine miles distant at 6:00 a.m. Stopped at the Ranche of Hay and Thomas, ex-surveyors,[33] who were thrown out of a job by the retirement [termination] of Dr. Reed and the succession of Dr. Latham as Surveyor General. They have a fine sheep ranche; also a large number of horses and mules. Are busy now shearing sheep.— Reached Cheyenne at 9:00 a.m. Met Jos. Carey [a prominent cattleman and politician] and Gillen, Kimball and Woods of Omaha. Found letter from Miss H. Also from Aut— Found gun, axes, grindstone and baking powder all right. Tested chain; mailed letters; bought lots of things. Got a dinner at R.R. House—$1.00** and beat the

---

*This north-south range of mountains was renamed the Sherman Mountains in honor of the Civil War general. The summit of 8,000+ feet, at Sherman, Wyoming, is the highest point on the entire transcontinental railroad.[21]

**About $25.20 in 2022, per measuringworth.com purchasing-power calculator

hotel keeper about 75 cents then— Saw Warner at dinner— Started home at 4—reached camp at 6:10 p.m. Boys got in from timber 12 miles distant. A rough country west of us. Plenty of water and more wood. Signs of Indians. One seen near camp— Got a splendid letter from Alice. She is at San Jose for her health. A bad cold and cough. Perhaps it is worse than she tells me but I hope not— I haven't written just as I should; but I will make ample amends next time which will be tomorrow. Camp was so dull and I tired that I wrote a dull uninteresting letter, but will do better— She deserves the best that I can do in writing or anything else.

Tuesday, 17th

Lay in camp all day. Jap Corey and his cousin visited us— Campbell and I took a hunt after 4:00 p.m. Returned gameless—

Wednesday, 18th

With Arthur and Texas and a span of mules started for town. Changed teams at Thomas' Ranche to try one he had to sell. Too small and too high, $275.* Arthur went to the post with his cousin Capt. Wessels who sent him to camp in wag. with an escort of cavalry.

Thursday, 19th

Rode a grey pony to town belonging to Hay and Thomas. Price $80.** Too high. Reached camp at sunset.

Friday, 20th, 1873

Went to town with a team and Scott, Campbell and Pattison. Rode a black pony of H. & O. Like him pretty well. Price $60. Got caught in a hail storm. Reached camp at sundown. Brought in large stone for Astronomical station—a foot square, seven ft. long, price $12.50. On 19th Campbell and Pat killed antelopes.

Saturday, 21st

With Lew, Al and Geo. Scott went to town. The eastern train brought the long expected level, C.O.D. $84.20, an outrageous price. Had new spring made for large transit. Got stone hammer. Letters from Aut. Heard from Supt. Sickles through Sur. Genl. Latham. Nothing definite. Rode home with Thomas Campbell. Killed two antelope. Found that Matt and Dick had almost finished dressing the stone shaft—[$]25 saved thereby. Weather very hot in Omaha and the East—but pleasant here— Mem.— on the 20th H. F. Clark, Prest. U.P.R.R. died very suddenly.

---

*About $6,940 in 2022.
**About $2,020 in 2022. $60 was about $1,500 and $12.50 about $315.

*The first of seven astronomical monuments erected along
the boundary, this one at Lone Tree Creek. Drawing
by Robert Swaim, artist and topographer.*

Field Notes of the Survey of the South Boundary of Wyoming

Thursday, 26th

Have spent this week in getting ready to move, and at 9:00 a.m. pulled out. Made ten miles on the line, camping at a spring— Lon went to Cheyenne. Saw Sickles. He will do nothing for us.

Friday, 27th

Started for Dale Creek thinking it was 12 miles. Found the country very rough. Crossing Box Elder canon, on the bank of which the 62nd mile came— Had team on line till 1:00 p.m. Ate lunch. Ran till sundown making 9 miles and no sign of camp. Found team awaiting us near old saw mill. Reached camp at 10:00 p.m., 15 hrs. since breakfast.

Saturday, 28th

Did not move camp. Went with team to work. Was until 4:00 p.m. running 5 miles coming out— South of camp—very rough— Wrote to Aut & P.M.'s. [Post Master's?] We are now south of Sherman, the nearest station. Will send up tomorrow and when we reach the Laramie River Campbell and I will go to Laramie, 40 miles.

Sunday, 29th

Left camp at 7:00 a.m., crossed Dale Creek on 1st miles (69th). Very rough. Took lunch at 3rd mile—brought out by Lon— Made 5 miles camping on Fish Creek at 73rd mile. Which mile crosses a mountain too high for chaining so we triangulated.* Received letter from Alice. Only one that came— Weather all fine—nights cool—Line timbered with pine, hemlock, birch and Aspen.

Monday, 30th

Ran 4 miles camping at McGreavy's tie camp near Diamond Mt. Reached camp at 7:00 p.m. Boys killed a yearling elk. Stood guard— rained in p.m.

Tuesday, July 1st, 1873

Ran line 4-1/2 miles. Very rough. Heavy timber. Thermometer 48° above. Camp in deep cañon at foot of Boulder Ridge Summit of Black Hills.

Wednesday, 2nd

Ran one and 1/4 miles working ten (10) hours. Heavy timber. Camp near line.

Thursday, 3rd

Took an azimuth last night. Byers got his back up because we changed him from the teams to the line and left. Moved camp 4-1/2 miles west to the plain. Ran the line same distance leaving timber on the 85th mile. Dick killed an antelope. Billie went to Laramie.

Friday, July 4th

97th anniversary. Pleasant and cool— Didn't work. Billie returned at 11:00 a.m. bringing letters and papers. Received letters from Wiltse, Aut, Miss H. and Judge W. Wrote to D., Miss H. and Alice— Are now camped on south edge of Laramie Plains. Snow capped Mts. to N. W. and S. W. and W. & S. Black Hills behind us, Mts. ahead.

Saturday, 5th

Left camp at 10:00 a.m. Ran 7-1/2 miles. Country rough, but well watered. Camped on small stream at 4:30 p.m. After supper, Bert and I mounted on mules started to explore tomorrow's line a little. When just out of sight of camp, over a hill, dismounted and fired at some antelope. I killed two, the second at two hundred yards running. Our mules ran back to camp. The boys thought we had been attacked and turned out to help us. Got our mules and proceeded on. Returned to camp at 11:00 p.m. On guard.

---

*When triangulating, surveyors measure a "baseline" to serve as the first side of a tri-angle. They use the angles of this triangle to calculate the lengths of the other sides.

Sunday, 6th

Left camp at 6:00 a.m. Reached Poplar mountain at noon. Quite heavy poplar timber on top of Mt. Pattison saw a bear— Billie failed to find us with lunch and water and we ran to the Big Laramie, which we reached at 6:30 p.m. without either. Weather pleasant. Reached river on the 103rd mile.

Monday, 7th

Lon, Billie and Mack went to Laramie 35 miles away. We are stopping here to establish an astronomical station. Laramie River is about two chains wide, swift running, clear water and pebble bottom— MacConnel got good observations early in the evening. Pat got an antelope.

Tuesday, 8th

Wrote letters home and sent them up by a stranger. Lon returned at 6:00 p.m. Bringing some additional supplies. He applied for an escort to Gen. Ord to come down here from Russell and follow us. Found a stone on west side of River for our monument. Boys got it in shape for planting.

Wednesday, 9th

No observations last night— Too cloudy. Campbell and I went out west to explore the line. Got caught in a rain. Killed a young antelope for dinner (by Bert) and ate most of it. I killed a buck before leaving camp, near the tents; also killed a buck while out exploring because he had a queer looking head— Found it was owing to a crooked horn. Found plenty of game—all antelope. Found the road quite rough and heavily timbered. Reached camp at 6:00 p.m. If the Prof. gets "good stars" tonight we may get away tomorrow.

Thursday, July 10th

Can not move today, as Mac– wants another night to work in— Took mail down to a ranch near here and left it. Campbell and Ben went back on the line to make some corrections. Heavy rain and hail in p.m. Set 2nd Latitude monument at 103rd mile. 27 chs.* west of Laramie River. Sand stone with large mound of stone.

Friday, 11th

Lon with the party who run the line left camp at 7:00 a.m. to proceed with the line. Lon will run to next station and I run camp. Crossed the Laramie 1-1/2 miles north of camp, got the team upon the level by dou-

---

*Surveyors' chains are 66 feet long, so 27 chains = 1,782 feet west of state boundary marker (mile post) 103.

bling and camped at 12:00 M. for dinner on small stream running east. The boys ran three (3) miles before dinner and 1-1/3 in p.m. returning to the camp at night. Storm of wind and rain at sunset. Killed an antelope.

Saturday, 12th

Boys were on line at 6:30 a.m. Arthur and I took a hunt from 6:30 to 9:00 a.m., killed nothing. Took dinner to boys and had camp moved along the road. Met them and follow road running up Douglas Creek just north of line. Camped opposite the 110 links and 10 chains point, on N. side Douglas Creek. Took an Azimuth in the woods on the line early in the evening. Dick quite unwell day before yesterday. Nearly well now but has a sprained or swollen wrist and stays in camp. George Scott taken quite sick this morning—an attack of bilious fever I think.

Sunday, 13th

Very cold last night. Mercury only 28 degrees above half an hour after sunrise. Boys left camp at 6:15. Took bay pony and started west to scout the road. Went nine miles from which could see the North Platte bottom—Summit of Medicine Bow Mts.—four miles west of here. Reached camp again at 10:00 a.m. Had a good ride. At 11 took dinner to men on line. Cannot move camp nearer to the line than we now are, so will remain here. Men made 1-3/4 miles on line. Very heavy timber. Ben killed a deer.

Monday, July 14th

Cold again last night. Thermometer this morning at 5:30, only 24 degrees above. Took dinner to boys on foot. Moved camp west over summit of Mts. and camped in a little open valley 20 chs. E. of 114th mile on line. After making camp went out looking for a way over the Mts. Killed two antelope.

Tuesday, 15th

With Billie left camp at 6:20—mounted on mules—took old road south through a little valley; eight miles from line entered North Park, which is simply a large basin or open park, without timber. Surrounded on southeast and west with snow capped mountains and bare Mts. on the north. The North Platte rises in the Park which is about 15 miles in diameter I should think. We found a pass out of the Park over a Mt. to the Platte and a crossing over the river. After which we returned to camp over the mountains. Each killed a black tail deer coming in. Reached camp at 3:00 p.m. Too late to move camp. So sent Fred out to find the men and pilot them in. He got lost in woods, and but for meeting Bob the whole party would have slept out. It was impossible to get camp much nearer the quitting place for the men— they made about three miles of line.

Wednesday, 16th

Packed two mules and the bay pony with provisions and blankets and sent them on the line, as the men will sleep out tonight. With the camp started at 10:00 a.m. to go south into the Park. Reached and crossed the Platte before 5:00 p.m. Drove north two miles and camped on small stream, using sagebrush for fuel.

Thursday, 17th

Found the line two miles north of our camping place at 9 o'clock a.m. The boys reached the river early this morning and crossed with no greater losses than that of a pick, spade and ax, which Pattison lost in crossing. Made camp four miles west of the river on small stream at foot of mountain range. Camped at 3:00 p.m. After which took a mule and scouted west for a road over the Mts. Found a tie cabin three miles north of line in timber. Camp near 124th mile and four chains north of line. [He probably means a cabin at a camp where railroad ties were cut.]

Friday, 18th

Broke camp at 8:00 a.m. Drove north and crossed the Mt. A rough road and hard work. Camped at 3:00 p.m. 3 chs. north of line and 10 chs. west of 130th mile post on small swift stream running north.

Saturday, 19th

Left camp at 8:00 a.m. to move west over another mountain range. Had a hard ascent to make, requiring eight mules to take up the lightest load. At 1:15 p.m. was about 10 chs. W. of camp, 40 chs. south and 15 chs. higher. Camped at 3:30 p.m. on swift running stream, going north with a similar one 20 chs. east of us and Mts. all around us. Raining all p.m. The camp is on the 133rd mile. Took an azimuth. Lon killed an antelope.

Sunday, July 20th, 1873

Did not work. Lon and I rode over the Mts. to look for a way over with the teams. Found an old blazed road. Much speculation as to who made it. Ate our lunch on a snow bank 10,000 ft. above the level of the sea. Mosquitoes very bad there. Boys picking wild strawberries in camp at foot of Mt. Campbell killed an antelope. Rained in p.m.

Monday, 21st

Lon and party went on with line. Billie going out with pack mules to supply them bed and board. Went with Neal to clear fallen timber from the road. Hunted in p.m. George Scott still sick but improving. Pattison

Surveyors on the "line" in snowy mountains in summer
Allyn Collection, 1904, Riverton (Wyoming) Museum

came in feeling unwell. The change of climate is too great for some of the boys. Line running through heavy woods, 2-1/2 miles.

Tuesday, 22nd

Rose at daylight to hunt, as the boys must have game on the lines. Came into breakfast at 5:00 a.m. Left camp again at 5:30 and in 20 minutes had an antelope. The largest yet. Weighing over a hundred pounds dressed and very fat. Rode out on line. Found the boys eating dinner on a snow bank with a smudge [smoky fire] to keep off the mosquitoes. The line crosses the road on the 138th mile. Continental Divide. We will move tomorrow.

Wednesday, 23rd

Broke camp at 7:00 a.m. Took dinner on side of mountain. Crossed over summit and camped on small stream 1/2 mile S. of 139th mile post. Billie came in with his pack train and took out a new supply of provisions.

Thursday, 24th

Left camp at 6:00 a.m. and prospected for the road which we have been following. Traced it to a ravine where it crosses our line. Broke camp at 10:00 a.m. Reached the line and camped a little north and a few chains east of 142nd M.P. [mile post] on which mile the road crosses the line to the N. Quite a stream just north of camp running west which we take to be Little Snake River. Mts. all around us. The men on line came into camp and it seemed quite a reunion. Had a slight touch of a mountain thunder storm near dark. The thunder roared and crashed through the valleys in a terrible manner.

Friday, July 25th, 1873

Left camp at 6:15 a.m. road hunting. Found a camping place on a small stream running north on the last 1/2 of 144th mile btwn. two N. & S. Mts. Killed a black tailed deer just in the place for camp. Broke camp at 10:30 and moved over Mt. and camped at 3:30 in a hailstorm. Yesterday, our line ran along a stream which it crossed five times. Today over a high mountain. The line is running through heavy timber and the men make but two (2) miles per day. Slow progress, and cold nights approaching.

Saturday, 26th

Moved west and camped on stream 50 lks. wide running north—1/2 S. of 145th post. Rained in p.m. Billie went out to line with his pack train. Had difficulty in tracing our old road.

Sunday, July 27th

Broke camp at 7:00 a.m.— Dinner on stream running north about a mile north of the line. Quite a heavy rain about noon. At 2:00 p.m. the teams moved west and I took bread and venison and started S. to the line which I readily found. Ben being unwell came back to camp with me. Camp about north of 149th post—1-1/2 miles.

Monday, 28th

Left camp on pony to find road at 6:00 a.m. Traced it south over a high mountain and fortunately found the line on S. side. Took Billy and his pack mules and returned to camp at 12:00 m. Was camped on Line at 5:00 p.m. MacConnel went out to the line to assist in taking an Azimuth. Billie and outfit also went out. Matt and Dick came in to camp. Rained in p.m.

Tuesday, 29th

Left camp at 6:15 a.m. Found that our road runs on south from here to a range of Mts. and is of no further service so we must chop our way through. The field party are now two miles ahead of us. In p.m. went out to line and a mile beyond the party, from which point I could see an open country ahead extending to a range of Mts. perhaps fifty miles distant. Reported the discovery to the boys and there was joy in camp. After working three weeks in heavy timber an open prairie looks beautiful. Marked a road back through the woods for the boys to chop out tomorrow for the teams and we will move on. Thermometer below freezing in camp this morning while in the other camp on the Mts. at an elevation of 10,000 ft. it was 47 degrees above zero. Dick sick this morning but went on the line this p.m. Texas in camp sick. MacConnel still on line and Matt in camp.

Wednesday, 30th, '73

Left camp at 6:00 a.m. Reached the line at 8. Found Lon taking a long sight over all the timber ahead of us—probably two miles. Traveled a while with Billie and his train hunting a passage down the Mt. Found none. While I was gone, the boys were chopping out the road— Got back to them at 2:00 p.m. Found them about half way along with the teams. Road steep and through timber— Lots of chopping. Billie came in for "grub" at 4:00 p.m. Had seen nothing of them since morning. There is some danger of their laying out tonight. Went into camp near 152nd post at 6:00 p.m. Have discovered no way down the Mts. yet. Must find one tomorrow.

Thursday, 31st, 1873

Left camp at 6:00 a.m. Blazed a road to foot of Mt. Returned to camp at 9:00 a.m. and with three of the men went to work chopping out a road. Ben and Lew came in from line to help. Lon and party are out of the woods. I wish we were. The way looks pretty bad over the Mts.

Friday, Aug. 1st

Left camp at 6:00 a.m. while the men were clearing the road to the foot of the Mt. Blazed a road around the south side of the same. At 10:00 a.m. Bert, Dick and Pat came to us to help us over— The remainder of the line party being in camp awaiting us. Passed over the highest part of the Mts. and camped on low divide on line near 155 M.P. Stood guard 40 minutes apiece.

Saturday, Aug. 2nd

Broke camp at 7:30 and started down the Mt. Met Lon about 11:00 a.m. Reached Snake River [today's Little Snake River] at noon, crossed it twice and at 2:30 reached the other camp. Quite a reunion, having been separated a week. Our pass over the Mts. was a rough one and long to be remembered and now we can sing "out of the wilderness." An old miner named Duickl stayed with Lon's party last night. The first man we have seen for over a month. Two other miners with us tonight. They are at work 22 miles south of here on Henz Peak or what used to be the Bear River diggings. Not much gold, about wages. We apparently have an open though broken country ahead of us and hope to make better time hereafter. We will run another day and then put in a station. Are now camped on Snake River. Lon and I scouted ahead a few miles this p.m. and Lon killed an antelope. Campbell did also. "Ain't I glad I'm out of the wilderness." Karner, a miner working at Henz Peak, went east to the divide on south end of North Park prospecting with Perkins. Both young men. About July 25th accidentally shot himself through the leg. His companion returned to camp for help and upon returning found him dead. These facts given us by James Carroll, a miner and friend of Karner's.

Sunday, Aug. 3rd

Moved camp west about 5 miles, crossing the Snake River twice and driving up a steep mountain side camped on line at the 163rd mile post on plain near Sheep Mt. and a few miles S. E. of Battle Mt. where the Utes and Arapahoes or the latter and trappers which lasted ten days [*sic*]. Nothing definite about it. Erected post for observations as we will put in a station here. Lon and Texas caught a fine string of trout and Pat killed a goose.

Monday, Aug. 4th

Trout and cornbread for breakfast. Spent the greater portion of the day hunting a stone suitable for the monument at this place. Found one and got it to camp all right. Max went out in the morning on Sheep Mt. just west of here and killed a mountain sheep and an antelope. Lon went out in p.m. after supper and killed a sheep and a black tailed buck. Professor got some pretty fair observations last night. Cloudy and rainy at dark. Boys caught lots of trout.

Tuesday, 5th

Went trout fishing. "Caught 'Em you bet." (Washed out clothes and mended my breeches. confidential). Campbell killed two antelope. No stars last night so the work of the night before is worthless too.

Wednesday, 6th

Lounged about camp. Wrote to Nellie Wakeley. Good observations last night. Campbell and I strolled over to Sheep Mt. After supper. I killed a young buck on the steep side of the Mt. Shot him through the head and heart.* Campbell wounded one. Was on guard last night.

Thursday, 7th

A duplicate of yesterday. Weather pleasant. Wrote to Alice. Went out with Lon in p.m. He killed a black tailed buck. Have high living nowadays and no work. Deer, antelope, sheep, geese, trout and grouse, breakfast 8 and dinner 3.

---

*A fuller version of the story was later published. See p. 231.

Friday, 8th

MacConnel completed his observations last night. Today we will set the stone and move on— Weather fine— Wrote home— Later. As we couldn't get started today, it being late when Mr. McC completed the reduction of his observs. We concluded to do nothing until tomorrow. Cloudy at sunset.

Saturday, 9th

Found our line 252 ft. south of our tent. Set stone shaft with huge old mound and elk horns on top. Lon went on with line. Left camp at 11:00 a.m. Camped on the river on W. side of Sheep Mt. (which we crossed on 165th mile) near the 158th M.P. Explored Battle Mt. on a mule, Reached camp at dark. Raining. Lon killed a she black bear.

Sunday, 10th

Breakfast at 5:00 a.m. Men left camp at 5:30. Camp in motion at 6:30. Camped at 2:00 p.m. on the river 20 chs. N. of 175.40 M.P. Killed an antelope. Supper at 5:00 p.m. No dinner.

Monday, 11th

Broke camp at 6:00 a.m. and moved down Snake River. Three miles from camp found Reader's Ranch. An old Galenian. Bought of him flour, baking powder, thread and buckskin. Two (2) miles further found Slater & Brown's Ranche. Jim Baker, the old partner of Bridger, also lives there. The latter with three teams just starting for Rawlins* for winter supplies. Sent in mail. Learned that Bridger's Pass is about twenty (20) miles north of where we crossed the Mts. and the settlers very much surprised that we could cross elsewhere. Four miles below Slater's is Perkin's store. Bought of him baking powder, tobacco and pick. Went south to line on pony. Found it 1-1/2 miles south of river. Came back, took on wood and water, crossed river and struck S. W. to the line. Made dry camp in sagebrush at (186) M.P. Men made 11 miles on line. Raining at dark.

Tuesday, Aug. 12th

Broke camp at 6:30. Took dinner on the Snake—where the line crossed at 192nd M.P. In p.m. went S. around a bend and camped at 6:00 p.m. on S. side and on line at 197 m. 20 chs. Took an Azimuth in evening.

Wednesday, 13th

Broke camp at 6:30. Brought teams on line to the river which we crossed on the 1st 1/4 of the 204th mile. Had dinner near 204th M.P.

*Rawlins, Wyoming, named after General John A. Rawlins

Then turned north to get around the bluffs. Got about four miles N. of line. Got back to the line at sundown. Camped on dry creek at 208 m. 20 chs. Have now averaged nine (9) miles on line from last station. The country here perfectly worthless. Nothing but sagebrush and greasewood. Soil sandy clay.

Thursday, Aug. 14th, 1873

Neal, Al and Geo. left camp with the stock at 4:00 a.m. to take them down to the river to water and grass. Boys left camp at 6:00 a.m. Stock returned at 9:30. Broke camp at 10:15. Country very rough and timbered making it difficult to get the team along. Reached the party at 5:00 p.m. in dry ravine at 217th M.P. Lon and I went in search of water. Found none. The Muddy which according to the maps should come in here does not appear, but instead we found a dry bed, fortunately have about fifty gallons of water aboard, enough for the men but the stock must go dry. Took an Azimuth.

Friday, Aug. 15th

Left camp at daylight with George, Al and Neal and the stock to go to the river for water. Found the distance to be over ten miles. Filled our barrels with water. Got a post for the large transit and returned to camp at 1:30 p.m. Billie who had gone west on a mule at daylight returned to camp at 9:00 a.m. having found water six miles ahead. The line had gone on. Broke camp at 2:30 p.m. Camped at 223rd M.P. on small sulphur spring; erected post for observations— Had supper and went to bed.

Saturday, 16th

Mr. MacConnel had a good night for work. Left camp at daylight on old Jim to scout country ahead. At 12:00 m. came to deep canon with small stream of water at least 20 miles from camp. Turned my face campward, found my canteen strap broken and it gone. Canon too deep for a descent. A rain coming up, I spread my rubber coat and caught a pint of water. Ate my lunch—a biscuit and rode on. Reached camp at 5:40 p.m. having been in the saddle just twelve hours and ridden at least forty-five miles. The country here a perfect desert. No wood, grass or water. It behooves us to make good time to Green River fifty miles away. Our supplies are getting low. No game here at all but rabbits. An old road runs west about 20 chs. north of this camp. Suppose it to be the old Cherokee trail upon which they returned from Oregon 18 years ago. It runs nearly west and we must follow it to get through the country, which is badly broken west of us for thirty miles where we come to the Escalante Mts. an unknown country as yet.

Sunday, 17th

Another good night for observations and for me of rest and sleep. Wrote to Stebbins and read Shakespeare and so forth and rested mostly. A beautiful day, but a terrible place in which spend it. Surely "the sound of a church going bell these valleys and hills never heard" and never will they hear a more melodious sound than the howl of the coyote or the dismal cawing of an unfortunate crow. Several of the boys are hunting and their united endeavors secured one poor little rabbit.

Monday, 18th

Breakfast at 6:30. A good night for observations and Mr. MacC completed them. The first time we have had three successive clear nights.

Sunday, 24th

Since the last entry as above much has transpired out of the usual routine of our monotonous life but nothing serious or very alarming. Upon reducing the observs. of Sunday night it was found that the instrument was out of adjustment, therefore another night's work was necessary. On Tuesday these observs. were reduced. We found the line 92 ft. south. Set the monument at the 223rd M.P. A stone 12 x 14 in. 10 ft. long. Corrected back and made ready for a start. On Wednesday, left camp at daylight [illegible] and teams. Shot two young sage hens as we were starting. Even these are a delicacy in this barren and desolate country. The men made 17-1/2 miles on the line stopping on high bank of Vermillion Creek which I visited last Saturday. I took dinner to men on the line, and the campmen misunderstood my instructions and went three miles too far west on a road running three miles north of the line. Came back and down to line which we reached two hours after dark. Had supper at 11:00 p.m. Went on guard at 2:30 a.m. On Thursday morning left camp at daylight on pony to try and find crossing over the canon before us. No description can give an idea of the magnitude of these canons. Returned at noon without finding a pass. In p.m. the men ran the line ten miles west. Mr. MacC accompanying them. We took team back to the road. I proceeded, then about an hour crossed Vermillion Canon and on the road two miles west of it discovered a troop of some kind galloping toward me about two miles farther west. From close observations thought they were Indians; rode back and corralled teams on east side of canon— Sent Fred out to tell the men where camp was, though we had previously intended camping on the canon and having the men walk up to camp. Billie and I went out again on the road but saw no signs. The men on line had seen elk signs and probably the troop I saw were elk. Mr. MacC did not come in with the line men and we feared he would lie out. After supper Bob took a light and went to pilot him. Found him at 12:00 m. about five miles S. W. of camp in a canon containing good water. Had a fire and was comfortable but hungry. Would not come in, fearing to carry his chronometer through the brush at night. Bob reached camp at 3:30 a.m. Friday. After breakfast, Bob took some provisions and coffee and went back to find Mac as he had intended remaining where he was until the line men came out— We moved west about four miles on road; then turned south, and at 11:00 a.m. struck stream, the Vermillion running E. then S. high steep banks. Built a bridge. Just as we finished dinner, MacC hove in sight on the trail. Had not waited for Bob but went to our old camp and followed us in—twenty four hours without eating and laying out in a rainstorm. Had not seriously affected him. In p.m. the line men went south and E. to where they quit work and ran few miles of line. Could not move camp, so they walked in three miles. Saturday the 23rd crossed on our bridge. Moved camp S. W. across from Big Creek on the S. side of which we camped at the 249th M.P. Took an Azimuth. Saw and wounded an antelope. Ran him three miles with a mule but did not get him. Good grass and water near and quite a change from the desert proper, though we are hardly out of it

Sunday the 24th broke camp early. Got teams to top of bluffs on west side of creek at 10:00 a.m. The men ran the line three miles and at noon were stopped, or rather the teams were, by a huge canon. Suspended work and went south around it. All hands except Dick. He followed along the line and killed two antelope and now at sundown we are anxiously expecting him in. Are camped about a mile south of the line and probably about 254th M.P. A mountain lies to the west of us and we don't know what the country is beyond it to Green River. Hope for the best though, for provisions are very short. Sugar gone several days ago. Saw many deer and antelope today. Also mountain sheep.

Monday, 25th

Line men left camp at sunrise to go East to canon which stopped us yesterday. On the east side of the canon lies the scene of the great Diamond Excitement of last winter.* Numerous claims are staked out but unoccupied. The country is wholly barren and the only hypothesis upon

---

*In 1872, several Kentuckians perpetrated a hoax on group of San Francisco bankers. Even jeweler Charles L. Tiffany was duped in "arguably the biggest swindle in the history of the frontier West"[22]—$650,000, about $16.4 million in 2022. A "Diamond Field" still appears on U.S. Geological Survey maps despite the absence of diamonds.

The field is on the state line between Wyoming's Sweetwater County and Colorado's Moffat County; the only town in the vicinity is Hiawatha, Colorado.

which diamonds could be expected would be that of the hunters' coon dog— good for nothing else imaginable. These diamond fields are on the 251st and 2nd miles of our line, partly in Wyoming and partly in Colorado. I took old "Jim" and I scouted ahead for a road. Returning at 9 a.m. saw and chased a large black bear but lost him in the timber. Just as camp was moving, saw him again north of camp on the prairie. Gave chase again on a pony and succeeded in running him into the teams. He passed very close to Max and Arthur who gave him a shot each, breaking his fore leg. He did not fight but succeeded in escaping. Line men made 8 miles and we camped in a beautiful grassy valley. Quite an oasis in this desert. This is the head of a stream running into Green River.

Tuesday, 26th

Broke camp at sunrise. Killed a buck antelope just after starting. Stopped for dinner on a mountain which rises 2000 feet in 1-1/2 miles. Drove teams up the east slope. Scouted ahead and found roads down the west slope to the southwest. Line ran 7 miles. Camped opposite and about 3 miles south of 167th M.P. Men ran onto a large black bear coming in. No damage done.

Wednesday, 27th

Broke camp at 7 a.m. At 10 a.m. struck Red Creek, which is properly named. A small stream running south into the Green River in Brown's Hole, which is five miles south of the line. Camped on Spring Creek which is about 280th mile. The line was run to 273rd M.P. Left team and lunch for men on the hill 6 miles east of camp. Green River, according to our map, should have been at the 273rd mile corner but it is apparently several miles to the west. Grub is about played out and guess will have to start for town tomorrow at any rate. Built fire after dark to guide men to camp. Spring Creek here runs on top of the ground while a few rods above or below it runs through a deep cut.

Thursday, 28th

Lon and I with Al and a team and a saddle mule with one day's rations started at 7 o'clock for Green River. Went west ten miles on a road when we struck the river. Crossed first channel but failed on second one—too deep. Apparently this road does not go to the station. Turned back to take a trail which we saw on Red Creek. Passed camp at 3:30 p.m. Had lunch of coffee and mush*—and pushed ahead. The boys are left with nothing

*A thick porridge usually made of cornmeal

but a bushel of beans and a keg of molasses. They won't starve on this, but it's pretty hard living. Campbell is running line and on the hill west of camp met the team with half a deer aboard, which Lon killed 800 yards distant. A good shot. This will help the boys out a little. Reached Red Creek at dark. While hunting a camping place was astonished to hear the shouts of herders "rounding up" cattle. Followed up the sound and two miles south found a herd of 1300 cattle and ten drovers. Had supper with them and learned that Green River was 60 miles away and the road ran up from Red Creek, as we supposed. Also Mr. Richards* here who has a cow camp three miles north.

Next morning, the 29th

We went to his camp for breakfast. He kindly offered to lend us bread and meat to last us and our camp till we got back. We left note in road for Billie, who is coming over, telling him where to go for rations and to bring another team out ten miles north of Richards' to meet us, as the road from there is bad. Reached the Poplar Grove on the high divide 35 miles from the station about sundown. Here is wood, water and grass in the midst of a desert. A splendid camping place. Made a good supper on potatoes, bread, coffee and young sage hens, four of which I shot with a rifle on the road.

Saturday, 30th

Was on the road at 6:30 a.m. Reached Green River at 2 p.m. Found an immense amount of mail. Everything all right at home. No bad news at all. It seems impossible that so little of importance has transpired in two months, the time which has elapsed since we last received mail. In the hurry and excitement of an active participation in the daily life of a large city, one cannot frame a just estimate of the importance of passing events, but isolated as we have been—cut off from all communication with the world in general for two months, then to have the detailed history of that time laid before us in the unbroken files of a daily paper and we can form a full and correct estimate of the day's doings. In Omaha the papers are wonderfully alike; suicides, assaults, robberies and arrests make a large portion of its daily history. Nor is this confined to our city alone. The Associated Press dispatches are mostly adapted to Police Gazette use. After reading all the news, we are better contented with our exile than before. Although isolated as we are, we seem to be playing fully as an important a part as the majority at home. Received full report from Aut,

---

*Probably George Richards, whose name and brand ad appeared in the *Brand Book* for 1884 and in later Sweetwater County newspapers.[23]

with papers in abundance; also letters from Father, Mother, Alice, Delia [Alice's sister] and Nellie B. Got our freight from depot. Bought flour, sugar, potatoes, clothing for the boys &c. Expended $200.00 in short order. Had wagon loaded at 6 p.m. Took supper at R.R. eating house—the poorest on the road. Saw Reynolds and Goodwin in mail car going down. Sent in trunk and Lon's watch by Goodwin, i. e., the latter by him, the former by express. In the evening, wrote until 3:30 a.m. on Sunday, Aug. 31st. Slept until 5 a.m. Had breakfast, and Lon with team started for camp. I remained with "Johnny" the mule to get some new axes ground. Found that a registered letter had come that morning for us. Containing draft from treasury department for the survey of boundary of Pawnee Reserve.* Could not get it cashed in Green River. Endorsed and sent it to Aut for payment [via postal money order]. Had dinner at eating house and at 1 p.m. started after the team. Caught them at 4 p.m. By driving until 10:20 p.m. made Poplar Grove again. Found Bill Tabor, a noted hunter, here and another man camped there. Saw Johnson and Ed O'Sullivan on mail car this morning. They are fine fellows. Also saw Matt Hyde.

Monday, Sept. 1st

Went on the road at daylight. Met the other team near Tabor's, just the right place. Divided the load and proceeded on our way. Camped with Richards on Red Creek.

Tuesday, Sept. 2nd

After taking a lesson on the "Diamond Hitch" used in packing, moved on for camp, which we reached. at 4 p.m. and were gladly welcomed indeed. The boys were again down to beans and molasses, but were cheerful. Brought in a. heap of mail. Campbell fired a couple of shots into a bear coming in but without doing him serious injury. Had a good full night's sleep.

Wednesday, Sept. 3rd

For myself a day of rest. Much needed for we had a long hard trip. Lon is quite unwell but nothing serious I think. MacC. got a few stars last night, the first at this station. Boys fishing and washing. No game here. Ben killed a fawn while we were gone and carried it ten miles to camp. No game nearer. Wrote letters and sent over to Richards' camp by Billie.

Thursday, Sept. 4th

MacC. got a few more stars last night. Went and found stone for mon-

---

*Richards had finished the resurvey in May. See pp. 246–47.

ument which Matt is now working. Did our washing. Billie returned at 2 p.m. and Smith came with him. Took dinner and went on to a hunter's camp a few miles west of here.

Friday, Sept. 5th

Breakfast at 7 a.m. A beautiful morning but rather cool last night as I found on guard. MacC. got sufficient stars last night to determine our location and now as soon as he has reduced his observations we will correct back as far as necessary, cross the river and propel. We are now camped on the 289th mile, leaving but 80 miles to run and good assurances of an open country half way at least.

Saturday, Sept. 6th

Gave MacC. another night at station all right now. Campbell and Billie went back 17 miles to correct. The boys have the monument planted at the 289 mile and we have the team on the west side of the river and will take dinner on the bank.

Evening, Sept. 6th

Got the line across O.K. and made five miles, camping on the line and on the east bank of Henry's Fork. This is a clear, swift mountain stream, running over a gravel bed, skirted with timber and easy to cross. This is the most picturesque and convenient camp on the line thus far, and the only good camp since leaving the Snake River, nearly a hundred miles back.

Sunday, Sept. 7th

Broke camp at 6 a.m. the line crossing the river near camp. Moved teams up the Fork about five miles and stopped for dinner, or rather to give the cooks a chance to bake bread. On the way up crossed the stream several times, once the first time near the ranch of Charley Davis—(supposed to be) just south of which the line runs. At 10:30 o'clock took a pail of lunch—canteen of water and one of molasses and mounted on a mule went South to find and feed the men. A Mexican herding for Joe Baker accompanied. We mounted on a stallion to see how it was done. On the way out his horse bucked him off and got away but he caught him and went on his way. Returned to camp and moved up opposite Baker's ranche and then struck South to the line. We men made 11-1/2 miles and we camped at dark one half mile North of the line near a pine mountain. A dry camp. Found dead deer near camp.

Monday, Sept. 8th

Broke camp at sunrise. Took dinner on a little stream, the third within one-half mile, on which is thick underbrush through which we had to cut. Lon being troubled with a sort of diarrhea, I ran the line 5 miles in P.M. making a dry camp without wood, burning a, couple of posts. Camped on the 317th M.P. Took an Azimuth. Killed an antelope in A.M. Yesterday is the first Sunday that ever passed without my knowing it was Sunday. N.B. Crossed Beaver Creek on the 314th mile, several streams in a narrow bottom all skirted with thick willows.

Tuesday, Sept. 9th

At 4 a.m. Neil and Ben took team and went South to the mountains for wood. Had breakfast at 6 a.m. Crossed a fork of Henry's Fork at 10 a.m. Stopped at noon on another stream for dinner. Made ten miles by 2:45 p.m. which brought us to a top of a high bluff at the fork of which runs another fork of the Fork. Dick and I went a foot to the east edge of a mountain range three miles west and gave Lon a long sight. Saw an elk and three deer. Found the country rough and heavily timbered. Will have to put in a station where we are on the bluff; send the team to Evanston and go through to the corner 43 miles with pack mules.

Wednesday, Sept. 10th

Got a post and some wood. Moved camp over to the 327 M.P. and set up for a station. Went out west three miles hunting. Found nothing. Lon killed a deer and the boys caught lots of trout.

Thursday, Sept. 11

Went out hunting stone. Could find nothing. Will have to go back to Henry's Fork tomorrow.

Friday, 12th

Started Campbell, five men and a team back to the Fork for a stone for our monument. Dick and I went fishing. Got back at sundown tired, wet and hungry, but with fish enough for breakfast. Lew and Ben went out and brought in a deer which they killed yesterday. The stone hunters not yet returned.

Saturday, 13th

Nothing doing today. Lon and Arthur went fishing. George also. Brought in a fine string of trout. No sign of the boys yet. They must have gone a long way back. Tonight is clear and this makes the third good night for observations. Tomorrow we can put in the monument if the boys return, and on the following day move on. Wrote letters to Delia and Alice today.

Sunday, 14th

Another Sabbath which probably would have passed unnoticed, had we not been in camp. Weather very fine. As pleasant as September at home. Spent the morning in packing some of the mules we will use who were strangers to the business. Ben and Billie are busy getting the provisions, etc., ready for trip. The boys returned at noon with a good stone, which they found on Henry's Fork about twenty five miles from here. Pat killed a black-tailed buck, so their provisions held out. Spent the P.M. in getting the stone marked, drawing stones for the monument and getting ready for a start tomorrow. MacC. finished his work last night.

Monday, 15th

Matt finished marking the stone this morning and at 9 a.m. I moved out with the line, taking 8 men, 4 pack mules and 2 saddle horses, each man carries a gun and ammunition. The pack train overtook us four miles on our way. Did not stop for dinner. Ran the line 4-1/2 miles, and camped in a little grassy glade at 4-3/4 miles. Made a bivouac by cutting boughs and setting them up leaning against a long pole supported between two trees. Dug a little spring just behind camp. No running water. In unpacking the mules Ben (the cook) made the unwelcome discovery that instead of a sack of beans he had brought one of green coffee. The teams are well on their way to Ft. Bridger ere this, so we will have to run on bread, meat and coffee. We have one canteen full of molasses, but have agreed to not use any until ten miles of this check is completed. The country is not very rough but thickly covered with pine timber, much of which is dead. Have a big camp fire in front of our bivouac, by the light of which the boys are playing euchre, posting diaries, etc. Will stand no guard tonight nor until we see signs of Indians. A slight sprinkling of rain today, but perfectly clear now.

Tuesday, 16th

Had a fair night's rest, but being unused to quite so much ventilation, not as good as usual. Breakfast of venison, bread and coffee at 5 a.m. and on the line at 6. Chopped three fourths of a mile to the edge of the bluff from which we got a sight 1.50 m. chs.* across Smith's Fork of Green

---

*Here and afterward, Richards sometimes wrote the *m* and *ch* or *c* above the figures, which must indicate miles and chains.

River—a stream similar to Henry's Fork where we last camped upon it. Crossed this fork on the 334th mile. The valley is wooded and the hills upon either side descend to the stream in a succession of "steppes" or level plateaus, upon which are large lakes of living water, clear and cold with a gravel bottom inhabited by fish and beaver. From the 333.50 M.P. looking E. and N. E. seven of these lakes are in view all on different elevations, with the steep mountain sides around them covered with dense pine forests, the open plains away to the North, and the high, rugged, snow-clad mountains to the South, making the landscape one of unequalled beauty in my experience. Made three miles and four chains stopping at 5:45 p.m. at 333.68 M.P. Had a good dinner brought out by Billie, which I carried a mile to the boys. Camped in the woods near a spring and grassy valley. Lew killed a deer at sundown, which came just in time, as we had used the last of our venison. Salt meat is not good to work on. Ours is a good specimen of a camp in the woods tonight. A bivouac of boughs, with a roaring fire of pine logs before it. Heavy timber about us. The mules on one side, tied up for the night—their packs on the other. A dressed deer ornamenting a tree near by—and the boys around the camp fire, having their regular evening game of euchre. Weather clear and pleasant.

Wednesday, 17th

In the woods all day. Camped at 335.40 but got the line up to 336. Weather cool but clear.

Thursday, 18th

Was on the line at 6 a.m. From the 336.40 M.P. got a sight of 2.65 M.P. across two streams and up on the side of a mountain. Set the 338 M.P. one chain east of a well traveled road running N. & S. Camped near the 339.25 M.P. the chainmen being about a mile behind. The sky became overcast with leaden ominous looking clouds this P.M. and there is every indication of a long storm. The equinoctial is in order any time now. Placed our camp in a well protected ravine, with a view to standing a storm, if a hard one sets in, we can build a log cabin pretty "sudden." Wrote a note to Lon. Would like to get an Azimuth tonight but it is too cloudy.

Friday, 19th

We escaped last night with only a slight sprinkling of snow and rain and this morning is clear. Guess that is all we will see of the dreaded equinoctial. The chainmen and Billie went back and chained up. Sent my note to

Lon by them, to be stuck upon a post in the road, trusting to the cold charities of the world for its being more properly posted. Pushed on with the line. The timber large and thick. First 1/2 mile through quaking aspen, much worse than pine for running. Only made 1-1/2 miles, camping at 340.57 M.P. where I took an azimuth. No water near camp. In hunting for a spring just before sundown, surprised and killed a very large buck. Got Dick to help me load him on a pony and it was hard work for both of us. We estimated the weight dressed at 300 pounds. His horns are 7-pronged, bare of velvet, and very sharp. The country today was ascending to the 340th mile, where I think we reached the summit of the Uintahs on our line. Elevation 9,950 feet. Timber heavy but no snow.

Saturday, 20th

Had an unexpected rain, hail and snow storm last night, accompanied by lightning and heavy thunder. Several trees were struck with lightning near us. Now at 11 a.m. after the sun shining all the morning, snow and ice lie thick upon the ground. The weather seems like November. Dinner at 2 p.m. at 342.23. Got a long sight, or two rather, from the same point. The first in the bottom on the west side of Black's Fork, at which we camped. The other about a mile west on the mountain side.

Sunday, Sept. 21st, '73

Cut through the timber 23 chs. east from camp and set the 343rd post, then ran west through the timber setting the 345th post at sundown near which we camped. The line crossed Black's Fork at 343.15 M.P. Billie and Matt went down stream a mile from our camp of last night to a tie cabin and ground some of the axes. Quite a large number of men employed here getting out [railroad] ties, which are run down stream at high water to the U.P. Last night was the coldest we have had in these mountains. Water froze four inches deep, within ten feet of our camp fire which was burning all night.

Monday, 22nd

Rather warmer last night. Slept well beside the camp fire. Made 1-1/4 miles before dinner, but in the P.M. struck some large dry pines "on line" which checked us somewhat. The trees were over four feet in diameter and about 110 feet high and perfectly straight. Heard a steam whistle last night which we suppose to come from a saw mill to the south of us. This is the first indication of civilization that we have seen since leaving Cheyenne. All the people that we have seen in the scanty settlements through which we have passed, seemed entirely destitute of ambition, satisfied with game enough to eat and nothing to do but hunt it. Took an azimuth this evening at the 347th post. Have run 20 miles in eight days, or an average of 2-1/2 miles per day through heavy timber.

Tuesday, 23rd

Took dinner on the west side of a road running south to Coe & Carter's saw mill which is a mile from the line. Sent a letter to Lon by the superintendent of their work. Camped for the night near another saw mill in which Dick Carter is part owner and so also is one Scott. Made 2-1/2 miles, camping at 349.40 M.P. The timber on the mountains to the south of us is all on fire, making a splendid spectacle. Learned from a man in charge of the saw mill, which is not running now, that we have but five miles of timber before us. This is glad news to us, for this timber business is slightly monotonous and camping out without tents at this season is not very pleasant.

Wednesday, 24th

We were at work early, but were delayed a long time by a large dead pine tree, that centered on its stump and was so supported by the branches of surrounding trees that it would not fall. Made 1/2 mile before dinner. About noon the fire which has been steadily bearing down toward the line and the saw mill, crossed the little stream that the mill is upon, about 5 chs. south of the mill, so that probably it escaped, but the one belonging to Coe & Carter seems to be right in its line. Made 1-3/4 miles by sundown, through heavy timber, but the prospect ahead is a little better. May get out of the woods tomorrow.

Thursday, 25th

Made almost 3 miles today by getting a 1-1/2 mile sight. Country rather rough and cracked up by land slides. Camped at 354.10 M.P. A great deal of wood chopping is being done near here and some charcoal burning. Are out of venison now and running on pork, bread and coffee. Plenty of game in the woods but we won't take time to hunt it. Took an azimuth this evening on the 354.10 M.P.

Friday Evening, Sept. 26

Hurrah! We are out of the woods and the end draws near, i. e., the west end. The 357th post came just on the west edge of the timber. We are now encamped on the west bank of Bear River, which we crossed at 358.30. Another stream almost as large crosses the line at 357.50 M.P., is

40 lks. wide. The bottoms bordering each stream are about 30 chains wide, and covered with a heavy growth of willow, but at present are not marshy. The streams are clear, swift running with gravel bottom. Are camped near the 359th post, which leaves but 9 miles to run, which we will do tomorrow, and then, Ho! for Evanston. Crossed the highest point of the Uintahs (on the line) yesterday on the 355th mile. Elevation 10,200 feet. Snow near the line.

Saturday, 27th, Evening

Hurrah! again. The "west end" so long looked for and anxiously expected is now behind us. We set the 368th post at 5 p.m., having run 9 miles, all open except 5 chains of quaking asp. The 366th mile passes over two very high backbones or hogbacks but the post comes upon a flat on the west side of them. Are now camped on a little stream 20 chains west of the 368th post. No timber near and we are burning sage brush again. Quite a high mountain rises just west of us and between the streams at its base runs an old well travelled road, which we suppose to be the old Mormon trail to Salt Lake. The weather is still clear and pleasant though cool. Lew killed a black-tailed fawn this morning.

Sunday, 28th

Slept rather cold last night. Was on the road at 8:45. Camped for dinner on Bear River. The road thence bears N. E. pretty strong, probably being somewhat longer than a mile across the country would be, but as we do not know the location of Evanston with relation to our terminal point, it is our best plan to follow the road. Came to the R.R. at 4 p.m. a short distance west of Hilliard station formerly known as the Tie Siding. Camped on Bear River again at the old stage road crossing and near a large ranche now deserted. Its owner made a fortune out of it and lost it on a tie contract, one of the victims of the railroad.

Monday, 29th

Was in motion at 7 a.m. Forded Bear River, all taking off our shoes and the pebbles and sand froze to the soles of our feet. Reached Evanston at 10 a.m. capturing our camp, as the boys were not aware of our proximity until we announced our arrival with a yell that would have done credit to a band of Comanches. Lon has been unable to open communications with Prof. Safford, and could not learn his whereabouts until today, consequently nothing has been done here. Otherwise, we are as near done as we expected. The Treasury Department has sent us draft for the main Pawnee work, so we have funds to run on. Sent the draft to Aut to be cashed, when it returns will pay off the men we can not use and await patiently. Safford is at Bismark, Dakota. Lon paid off and sent home Arthur, Al and Fred on the 24th. The U.P. Co. gave us half rates on tickets for the boys to go home upon. Found letters here for me from Alice and Miss Hurley and Judge Wakeley. In P.M. shaved for the first time on the trip. Changed my clothes and wrote to Aut.

Tuesday, 30th

Received amount of draft from Aut by express. Got answer from Safford. He cannot come till Oct. 20. Learned yesterday for the first time of the failure of Jay Cooke and Co. and the general financial panic.

Wednesday, October 1st

Paid off and sent home today Campbell, Dick, Billie, Lew, Pat, Max and Neal. (Saw Dr. Reed on platform on Monday.) Evanston is quite lively R.R. town but a dull place to loaf in. Wrote to Alice.

Thursday, October 2nd

Nothing doing. In evening, Lon and I looked through the Chinese department* of Sisson, Wallace & Co.'s store, accompanied by Mr. Hopkins, one of the firm. Purchased some trinkets. In P.M. rode over to a [coal] mining town called Almy, a mile west of Evanston.

Friday, October 3rd

Started to run a line from an observatory** here south to the bdry, with Matt and Bob flagmen, Ben and Geo. with the teams. Made about eleven miles and camped on a high divide. Weather cool.

Saturday, October 4

Continued the line and intersected the south boundary about the middle of the 364th mile. Set a post at the point of intersection and Mr. MacC.

---

*Created for the large numbers of Chinese who came to work on the transcontinental railroad and then in the coal mines. At this time there were about 100 Chinese in Evanston, perhaps one-sixth of the new town's population.[24]

**The astronomical station to precisely determine longitude for the western terminus of the south boundary was situated near the railroad station at Evanston in order to receive telegraphic time signals from the astronomical observatory at Salt Lake City, sometimes referred to as Brigham Young's observatory. When the latitude and longitude were determined at Evanston, the meridional distance (due south) to latitude 41° could be computed to the Utah/Wyoming parallel, then the distances along the parallel could be laid off to the west to set the southwest corner of Wyoming.[25]

began his work of determining the latitude of the bdry at this point.* Weather clear.

Sunday, 5th

Clear and pleasant. Am somewhat unwell with a diarrhea, the first indisposition of the trip for me. Matt went to town.

Monday, 6th

Weather clear last night, good for observations, but cloudy tonight and a little rainy. Ben went south to the mountains deer hunting and came back about 11 p.m. without having killed anything. Feel somewhat better this evening.

Tuesday, 7th

Clear in the morning but clouded up soon and snowed and rained alternately all day. Took Buck and went hunting. Was out until 4 p.m. Saw game but did not get a shot. Very disagreeable. Put up a stove in the cook tent today. Snowing hard at dark. Two nights that Mac could do nothing.

Wednesday, Oct. 8th, '73

Clear and pleasant this morning. The mountains all around us are white with snow but we escaped with very little. Ben went down to the mountains hunting. Saw about forty deer but killed none. Weather fine.

Thursday, 9th

Weather good. MacC. got some stars last night. A stranger from Nevada came into camp hunting a team and boy that are at work in the mountains somewhere. Asked him to stay over night and he gladly accepted, being tired and hungry. Lon and Matt came into camp in time for supper. Couldn't stand it in town any longer. Brought us mail from home.

Friday, 10th

MacC. finished the reductions of his observations this morning at 10 a.m. and Geo. and Matt with ponies went east correcting. In the P.M. Lon, Mac, Ben and I ran the line from Mac's station west to the 367th M.P. returning to camp at sundown. Bob still sick, apparently.

---

*Although the latitude was determined at Evanston, a subsequent latitude determination at the border did not require ultra-precise time as was required for the longitude determination. The sidereal (star time) and solar (civilian time) chronometers would provide adequate time for the latitude observations to verify that the south line had been accurately surveyed to establish the 41st parallel.[26]

Saturday, 11th

Broke camp at sunrise. Lon and I on ponies went west to build the mounds along the line, the teams and men going on the line to town. We reached Evanston at 4 p.m. and got dinner at a hotel, the teams getting in at sundown. Got letters from Judge W. and Alice.

Sunday, 12th

Took the 2 p.m. train for home with Geo. and Bob. Dinner at camp, supper at Green River.

Monday, 13th

Breakfast at Laramie, didn't feel well, headache, so didn't eat dinner or supper which we stopped for at Cheyenne and Sidney.

Tuesday, 14th

Breakfast at Grand Island. Dinner at Fremont. Reached home [Omaha] at 2 p.m. Found election red hot. Voted. With Bob, Arthur, Campbell and Aut had a visit in evening and some oysters.

Wednesday, 15th

Bob went home. Election good. All Republicans elected.

THIS SURVEY determined that the 34th meridian fell about half a mile west of Evanston, not in town as Daniel G. Major had determined in his survey of the Utah-Idaho boundary in 1871.* Surveying for latitude, Major could employ a field chronometer, while accurate observations of longitude required a telegraphic connection with a point whose longitude had already been established. For the 1873 survey, that point was Salt Lake City, about eighty miles west of Evanston on the Union Pacific Rail Road. (See footnote on p. 110.)

When Prof. Safford arrived, he took observations at Salt Lake on November 2, 3, 4, and 6 while MacConnel did the same at Evanston. They

---

*Major had established the line "in the street on West side of Evanston Hotel and about opposite a chimney on the West side of roof of same 18 ft. from the West side of the Hotel," wrote Lon in his 1873 notes.[28] In regard to the monument for the Wyoming-Utah-Idaho corner, he wrote in his 1874 field notes,[29]

> The observations for the location of this monument at the intersection of the 34th meridian with the 42nd parallel were also made at Evanston in 1871 by Mr. Daniel G. Major. Mr. Major's station was located about 1478 feet east of mine. His determination locates Evanston about 19 chains farther east than mine. Deducting this difference from 55.70 chs. leaves the line west of initial monument about 37 chains [.46 mile].

switched places and repeated the process on the 10th and 11th.

The observers exchanged stations to eliminate the "personal equation" that might lead to error, as had been done between Greenwich and Brussels, New York and Albany, and various other places both in Europe and America, Lon wrote in his field notes.[27] As noted earlier, surveyors measure the time it takes for a specific star to cross two meridians. A timing mistake of one second would cause a surveying error of 1,167 feet on the ground.[30] Among the instruments used was a Mean Time (solar/civilian time) Chronometer belonging to Brigham Young, the Mormon patriarch, to compare readings with Lon's Sidereal (star time) Chronometer.[31]

A red sandstone monument was carved in Wahsatch, Utah, delivered to the site,[32] and duly installed. Lon paid off the remaining members of the party, and in a letter of November 8, 1873, he grumbled to Will, "I hope I have enough left to get me out of this 'blasted country.'"[33]

Once home, he set to work on the field notes for the Land Office. Just two months later he had finished two volumes comprising 360 handwritten pages of surveying data such as astronomical readings and description of the country at each mile. By January 22, 1874, he had delivered them, and was able to crow to Will,[34]

> My notes were highly complimented in the Land Office and the [topographic] profile takes <u>amazingly</u> and is <u>new</u> to all of them. I saw the maps of that East line of Nevada or <u>West</u> perhaps the diagonal one anyhow. It is same scale as ours, but on continuous cloth backed paper. It is not <u>near</u> so well executed as ours to my notion. They liked the plan of single sheets because more easily handled. I think we ought to have put it on cloth backed paper though. Mr. Burchard [Congressman Horatio C.] went with me and I <u>think</u> we captured the whole institution, and all promised, from Comr. [Commissioner] down, to put it right through.

One of the Utah sides of the boundary monument set by A. V. Richards in 1873. It was the only state boundary corner marker installed by him that was still standing a century later. The story of their "remonumentation" begins on p. 157.

Andrew Johnson, 2019, hmdb.org

Survey of the Western Boundary
of Wyoming Territory, 1874

Background

ON THE SOUTHERN boundary survey, William A. Richards gained the additional knowledge and toughness he would need to tackle the more rugged western boundary. His brother Alonzo (Lon), the survey contractor, felt confident enough in his 25-year-old younger brother to turn over the most dangerous stretch to him. It was a grave responsibility: Significant errors, or the loss of mules or equipment on a mountain or river, could cost Lon dearly. Will and the party had to continue marking every mile accurately despite the high mountains, deep canyons, and dense timber. They would endure storms and icy temperatures, and somehow cross the unbridged rivers and canyons.

This survey was to follow the 34th meridian of longitude from Wyoming's southwest corner to the Montana border. With no telegraph stations available to help the surveyors stay on the meridian, they would have to rely on a transit that Lon had custom-made for this assignment. (Its photo and specifications are on p. 250.) The accuracy of the transit and other instruments was confirmed by a test that used the Evanston telegraph station. The new transit could also measure across rivers and canyons when the distance could not be chained directly[1] and would be particularly useful in locating the Wyoming boundary's point of intersection with the Idaho-Utah border. When the Richards party arrived there, Lon discovered that their line fell about seven-tenths of a mile west of the one established by Daniel G. Major in 1871.[2] They set their own marker and moved on, leaving Major's in place pending confirmation.

This tri-state "corner" happened to be near the point where the land became too rough for wheels, about one-third of the way to Montana. After this, the supplies would have to be carried by pack mules. Lon had decided that he would turn back with the wagons once they became impractical. He wanted to return to Omaha anyway, to scare up further contracts and be with his family—even though as contractor he was supposed to stay with the survey the whole time. At the end of August he would return with eminent astronomer Augustus MacConnel of Cambridge, Massachusetts, to confirm the terminal point of the boundary and set the monument for the northwest corner.

Will's diary begins when he was left in charge of the survey.

Saturday, June 20

11 A.M. Waiting at sight mound on hill east of camp for [flagman] Dick to get on line [illegible] across Thomas Fork. Roney on the bank sight and the pack train on line going down into the creek bottom. We are now at the 96th mile on the W Bdry. At this point the line becomes impassable for wagons as we intended sending them back as soon as they [illegible] here [illegible] yesterday with the party [illegible] camp and rearranged our outfit some to pack it all. Billie went to Montpelier the day before for mail and started yesterday but soon came back as he found it impossible almost to get out of the willows and sloughs that cover the creek bottom— In the P.M. Lon and I started to go north on the line to prospect the country a little. Crossed the stream but could not find a crossing for the pack train and spent the entire afternoon floundering through marshes and tangled willows, leading our horses, and often waist deep in water— Did not succeed in finding a crossing, and barely reached camp before dark, wet hungry and more tired than we had been before on the trip— This morning Lon went back with the team taking all our surplus baggage— He will remain at Omaha this summer and with Prof. Safford [the astronomer who confirmed the 1873 boundary terminus] meet me at Bozeman on Aug. 20th provided we get there. We made the happy discovery yesterday that no Latitude station is necessary at the Summit of the Rocky Mts., only one required at the terminal point. This is good luck surely. Although we have had the Instructions a year they had never been

---

Crew Members Mentioned in the 1874 Diary

Some of the men were veterans of the Richardses' surveys in Nebraska and the previous year's southern boundary survey. Their full names are taken from field notes or letters and matched up with names from diary where possible (in brackets).[3]

TOPOGRAPHER Porter P. Wheaton

FLAGMEN Richard L. Rossiter [Dick], Charles J. Roney

AXEMEN T. H. Ballard [Tom], Thos. Barry, C. Bordway [Charley?]

CHAINMEN Thos. E. McLeland [Mac?], W. F. Reavis [Frank?]

PACKERS W. H. Bordway [Billie], George A. Scott

COOK B. F. Morgan [Ben]

---

correctly interpreted before— We are well equipped for a two months trip and do not expect to be longer than that in reaching Bozeman— I received a letter from Nellie [Wakeley, a friend] yesterday and wrote a long one to Alice [his fiancée, Harriet Alice Hunt]— The idea of being for two months altogether shut out from civilization is not very pleasant, but it comes in the line of business and we do not complain——Evening. Sitting by the camp fire— We succeeded in getting the line flagged to the divide or high mountain north of the creek & chained 3ms 30chs. [miles, chains] making 99m 30— The boys followed up the creek about three miles till it runs through a narrow cañon with perpendicular walls 700 ft high where they found a crossing at 3 P.M. but the mules were so tired that they were compelled to unpack & go into camp— The little black mule fell down a hill and landed heels up against a fallen tree—and if that had not stopped her she would have gone into the stream. Billie came out to the line and we came into camp which we reached at sunset. We are all right tonight have did all we could in one day, now sitting around the camp fire taking a smoke, both of tobacco & pine logs— The elevation of the creek bottom on the line is 7500— one mile north 8550—

Sunday, June 21st

Breakfast at 6 A.M. Packed up by 8:30 & started East up the Fork on the N. side— Went around the point of the Mt. & took up a cañon bearing toward the line— the chainmen & moundmen went to the line the same way we came in last night, down the stream— Our cañon proved pretty rough for the pack mules, but no accident occurred. At 2 P.M. we struck the line, where I am now on a high peak. Have set Dick ahead [on the line], set the 100th mile [post] to the South and am waiting to set the 101st to the North— It has been raining off & on all day, but no one paid any attention to it nor has anyone objected to working on Sunday. Billie fired at a black tail deer yesterday but missed, and this morning as we were packing up a very large Cinnamon Bear came and sat on a hill about 20 chains from camp and overlooked the proceeding. Two of our hunters went after him but returned bootless, & if they had found him they might have been headless. Camp is near and we will do but little more today— Evening. made 1m 50 chs. today camping opposite the 101st M.P. Raining at sundown. In scouting ahead for a way out tomorrow—this P.M. Billie passed within 70 yards of another large bear who stood up and looked at him. As he had lost no bear he passed on—[sic]

Monday, June 22nd.

Was on the line at 6:30. Began raining at 9 and continued until 2 P.M.

In consequence of which we made but 2m 33c [chains, about .41 mile] and a mile of that was through timbers which we chopped. The packs also slipped badly and nearly every one had to be repacked. Old Jim [a mule] tipped over on a side hill but did nothing worse than smash a water pail, which is bad enough in this country— We are all wet & tired tonight but like [Dickens's] Mark Tapley "jolly still." Have two good camp fires going —Nothing but Mts ahead but think we can make a good run tomorrow—

Tuesday, June 23rd.

Broke camp at 6 A.M. Clear & warm, though we had a severe rain & hail storm last night. We were camped in the timber and the boom of falling trees, was not pleasant with the thought that one might fall across our tent, the thunder roared fearfully and its reverberations through the cañons was deafening, several trees were struck with lightning near camp but the morning showed us still uninjured, though our slumbers had not been remarkably peaceful. We have made a good run today, for the country and did considerable chopping made 5.27 camping 1/2 mile W. of 108.60 Passed the summit of the divide between Bear and Snake Rivers at Alt. 9,750—Was very much annoyed in the P.M. with mosquitoes. Dick gave me a sight of 1-3/4 miles and while waiting for me to come up went into the timber to look for Elk. Heard a great noise in the bushes on a side hill near & saw a large brown bear coming straight for him. Without any unnecessary delay he climbed the nearest tree & when safe among the upper limbs looked for his bear but he had departed perhaps worse scared than Dick. We see plenty of tracks & "indications" of game but as yet have killed nothing but grouse of which we have a couple for breakfast every day, though we shoot them only with Winchesters or revolvers—

Wednesday morning 24th.

At the line at 6 A.M. an open country before us for about twenty miles, badly broken but no timber— The snow clad mountains are gradually closing in upon us and in a few days we will be in their midst— Dinner at 2 P.M. at the 115 mile, on a clear stream 35 lks.* wide flowing E. Have made 6-1/4 miles so far today over (One of our tormentors above—) a rough but open country— The train still behind us— Charley brought out our dinner— Alt. 7750— 9 P.M. 10-1/4 miles run today, camp at 119 M.P. Every body well tired— Roney, Wheaton & Charley now out taking an azimuth.** I passed on that item as carrying the transit as far as I have

---

*Links. A chain has 100 links 0.66′ long, so 35 links = 19.25′, 20 = 11′, 10 = 5.5′, etc.

**The azimuth is the "direction" of a line with respect to the meridian (or true north).
  —Dr. Stoughton. See his article, p. 265.

today over a rough country almost makes a day's work. Wheaton was busy with topography all day. [I did not touch it.(?)] Alt. 8800.

Thursday June 25—

Left camp at 7 A.M.— Weather splendid but mosquitoes very troublesome— 10 o'clock A.M. — From the 122nd M.P. a settlement is in sight about four miles to the N. W. in a little valley running S. E. Think it is the Salt Works we have heard of. Evening.— At 12 M. stopped for dinner at 124.24 on Smoky Creek a branch of the Salt River— Being anxious to learn something of the country before us we stopped at this creek. The pack train came up at 2 P.M. and we went into camp after which Billie & I took a couple of mules and started for the cabins we had seen. Found them to be the Oneida Salt works owned by Mr. White. The salt water is found four feet below the surface, three vats are worked holding probably 8 barrels each and 4500 lbs. are turned out every 24 hrs. All of this section of the country, Montana & Idaho is supplied from these works— 4 ox teams loaded with 16000 lbs. [sic] each started for Helena Mont. this morning—The salt is of a superior quality— The men at the works gave us very encouraging report of the country ahead. Said Snake River was fordable, that there was but little timber and no hostile Indians. All of which we took with a grain of allowance. We ground two axes that we took with us. I wrote a letter to Alice and one to Lon. Just a few words to tell of our progress, & we came back to camp. The boys had done considerable fishing but nine trout was all they could show, but they were nice ones. A trapper had passed by while we were gone whose report of the line ahead was so different from the one I got at the Salt Works that after supper I rode down to his camp about 1-1/2 miles below ours. Found him living in an Indian Lodge, with a young and clean looking squaw, and they had a pappoose, & three dogs and nine ponies. He gave rather a discouraging account of the country before us more especially of the rivers— First Salt River, no ford, then John Gray's River ditto worse than the Snake no ford very swift &c, then Fall River do. [ditto]— & heavy fallen timber— Well that's where our line goes and where we'll go or "bust." He also gave me a few notes concerning Prof. Hayden* that did not sound as well as his report— He thinks him a good deal of a fraud— guess I can go to bed pretty well now, and some more convenient time figure over the "how" we are to cross those streams— Ran 5m 30chs. (530) yesterday—

---

*Ferdinand V. Hayden, leader of the Geological and Geographical Survey of the Territories from 1867–79

Friday June 26, '74.

Trout for breakfast— Very cold last night water froze in camp. On line at 6:30 A.M. country very rough with scattering timber. Dinner at 129th M.P. Pack train ahead of us— Evening. Struck a few large trees on line this P.M. which retarded our progress so that we camped near the 131st M.P. having made just 7 miles. The line is still running in the bluffs on the west side of Salt River and about three miles distant therefrom— Weather cloudy threatening rain— Mosquitoes worse than I ever saw them before, but the nights are too cold for them to be about.

Saturday June 27

A light rain last night but clear & warm this morning— Struck Salt River bottom on the 137th. Two Shoshone Indians came out to the line apparently did not like the looks of the outfit as we were all well armed, and they left. Their camp is about two miles west of ours. We made nine (9) miles camping opposite & 1/2 mile W. of the 140th M.P. Stood a guard over the mules as Indians will steal—

Sunday 28, 1874

Did not work today, but we passed the time in washing mending fishing & resting. Do not like laying up on Sunday, it gives one too good a chance for thinking. The day passes slowly & night finds us not one day nearer home— Roney, Wheaton & Tom Barry took an azimuth. Clouds & dew kept them out till 2 A.M. Monday morning. Chronometer showed 23" [23 seconds] fast, a very great change. Very cold.

Monday 29, 74.

On line at 7:30 a little late as we gave the boys who were out last night a chance to sleep. Had some very fine trout for breakfast— Struck some thick willows on the 142nd mile & made but 2-1/2 miles before dinner. Struck a bend of Salt river on the 146th mile & offset us and it had considerable chopping also but made 8 miles & camped at sundown near 148th mile. Salt River 20 chs. E—

Tuesday June 30—74.

The 149th mile was all through light timber and 12 chs. beyond the post we came to a high steep wooded bank at the bottom of which runs Salt River— Went into camp on the bluff and started Dick and Frank down stream to prospect for a crossing while Billie & I went up stream for the same purpose— There is a valley or rather basin on the other side of the River, shut in upon all sides with high mountains. To the N. E. is a

*Salt River Valley in the vicinity of the Wyoming-Idaho boundary,
near Freedom, Wyoming*
Author photo, 2000

cañon between two of the highest peaks & it looks like a stream might be running through it. If so I think we will find it to be Snake River, and hope we will for we have expected to strike it in the grand cañon & in a bend & if it comes in here we will be fortunate— We took Hayden map as correct at first but have already proven it very incorrect. According to it we should now be across both Salt & Gray's Rivers & on the banks of the Snake, so our line shows his map to be about 15 miles out at this point— Evening— We found a place where we can construct & cross a raft & ford the mules & came in to dinner at 2:30 P.M. after which the boys began work on the raft. Dick & Frank came in at 4 P.M. had also found a pretty good ford three miles below camp. Frank crossed & as we had surmised found that the dreaded Snake is in the bottom before us— & their ford is just at the mouth of the Salt— There is no sign of a ford on the Snake though— I went out in the Mts. west of camp a few miles & from a high point could see the Snake away up in the Grand cañon, also quite a large stream running into it just where it leaves the cañon, which must be Gray's River— The good luck that attended us last year seems not to have deserted us, for although the Snake may be difficult to cross where we are, we have struck it at the most favorable point within 50 miles either way— With Wheaton & Roney took an azimuth tonight— finished at 11 P.M. Did not change the line perceptibly (nor did the last one) and the chronometer showed 21 seconds fast, both of which facts go to show that the previous azimuth was right and that the chronometer changed its rate from some jar or other similar cause—

Wednesday.— July 1st.

Finished the raft by 9 A.M. Dick & Frank swam across we threw them a line got the rope across ferried over the "stuff" set Dick across on line, the last of the men went over, the boys drove the stock across where they forded all the way and at 3:30 we sat down to dinner hungry wet & tired but across Salt River with which every body we have seen for 50 miles have scared us— Took a pony & rode over to the Snake & up to the mouth of Gray's River and the foot of the cañon, then down to the mouth of the Salt about 3 miles—near the latter place found a channel where I think we can ford, if not there then there is no fording the stream— Returned by sundown to camp which we left on the bank of the river where we crossed—

Thursday, July 2nd.

Ran the line over to the Snake River which we reached at 157 m 20 chs 30 lks. Triangulated* the distance back to the brow of the bluff on the S. side of Salt River from the first sight on this side making the Salt about 2.30 chs. wide— Moved camp to the mouth of the Salt which is the location of my ford which when tried proved too deep. Spent the P.M. in riding up the River trying to find a place for a raft— Found the trail of three men apparently prospectors and it being fresh followed it two miles up Gray's River hoping to find them thinking they might know something of the River— Did not find them & returned to camp at sundown. The Boys had caught a lot of very fine trout averaging about 2 lbs. each.

Friday 3rd.

Tried another place for a ford & raft but couldn't make it. As we saw a smoke last night some distance down the river. Billie & I went down there. Crossed Salt River just above its mouth after three trials. Three miles down the Snake we overtook two men from the Carribou mines who had come down to catch some trout for the 4th— They could tell us nothing about the Snake but invited us to go up to the mining camp & attend a dance that night. Said all the ladies would be there and several ladies from Soda Springs 50 miles distant. A press of business compelled us to refuse

---

*When triangulating, surveyors measure a "baseline" to serve as the first side of a triangle. They use the angles of this triangle to calculate the lengths of the other sides.

but if we had been sure of a crossing we or I at least would have gone for I think it would have been new & novel. We returned to camp at 1 P.M., had dinner then commenced building a raft, carried the timber for it 3/4 of a mile. Worked hard till sundown had supper and went to bed. With a sure prospect of a hard day's work on the 4th, while the result of it is still very uncertain.

July 4, 1874

The mental barometer of this outfit for today shows the greatest change of the trip— We were at work early stimulated for hard work with a good strong breakfast of baked beans, bread, bacon, trout, coffee & dried apples— No one seemed to feel very enthusiastic either

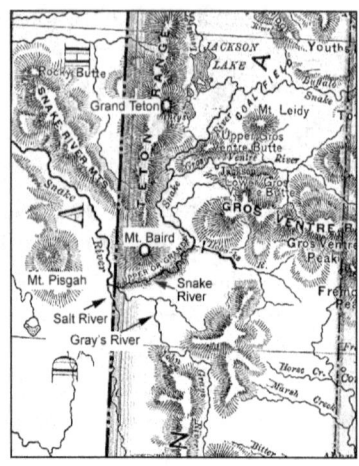

Rivers converging near the Wyoming-Idaho boundary
Annotated detail of 1895 map.[4]
Also see pp. 150–51.

on the subject of our national Independence or what was of more moment the success of our raft— We launched her safely she floated like a duck but when two men boarded her with poles their best efforts failed to get it 50 feet from shore. As this was the narrowest point we could find, and it was 450 feet wide there— We knew that rafting was a failure. We had thought of building a large one that would take our whole outfit at once, & cut loose from the shore near the mouth of Gray's fork, and make a landing where we could. We might have done this, but could not cross our stock that way. It would have been risking everything on a single chance and I determined to only try it as a last resort. When the uncertainty was past, relative to the small raft, every man seemed relieved, and the Barometer rose slightly— We went in to dinner in a light rain, no nearer across the River than when we first reached it— If we had failed, Ben, our cook, had not, and we had a dinner good enough for any 4th of July, the main features of which different from our usual fare, were corn bread, dried plum sauce & trout, the last however we now have at every meal, as they are very plenty in the Snake, large and easily caught. — After dinner as it still rained, we had a first rate game of casino. We were apparently in a tight place—with no common obstacle confronting us, but we kept our nerve, and like Mark Tapley were "jolly still"—but I will own that my jollity was a little forced, and of a melancholy nature—and nothing but force of will kept me from not exactly being "blue" but thinking of the good folks at either end of the Pacific [rail]road, and wishing that I was with them, and the Western Bdry. in Helena— About two o'clock Billie & I started to go across Gray's fork & try the cañon once & see how the route would be through it, as we half intended going to the upper end of the cañon to a crossing that we heard was there— That would have taken us at least six days. When about two miles from camp we came upon a newly made wagon trail—and if it had been a church I would not have been more surprised— We spurred on and soon came to the camp of four trappers & prospectors—from Gallatin City Montana. One of them had attempted to cross the Snake with a raft in 1868, was wrecked and lost all he had. We wanted to cross the river now, but as a matter of course, did not favor a raft. We finally made an arrangement that I would furnish all the men necessary and he would build a canoe and we would all cross. As has happened to us before (as at Green River) when it seemed that we could go no farther the way has opened before us. We returned to camp and related the story of our discovery, and the Barometer rose rapidly and it seemed a little like the Glorious 4th— We had thought of a canoe but none of us knew how to build or manage one, and at the best they are dangerous. It seems now that we would soon cross the old Snake—

July 5

Went out with Mr. Richardson, our canoe friend, and found a tree on the bank of the river large enough for a canoe—and set the boys at work on her under his direction, as it will take two days to build her. I concluded to go up to the mining camp on the Caribou. Wrote a letter to Alice, had dinner—started at 2 P.M. Billie going along. We got caught in a thunder storm when about half way—and got wet through— Reached the camp at sundown hungry wet and tired— The distance is 17 miles, 14 being up the Caribou creek which we crossed 13 times— got a good supper at a so called restaurant—for 75¢ but as we didn't like the looks of some of the loafers around the camp and thinking they might be in need of a mule, we came into the timber on the mountain— picketed our mules, built a camp fire, and for two hours have been drying our blankets & clothes— and I am writing with my pants & drawers hanging from a limb before the fire— Will reserve all comment on Iowa Bar till tomorrow and fix up our fire, don my clothes, roll up in a blanket and "retire" to dream perhaps of friends and home perhaps, or worse, perhaps of nothing.

Mem. On the 3rd Roney meandered the Left Bank of the Snake from the mouth of the Gray's River to the mouth of Salt River, Distance 3.m 12 chs.

Monday July 6, 1874.

Arose at sunrise a little stiff. We slept one on each side of the fire and while we kept it going we were warm and slept, but not very good. Went in to town to breakfast, then wrote a letter home. Bought a few things needed in camp, talked about the mines. The main camp is the one we visited called Iowa Bar. There are about twelve log houses there & five saloons, so many Bars that I could not distinguish the "Iowa." The only mining near the camp is gulch mining— washing out the Bar along the stream. Taylor's creek, Iowa & McCoy are the principal streams— Three miles west of the camp is Mt. Pisgah* upon which pretty good quartz ledges have been struck— & 8 claims are taken there now. I obtained a specimen which was taken from the Staunton mine— assays $2400.00** —from W. S. Norcross— Having satisfied our curiosity in relation to this camp we refused sundry & divers invitations to "Take something" & departed. Quite a "big time["] was had there the 4th— A lot of Mormon women, or "Irrigators" as they are called, came in from Soda Springs 50 miles distant & on the evening of the 3rd they had a dance at Iowa Bar, on the 4th went over to the other camp, 7 miles, on the head of Carribou creek & had another dance, on the evening of the 5. Sunday had another one at another camp, getting up at 12 M. to commence so they reported— the evening of the 6th they were to dance at Waumucks camp & on the 7th at Soda again. For one set of ladies that is doing pretty good dancing. Going down Sunday we were caught in a rain storm and as it cleared up, we saw the most beautiful rainbow possible to see— We were in a cañon and the rainbow was reflected or made against the side of the mountains to the east of us & not more than 500 feet away. We watched it almost spell bound until it faded away. I never expect to witness a more beautiful sight in nature. We were in a deep cañon, a small stream of clear crystal like water running at our feet while all around us rose the mighty mountains towering thousands of feet above us, some robed in green, some covered with dense black pine forests, while all were crowned with a wreath of snow, and spanning the largest one, the rainbow formed a crown upon its brow, that the grandest of earth's monarchs might well covet. The ends rested near its base on either hand & the Zenith of the cir-

---

*Now Caribou Mountain. Elevation 9,800 feet

**About $60,400 in 2022, per measuringworth.com purchasing-power calculator

cle illuminated the snow upon its summit with colors that no artist pencil could approach. We reached camp at 1:30 P.M. Found the boys & Mr. Richardson at work upon the canoe. In turning it over one side had split badly and they thought once of building another— but we will try & make this work. Went to camp at sundown in a heavy rain. Mush* & Molasses (made from sugar) for supper.

Tuesday, July 7.

A very heavy rain last night. The River this morning a good deal higher & very muddy showing a big rain above— Our sailors are now, at 8 o'clock, busy caulking the crack in our canoe with hot pitch, after which heavy canvas will be nailed over it and we hope to make the crossing today—

Mem— I learned at the camp that the trapper we found on Smoky Creek is known as "old Tex," the one we saw fishing on the 3rd is old Doc. Collins. The men who are with Richardson are Mr. Dix & Son & David.— I saw an old gray headed miner at the camp who came west in '49. He is now broke & intends selling his horses, taking the money and going home— A broken down discouraged old man, the mines & the greed for gold have made his life a failure— I learned after seeing him, learned from others, that he started from Hazel Green** in '49 & doubtless Father knew him. His name is Madden or something similar. — Evening—another failure. Richardson & Frank crossed the river in the canoe this morning but Richardson had a hard time getting back. Landed 15 chains below where he intended & came near being driven upon a rocky bluff by the current. It would be a long, hard and dangerous job to cross our outfit with one frail canoe, so we immediately began building another— By splicing two together we have quite a good boat which can be rowed. Richardson has put us in the way to cross but he is a good deal of a braggart & cannot do with a canoe what he led us to believe he could— Another heavy rain this P.M. and the river has risen considerably and is very muddy and full of driftwood—

Wednesday, July 8th— 9 A.M.

Breakfast early and boys at work. Canoe prospering finely, and we expect to finish it today. Weather beautiful— Evening— Canoe finished. We have fastened the two together and put on a pole on the outside in which pins are set for row locks. One of them, the first, the boys named

---

*A thick porridge usually made of cornmeal
**Hazel Green, Wisconsin, Richards's birthplace

the "Snake River Pioneer" and the other "Dictator" & put on the date, but Dick calls one of them "Louise"— & I call the other "Lizerr Jane." Guess we will make it tomorrow. Do not think a canoe was ever built quicker or better than this last one & Capt Richardson was not around at all. I left the boys alone this P.M. and went up Gray's River fishing— caught 14 fine trout. No rain today—

Thursday July 9.

7 A.M. A nice warm morning. River fell about two (2) inches last night. All ready to begin crossing our outfit. The comet which we first saw June 28 shone very brightly last night— Evening. Hurrah! We are across the Snake at 1:30 P.M. We had everything over but the mules— The canoes worked very well and Dick & I rowed them well together with Tom Ballard at the helm. We took about 600 lbs. of freight at each load & would be carried about 100 yds. below a point opposite the starting point in crossing. After unloading two men would pull the boat up stream to a point the same distance <u>above</u> our starting point. Dick & I would take the oars & shoot her into the whorf [sic]. It was hard work for us, for the current fearfully [sic], but we kept at it till all was over— Twelve round trips were made— In crossing the stock we first led the Gray pony across to try the water, & found it running nearly all the way. We then took the other gray & led him over & the boys on shore started the mules in, but they only swam down stream a short distance & came out again— The bank was almost perpendicular & the boys kept crowding them into the water until finally one struck across, then all tumbled in & started. It was an odd sight to see fourteen mules & horses, struggling against the current with only their heads above water. Some went pretty straight across while others drifted a long way down stream. It was quite an exciting time for me, for if they failed to make it there was a chance to lose money pretty fast on mules, besides the delay of the work. I felt relieved a heap when the first one touched bottom & came a-shore & soon every one was over & we were "on this side of the Snake" sure enough. We selected a long sandy beach for the stock to land on & it was lucky we did. At 2 P.M. we sat down to dinner well satisfied with our forenoon's work— We were just seven days in getting across but did it well & safely without losing any thing at all— No river has any terrors for me now, for I think we can cross any stream in this country— Our Capt. Richardson had nothing to do with our crossing but he and his partner complimented Dick & I highly on our rowing— I gave them the boat after we were through with it & they took it down stream & anchored it upon the S. side, & I suppose it will make a good many trips yet. After dinner we ran the line to the foot of the bluffs. The

S. bank of the River is 151.20.40. [151 miles 20 chs 40 lks.] & we camped opposite the 153 mile, could find no water in the foot hills though covered with timber & was compelled to send back to the river for a supply for supper & breakfast & we went to bed before it arrived without supper.—

Friday, July 10, 1874.

On line at 6:30 A.M.— & rough climbing to commence with. 12—noon—have run 1-3/4 miles this forenoon, through a little the worst mountains we have ever had. Have gone up 1500 feet in the last 1-1/2 miles, stopping for a tree to be chopped at 154.48— Pack train going around the point of the mountain to the west. No dinner today. Evening—Reached camp at dark. Supper at 8 P.M. Fourteen hours without eating & climbing the worst kind of mountains inclines one to relish his supper, & bean soup, ham, coffee & bread melted before our appetites like the dew before the sun. Now we are seated around the camp fire enjoying a rest & a smoke. Dick & Tom Ballard both unwell today. The effects of too much Snake river yesterday. We made 3-1/2 miles, camping a mile West of 156.40 at the junction of two mountain streams— The high range, snow capped, which has been in sight for 50 miles comes in tomorrow's work— This is very rough hard work, and if we keep up the average which we want to of 3-1/2 miles per day through here I think we'll reach Bozeman on time. The camp men saw a grizzly Bear, an Elk and a deer today but neither within shooting distance.

Saturday, July 11th.

Brought the line up to the brow of the Cliff on the S. Side of the main creek by noon & went in to dinner— The S. Slope of the Mountain is impassable for the chain men, so we ran a base line west from 157.31.85, of 34 chains & sent Dick with two men to the top of the mountain to get the line up and we will triangulate the distance. We can not get a sight on the highest peak because of an intervening peak covered with timber. As we have had no game yet & there are good signs around here, I let Roney go out to set Dick & run the base line & I went hunting. Came back at dark without having seen anything in the shape of game. Found that Roney took the west end of his base line from a point where he could not see the flag on the mountain & he came in long after dark, without having accomplished anything more than getting the line on the mountain— I ought to have known better than to have sent him to do the work, but will try & not lose any time on it tomorrow. Rained by spells this morning. Thermometer 76° in the shade at noon and we thought it very hot, while at home I suppose it is in the 90s.

View into Idaho from the summit
of what Richards called "The Bass"
Rick Baugher, idahoclimbingguide.com,
1999

Sunday, July 12.

Settled our breakfast by climbing the mountain to the line. Were two hours in reaching Dick's sight. Elevation of that point above camp 2875 feet, distance on line as triangulated 104 chs 10 lks, making this point 158.55.95. Now 12 m and we are chopping out some trees to allow a sight to the top of this range from whence we can see the top of the main range. Elevation here 9075 feet. Ben came up with dinner on time. We set the 159th mile post on the top of this mountain.* From here to the top of the next one it is impossible to chain, so sent Dick ahead to get the line. We will erect a pole here and triangulate back. Camp at the Western foot of the big mountain. Did no more than get the line to the summit of it. We have been running to this mountain from the 100th mile and I think it will be the highest point we will reach on this line. Its elevation as near as we can take it is 10300 ft. From it we have a magnificent view upon all sides. Looking back we can see the Salt River valley for 30 miles hemmed in on the East with the Salt River Mts. which are rough, snow clad & many of them higher than this point. On the West of it are foot hills gradually rising till they terminate in the Carribou Mts., the principal of which, Mt. Pisgah, contains quartz ledges, & at the East foot of which lies the Iowa Bar mines which we visited a week ago. To the N. W. we can see Snake River winding through the mountains for about 10 miles then the bottom through which it runs gradually widens out in a prairie bottom & the hills skirting it become lower, while away in the dis-

---

*This peak is just inside Wyoming and its summit is not on the state line. The Richards brothers must have corrected it when they retraced the line from the North, since Lon's detailed plat of the boundary (see pages 150-51) shows the mountain east of the line and aligning with the 160th milepost.[5]

It has no official name, according to the Idaho State Geological Survey office, but it is known as Mount Richards or Richards Peak on certain websites. Its elevation, about 9,600 ft., is lower than Richards's estimate. No other mountain peak is on the state line and has that elevation.

The Tetons from one of the few easily accessible points on the Wyoming-Idaho border. The largest, Grand Teton, was once known as Mt. Hayden.

Author photo, 2000

tance, showing dimly like a fog cloud, is another range of high mountains at least 125 miles away. Coming around to the east the view is limited to a few miles by the Snake River mountains of which this mountain (which has been variously named Mt. Richards, The Bass & Mosiah, and which we will know hereafter as "The Bass") is one. They are abrupt, badly broken, very rocky, sparsely timbered & mostly snow capped. Passing our line, which we cannot see for more than five miles ahead, we see the Tetons looming up— the largest is Mt. Hayden bearing 20° E of us from this point. It is the grandest looking Peak we have yet seen and towers far above all its fellows. Will reserve further comment upon it until I have had a nearer view. To the East & N. East of it we can see the lower country of the Yellowstone. To the East of us, a little north, we see a peak which we think is Mt Baird.* Taken altogether the view from "The Bass" fills my idea of mountain scenery. I was not satisfied last summer in that respect but have no more to say now. The country & surface immediately about us is peculiar. The mountain sides covered with finely broken rock which

---

*Hayden's map[6] showed a Mt. Baird just inside what would become Wyoming. The photo on the previous page is of a Mt. Baird in Idaho, the highest peak in the area.

it is impossible to walk over in safety, as half an acre of it is liable to slide out any time. The rock contains a large proportion of white sand & is not apparently of volcanic formation— though the numerous basins or craters would seem to indicate volcanic eruptions here at some previous time— As the sun is getting low will close my book & descend to camp, & finish this Sunday's work with supper then to bed— Total ascent today [4100?]* Distance on line about 2 miles Camp opposite 160 miles

Monday, July 13

Had to climb "The Bass" to work this morning just 2000 feet above camp— Took our dinners with us. Dick & Tom Ballard went from camp across the cañon to give me a sight on the next Mt. Am now waiting to set Dick. Have run a base line to the east of 14.86. from which I will triangulate both back to the 159th post and forward to the point where Dick will be set. The weather is beautiful, though more like September than July— The air is very clear, but there is nothing to see but mountains timber and snow— Would like very well to have a word from home & from Alice. There are a great many things that might occur in five weeks and we have heard nothing new since June 7th. I can only trust that all is well with them.— 11:30 P.M.— "Lying out" by a camp fire supperless & without blankets or coats will conclude the "Log" for today. Dick found a very rough road to the point he started for, so that by the time I had set him & taken the angles for the triangulation it was 12 m. A thunder storm had also come up, and as we were at an elevation of 10300 ft. we got the full benefit of it. We took shelter under a big rock and ate our dinners during the storm. We had no crockery or it would have been dropped & broken sure. The flashes of lightning followed each other in such quick succession, that there was almost a constant roar of thunder. We were surrounded by cañons from 2000 to 3000 feet deep, and the thunder roared & echoed & reached through them in a manner that was grand in the extreme, but as the lightning was playing around us, in such close proximity that our hair stood on end (but whether from electricity or fear I will not say) it had few charms for us. We could see the lightning below us, but the rain was certainly above us. Several trees were struck on our mountain and we half expected to see the lightning from the cañon attempt to climb a tree— When we left "The Bass" it was 3:45 P.M. Before reaching the front sight a distance of 1.m 18chs. we were overtaken by another

---

*Microfilm of diary is dark and murky. The 4 is possible and others may be 0s or 1s. Figures may be clearer in the original diaries, at the Wyoming State Archives.

storm which delayed us another hour. Dick & Tom went ahead about 1-1/4 to another divide. Had three large trees to chop out, so that it was 7 P.M. when we started for camp (having just succeeded in setting Dick) with no idea as to where it was, except that it was on the creek to the west of us, and the roughest mountains & deepest cañons intervening that I ever saw. We took down a cañon, walking over fallen trees & large boulders & through underbrush shoulder high, wet from the rain so that we met in a short time as we could be, and kept going until 11 P.M. when the cañon became so narrow & so filled with fallen timber that we could not travel with safety any longer, as I had the transit and Wheaton the chronometer— (Roney was with us too) (no joke intended) so we stopped to camp, as it was raining a little it was almost impossible to build a fire, the only timber we could find in the dark being partly green Fir— While hunting a dry pine log we saw the reflection of a fire above us in another cañon, and upon investigation found the five other men within 20 chains of us with a good fire and quite comfortably fixed— We accepted their invitation to pass the night with them. We have wrung out our clothes, put them on again and are now sitting around the fire the hungriest, tiredest, wetest but jolliest eight men that ever lay out on the mountains. Not a cross word has been said nor a complaining one— Think camp is not more than two miles down the cañon. The rain has ceased, our fire keeps us warm, and we will pass a comfortable night though we won't sleep much.

Tuesday, July 14.

Broke camp at early daylight. Found camp 1-1/2 miles below us, in the best place for us that it could have been— The boys in camp had breakfast ready in short order, and at 6 o'clock we were dry full & happy. Went to bed & slept till noon. Spent the P.M. in washing cleaning up arms &c. Rode out a few miles with Billie hunting. Saw nothing— Lying out makes us feel a little old today, and guess I'll go to bed. This is a fearfully rough country and we are having a hard time getting through it, but we <u>are going</u>, and have not yet given up reaching Bozeman on time— though we are making slow progress now. Have got the line up to the 162nd Mile Post.

Wednesday, July 15.

Left camp at 6 A.M. and was on line at 9. a.m. A long steep mountain to climb after leaving the cañon— Mem— We have named the cañon on the north of "The Bass" "Whang doodle* cañon," and camp Monday night

---

*A fanciful creature first imagined around 1850.—Wiktionary

"cañon camp," or camp calamity. Evening. Have had very good success today. Chained in two miles and got the line across the stream upon which we are camped about 1-1/2 miles ahead. The chainmen were stopped by a perpendicular wall of rock 250 feet high on the S. side of the stream, at 164.24. They erected a barked pole at the point and we will have to triangulate the distance back. The scenery today has been very grand. Upon either side of this stream the mountains rise to a height of at least 3000 feet and in some places almost perpendicular, while in others they terraced beautifully and cut out in a semi-circular form till they resemble a ground amphitheater. In many places the rocks have made a slide and at the distance we are from them those places seem perfectly smooth—evenly graded and of a variety of color that is rare indeed— The stream is a clear mountain brook 25 links wide, running rapidly over a ground bottom with numerous falls of from 3 to 15 feet. Taken altogether the scenery here is more grand and imposing, with a finer finish than any I ever saw on my trip across the continent last spring.

Thursday, July 16.

Our camp men decided yesterday that it was impossible to take our pack train any further up this cañon, which is our only way of keeping near the line. I told them we <u>would</u> go up the cañon <u>anyway</u>, so this morning left camp at 6 a.m. with every man but the cook, to make a way. [Underscores throughout are the writer's.] We moved immense boulders, cut down trees, graded hill sides, and made crossings on the stream with such good success that at 9 a.m. sent the men back to bring up the camp. I have just been up another cañon leading from the main one to the line and found it passable, also, so I think we are sure of getting over this range. Hope for a better country soon— at 2:30 P.M. the train came up. We're delayed by an accident to one of the mules (Dandy Pat) who tipped over backwards off a cliff forty feet high, made two complete revolutions lengthwise, and landed square on his back in the stream. Alighting upon the pack was all that saved his life, for it broke the force of the fall, also broke our large Dutch oven, busted a seamless sack containing sugar & 50 lbs. washed away, and smashed the pack saddle all to pieces. As it was too late to attempt crossing another range we went into camp and I took a pony and tried my hand at path-finding as I used to do last year— Was well paid for my ride and walk up the mountains, for I found that we must continue up this stream (which we now call sugar creek) for a long distance, before getting upon the line again— This is a little the worst country imaginable and we are having heavy work to get through it but we are

*Surveyors and their mules faced similar challenging terrain
on the Montana-Idaho boundary survey.*
Allyn Collection, 1904, Riverton (Wyoming) Museum

going yet— If our provisions hold out we will be all right. Hope to find game soon. Saw a great many fresh signs today of Elk, deer, bear & mountain lion. The boys saw two bear near camp—

Friday, July 17.

I was taken suddenly sick last night. Just as I was going to bed— Went out a little way from the tent and vomited fearfully & was too sick to get back, so lay down under a tree & after a while fell asleep. Awoke some time in the night and got to bed. Felt pretty weak this morning so sent Wheaton out with the Transit. Billie George & Charlie went up the creek to make a trail. Ben & I held the camp. From 164.75 triangulated back, set the 165 mile post— The chainmen managed by hard climbing to chain in the 166 mile, and also reached the creek on the north of that mountain which they reached at 166.m 60 chs. 10 lks— With the distance triangulated we made 2-1/4 miles today which is better than expected— We also have a sight ahead to commence from tomorrow. The boys all got in for supper, so we are all right for this day, though we know not what is in store for us tomorrow. All I want to do is to put in a fair day's work every night. This country cannot hold out all the way and when we reach better running we can make good time. A slight rain this P.M.—

Saturday, July 18, 74.

Started to work this morning as usual but played out before I reached the line & turned the transit over to Wheaton, and I went with the train, camped at noon at the forks of the cañon as we did not know which one would lead over the divide. With Billie, Geo. & Charlie started up the west one. Found it passable & Geo & Charlie went back while Billie & I went to the divide. Got caught in a hard rain but not so much lightning as we had on "The Bass," coming in I killed a fine cow Elk, as this is the first game we have had for five weeks we were glad to get it. Boys all got in before dark— The country ahead looks much better than that we have been running through—

Sunday, July 19.

Left camp at 6 A.M. Climbed a mountain 2200 feet above camp to the line. Ran the line about two miles to the top of the range, which we reached at 169m. 70chs. Did considerable chopping. The pack train had good luck and came up to a point a mile west of the line opposite the divide— & went into camp at 3:30 P.M. As we need an azimuth pretty badly, turned a right angle from the line and set a flag near camp, intending to take the azimuth there turn a right angle from it and run back to the line— Got caught in another thunder storm before reaching camp. The boys found the Elk all right near camp where we left it. It is splendid meat and very acceptable to us— Just at dark it clouded up and we could do nothing towards taking an azimuth—

Monday, July 20.

Ran about two miles the most of the way through timber. Did not leave the first sight until 10 A.M. as Dick almost got lost going ahead on the start. The train got down the north slope of the mountain without accident, though with some difficulty— Camped early in order to take an azimuth. Rode east a mile to the brow of the range from which point could see the Snake to the E. 10 miles. Mt. Hayden also in view very plain— This chain of mountains is running S. E. & N. W. following the Snake River. On the north slope, they are quite heavily timbered, while on the south they are quite bare and rocky— Streams are found in every cañon & ravine—

Tuesday— July 21st.

Roney, Wheaton & Frank worked till 3 A.M. this morning getting an azimuth. Roney is the slowest mortal it was ever my misfortune to be connected with— I won't help him any more & dislike to have the boys out all night but some one must help him— Only set Dick twice today but put in the 172-3-&4 posts and quit at 174.56 where we camped. Country still very rough but we <u>can</u> get the camp on line which is more than we have done since leaving the Snake river. The pack train had a hard day the flies being terrible, the weather warm and their road rough— They were packed from 8 to 4:40 could have made a mile more but stopped on account of them— "Pat" turned another sommersault down a cliff but did no damage— There has been snow on every divide for 15 miles and our altitude runs from 9300 to 9800 feet.

Wednesday, July 22nd.

Had considerable chopping on the line today. Camped on Teton Pass creek at 177.40. The horse flies worse than yesterday. The boys stopped at this stream at 11 A.M. and built smokes to keep them off the mules— Weather cloudy. We are descending slowly and the nights are much warmer. A cinnamon Bear came right into camp this afternoon but the boys failed to kill it although they fired several times—

Thursday, July 23rd.

Was on the line at 6 A.M. Had a good deal of chopping and three very deep cañons to cross. Made 3-1/2 miles and quit at 5 o'clock on account of rain at 181. miles. Came very near missing camp and lying out again. Rained hard until midnight, making the camp very disagreeable— Cooked supper in the rain and went to bed all more or less wet. Tom Barry shot a cinnamon Bear twice this morning but he escaped. Just before we quit we saw a black Bear coming through the woods to one side of us. Wheaton had my gun & I called to him to bring me it, when the Bear turned and came directly toward us. Frank rushing his gun and fired when the Bear was but 60 paces from us, and shot him right through the heart, and he dropped dead. He created quite an excitement for a short time—

Friday, July 24.

Everything wet about camp this morning, so that we did not get start- ed to work until 7. A.M. Grass & bushes wet making it very unpleasant— Ran 1-1/4 miles before dinner through small timber, much of it burned. Ben sent us out some Bear meat for dinner. It was first rate, almost as good as Elk— Evening. Had burned timber all the afternoon. Lost a little time getting a sight across a cañon. Ran 2-1/2 miles making a dry camp near 183.40. This is the third dry camp we have made on the trip— cool & cloudy. No mosquitoes nor flies—

Saturday, July 25.

On line at 6 A.M. Quite cool, very much like September. We are running along the foot hills on the East side of Pierres River [sic]— & Hole. It makes a large valley containing several streams, and a large beaver marsh. The country ahead looks better. Not very mountainous, but mostly covered with timber— Evening. We made 1-1/2 miles before dinner, which brought us to the edge of the bottom. Ran along the W. side of the same near the foot hills 6-1/4 miles in the afternoon camping on [blank space] creek at the 191.20. It seemed good to be running again on the prairie, and I think every man of us would be glad if it ran clear to the corner.

Sunday, July 26, 1874.

No work today, as this is a good camping place. Spent the day in washing, mending, hunting, fishing & resting. I caught a string of fine trout in the forenoon out of the Teton River on which we are camped. (The great Teton or Mt. Hayden is just E. of camp 16 miles distant.) After dinner Billie & I started for the mountains East to try and shoot a deer. I killed an antelope about a mile from camp, and we went on to the mountains. Went a little too far before turning back and got caught by the night on a side hill so thickly covered with fallen timber that we could not lead our horses through it nor could we follow our trail out in the darkness so we were compelled to leave them there and go to camp on foot— three miles, got in at 11 P.M. I did almost as much of a day's work as I would have done on the line, but got game & fish enough to pay for it, and we are now ready to strike for the "Corner." Weather clear & cool, no mosquitoes or flies, plenty of grass wood and water, and taken altogether it is the best camping place we have had—

Monday, July 27.

Breakfast with trout & antelope at 6 a.m. Billie & George went back after the ponies— Took until 10:30 to get the timber chopped out of the Teton River bottom. Left the prairie at 195.52 and entered a gently rolling country with scattering timber and numerous streams, making very good running. Made 6-1/2 miles camping at 197.50. Weather splendid. The pack train overtook us at 4 P.M. The boys got the ponies out of the timber by cutting a road for them. We have had a very fine view of the Tetons today. Mt. Hayden is the largest & is 13850* feet high, or 7450 higher than we were this morning— To the S. of Hayden are two others in line with it and probably 12000 feet high. To the North & a little East, is another very

---

*Richards or his source was close: 13,775 by today's reckoning.

rough ragged peak about the same height. We have taken several bearings to them and make their distance from the line to be 16 miles, though it looks no more than 10— Saw a good many antelope today and signs of larger game.

Tuesday, July 28.

On line at 6 a.m. a slight rain about 8, and little showers all day. Line ran through a gently rolling country, lightly timbered. Set the 200th mile post before dinner. Made 4-1/2 miles & camped at 202.10 at 4:30 P.M. on account of the rain. Stopped just in time, as it rained real hard soon after we got our tents pitched. Made a dry camp and packed water 1/3 of a mile from a cañon— On the 201st & 202nd miles there are quite a number of cañons, descend gradually from the South, while the North side is a per-pendicular wall of rock, of a porous nature like pumice, which we think to be a Basaltic formation.

Wednesday, July 29.

Rained all night and a while this morning so that we got started to work rather late, about 7:30. Ran all day through timber. Made 4 miles stopping at 206. camp 1/2 mile S. E. Another dry camp though within 30 chs. of water— Weather very fine, cool & clear— This is Aut's 21st birth-day [brother Austin C.] and I suppose he will celebrate a little. Would like just a little to be with him today—

Thursday, July 30.

Left camp at 6 a.m. Ran two miles before dinner which we ate at the 208th post on the bluff on the North side of the north fork of Pierres River— While eating dinner the pack train came up on the S. side of the river but could not descend into the cañon so went a couple of miles east to find a crossing. Mem. Roney's sale of eye glasses— Were delayed by a thunder storm until 3 P.M. from noon—And only ran one more mile quit-ting at the 210.9th post— Could find no water for camp so we all went with the train & had to go two miles N. E. & descend into a very deep cañon when we found a stream. Began to unpack just at dark, supper at 9:30. Cloudy. Mosquitoes bad again.—

Friday, July 31.

Reached the line at 8:30. Heavy chopping and lots of fallen timber to the stream on which we camped last night—which we reached at noon at 210. Took dinner on the north side of it, set in the 211 post and was delayed again by a thunder storm lasting two hours. Camped at 211.70 with a chance for a sight 25 chains long in the morning— Had supper before sundown. The nicest camp yet in a little opening in the timber—good grass & a nice spring near. We are now running through an undulating table land, covered with aspen and scattering pine with numerous openings. Making a beautiful country and good for running through. There are a great many old pony tracks, and I think a large band of Indians have been in here some time ago, perhaps wintered here. There is no game here now, but in the winter I think it would be abundant, now the game is all in the mountains to the east of us— Mosquitoes are very bad in the day time but quiet at night, it being too cold for them then. Mercury stands about 40° above at sunrise—

Saturday, Aug. 1, 1874.

On the line at 6 A.M. This is the third morning in succession that we have had wet clothes to put on to start with and it is getting slightly monotonous not to say unpleasant, with the thermometer almost down to freezing to put on wet pants, drawers, stockings & shoes, hope it won't rain today though now at noon it is very cloudy. Have had a good run so far set the 212-13-&14 post though we had but 10 chains to run on the 212th— Dick has gone ahead to get a sight across a cañon that will probably make another mile— We have 65 miles to run and to finish on time— Aug 20—must make 3-1/4 miles. This we can through this kind of country but I fear we will strike some heavy pine timber soon—

3 P.M. Put in third mile today at 2:30 P.M. At 215.11 came in sight of Fall River running S. W. Quit work at 6:30 at 216.11.48 in Fall River bottom made the best camp we have yet had, on a green grassy flat with small pines & hemlocks growing in little clumps upon it. With Fall just to the west of us— This stream is well named for it has a great number of falls upon it. Ten miles above our line are four, the highest of which is 40 ft. The river here is 3 chs. 35 lks. wide & very swift running over large boulders— One of these boulders in the center of the stream near camp is concave and the hollow is filled with a liquid as red as blood. The stream is too swift & deep to get to it or we would examine it. We have run 4-1/4 miles today which is good running for timber, and as we have made 25 miles this week will rest tomorrow— The bluffs on Fall River are formed in many places of massive boulders piled up from the bottom to the summit of the bluff and from a distance seem like a wall of masonry— Have seen a good many fresh pony tracks lately and today a party with 12 ponies crossed our line not more than 1/2 a mile behind us. We did not see them but the campmen saw their trail— Will stand a guard tonight & take an azimuth.

Sunday, Aug. 2nd, 1874.

As we were not to work today Frank & I got up before daylight had a cup of coffee & mounted on a couple of ponies started up the river determined to replenish our larder with some game or fish or stay out all day. The grasshoppers had been flying very thick & half a mile from camp we caught a box full off the trees for fish bait. Just as we were starting on we saw a moose about 1/4 mile ahead. We tied our ponies and crept up to within 250 yards & fired wounding him badly. We followed his trail about 1/2 mile and came in sight of him just starting in to swim a little lake 1/4 mile in diameter. The lake was surrounded by about ten (10) chains of grass & closed in all around with timber and mountains rising on three sides of it making a beautiful sheet of water. The sun was just rising over the mountains to the East, and with the Moose swimming for life across the lake it made one of the finest sights I ever witnessed. We ran around the lake to head him as he came ashore, but twice we thought we had lost him for he sank out of sight. When he reached the shore he was so exhausted that he couldn't get up the bank and I shot him in 3 feet of water — and dressed him in the water— We then went back to camp & sent out two pack mules after his quarters & head & horns. We estimated that he would have weighed alive twelve (12) hundred pounds. He stood six (6) feet high, his head measured 38 inches from the end of his nose to the crown between his ears. His horns were 4 ft 6 inches across from tip to tip, 6 ft 6 inches around the inside, the widest part of the webb 8 inches, will try and save the horns— The meat is as good as Elk— Got a good azimuth last night and we are all ready for a good run this week. No rain today nor mosquitoes—

Monday, Aug. 3rd.

On line at 5:45. Crossed Fall River at 216.18— triangulated it & crossed the party on ponies— Had fair running for timber— several marshes, set the 220th post at 5 P.M. and went to camp 1/4 mile east— Made four miles easy and have a good prospect for tomorrow. A little rain this P.M. & lots of mosquitoes.—

Tuesday, Aug. 4

On line at 6 A.M.— Had a good deal of open running across little marshes and peat beds on the two first miles, also struck one Lake 18 chs. wide which we triangulated. Made 2-1/3 miles before dinner but struck some heavy timber in the P.M. and quit at 223.55. having made 3.55. A slight sprinkle of rain, weather pretty warm & mosquitoes & gnats fearful. Billie saw another moose and the woods are full of signs of game of all kinds. Bear deer elk & moose— Four of the boys got lost in taking a short cut from the line to camp but got in before dark. I rather think they'll stay with the compass hereafter—

Wednesday, Aug. 5, 1874.

Left camp at 6:10. All made veils of mosquito netting. Got a sight of 1.20 & made nearly two miles before dinner, quite a heavy rain began at noon & lasted two hours, and we also struck heavy timber, quit at 6 P.M. at the 227th mile having made 3.25 today. The open timber quaking aspen & little meadows & lakes have given out and we have only heavy timber much of it dead & fallen. Camped on a little stream on line which runs only a few chains. The cañon in which it is bears S. E. another larger one is N. E. of us & the stream in it makes several beautiful falls about two miles East of us. We have only seen them from the line but one seems to be about 60 feet high—

Thursday, Aug. 6.

On line at 6:15 A.M. Heavy timber and slow running. From 229 MP could see steam rising from a hot spring about 1-1/2 miles to the N. E. Made 3 miles & quit at 4:30. Camp 1/4 a mile east of line near the hot springs which are opposite 229.70. Spent an hour inspecting the springs. They are located on the East slope of a hill ten chains from a stream 40 links wide running S. E.— We counted 18 that were running, some of them stand like a common large spring and range all the way up to those which are puffing like a steam engine. Some are heaving & roaring at a fearful rate— The deposits are sulphur, lime stone, alum. Got a few specimens from them—

Friday, Aug. 7.

Heavy timber all day. Worked hard & made 2.50. A good camp on a small creek near 233.

Saturday, Aug. 8, 1874.

Yesterday there were indications of a stream about 4 miles ahead, so we were on the line at 5:30 with the intention of trying to make it. The timber proved very thick and large and only by the hardest kind of work we succeeded in making 2.65 quitting at 235.35. The pack train passed us at 2:30 P.M. but failed to find the stream we expected, and had to go back two miles for water. We had supper after dark of bread, meat & coffee. Wanted to get an azimuth tonight but the line is 3/4 of a mile back or south of camp. The country has entirely changed within the last 2 miles, from a rolling grassy though timbered surface to a high sterile, rocky plateau, heavily timbered with occasional bare places or openings, all destitute of grass or water— This is the most desolate looking camp we have had, & to add to our comfort and insure pleasant dreams the mercury stands at 32° above (this morning at 26°) and while we were eating supper all the stock but 3 ponies disappeared & it's impossible to follow them tonight. I shall not let it keep me awake for there is no one to steal them & I know we can follow their trail in the morning and will find them at the nearest water. We have lately seen a great many large tracks which I think must be the mountain Bison.

Sunday, Aug. 9, 1874.

Billie went out at daylight took up the mules trail and found them about a mile S. E. of camp at a Little lake— Sent Wheaton out with the transit, & Billie & I went out North, to find the Continental Divide & scout the country. Found no water nearer than Thirsty Fork five miles ahead and four miles beyond that found the Divide, also found a lake just over the Divide. Nothing but heavy timber ahead and we must improve our time to the utmost in order to reach Bozeman before our provisions give out. Got back to camp at 3 P.M. The boys had got the line up to camp & we have everything ready for an azimuth tonight. Are camped at 236.10— Weather just like September.

Monday, Aug. 10.

Clouded up last night so that we could get no time stars, but we got Polaris & took the rate of the chronometer as shown at the last Azimuth station. This morning at sunrise the mercury stood at 26° above. We were at work early and had made 2.45 by 11 A.M. when it began raining. We built a bivouac with a big fire before it and ate our dinner. The rain soon changed to snow which melted almost as fast as it fell. We stood it about an hour then started back 2-1/2 miles to camp which we reached at 1 P.M. wet through and a little cold. I had told the camp men not to move from that camp if it stormed before noon, as we would rather walk back to a dry camp than to pitch our tents on wet ground in a storm, though nearer the line. It snowed hard nearly all the afternoon, the mules huddled together in the timber and we sat in the tents with our overcoats on, about five o'clock the storm subsided leaving the ground covered with two inches of snow, and before it melted we gathered up enough for us all to wash in which was quite a luxury as we have to pack water on a mule 1-1/2 miles and allow washing only in the morning. I read "Nicholas Nickelby" and played cards alternately all the afternoon & we went to bed warm & dry, thankful that we fared no worse. Ben on the line today— One of the mules "Kens" got one of her "hind" feet caught in a rope round her neck last night and when George found her this morning she was almost dead.

Tuesday, Aug. 11.

It was so cloudy and rainy this morning, and so far to the place where we quit yesterday, that it was 9:30 when we began work, we kept going pretty steady and quit at 6 P.M. having chained in the 241st M.P. a little more than 2 miles today, and leaving 35 miles to the corner— It is pretty evident that we cannot even get to the corner by the 20th inst. but we have enough provisions to last us till Sept. 1st of everything but meat. We hope to find game on the Madison but have been disappointed in the game in this country, or rather not in it. Camped on Thirsty Fork, a nice running stream on the line, but sinks 20 chains [1/4 mile] West—

Wednesday, Aug. 12.

Left camp at 6 a.m. Had good weather and open timber, so that we made 3m. 40chs., the line running right through camp, between the tents—which we reached at 6:15 P.M. Camp in an opening, a splendid place for an azimuth which Roney will take tonight. In scouting ahead of camp this evening Billie saw a Buffalo— We are almost at the summit of the Continental Divide or Rocky Mts.— A dry camp—

Thursday, Aug. 13th.

Roney failed with his azimuth last night. It was a very cold night and after taking one set of stars for time he moved the instrument accidentally before sighting on Polaris. As it was then about 1. A.M. I told him to give it up. I think trying to make an astronomer of him is like trying to bore an auger hole with a gimlet— Left camp at 6:30 running on the old azimuth. Left Mac in camp sick & Roney asleep— Reached the crest of the Mountains at 245m 56c 50l. Alt 8915 ft. The ascent is so gradual that it was difficult to find the summit. Took our dinner at the summit. Ran 2.40 & camped at the 247th mile post in the burned timber no water within two miles and very little grass for the mules. This has been a hard day on us. Heavy work and something affected nearly every man so that we had a headache & no appetite. Only 29 miles further. From a point near camp we can see across the Madison Basin to the place where the line ends, but it will be some time before we reach it as there is heavy timber all the way. Mercury this morning 24°.

Friday, Aug. 14th.

Began this days work by shooting "Juliet" our little black [illegible] mule, the best one we had. She caught her off hind foot in the head stall of her halter and in her struggles to release it broke the other hind leg between the hock & fetlock joints so badly that the bones were sticking through the skin. This is the worst piece of luck we have had but it comes at a time when it will not delay nor inconvenience us much— Sent Mac & Frank back to the summit to put in the corner. They set a post 9-1/2 ft long 15 inches square, 3-1/2 ft. in the ground & took 19 bearing trees. We ran three miles all though burned timber. Camped in a steep cañon containing green trees & good grass and 1-1/2 miles below (W) of camp a good spring. The boys went down & brought up a Keg of good water from it. We have had nothing but stagnant water for three days and were all beginning to feel the effects of it— Took an azimuth at 249.70 at the E. elongation of Polaris.— Weather fine

Saturday, Aug. 15.

On line at 6 A.M. Ran all day through dead timber. No water— Camp got in ahead of us and had some difficulty in finding the line, and we might have laid out again had not Wheaton found their trail while out hunting for water. Ran three miles, camping in the Madison Basin and about a mile S. of the river of that name. Went out while waiting for supper, with Dick & wounded an antelope but it got away as did my pony and I walked to camp. 23 miles more to run— Weather very fine—

Sunday, Aug. 16.

With Dick left camp at day light on ponies to try & kill something to relieve the monotony of our bill of fare.

Returned at 8 A.M. not having so much as seen an antelope, though signs are abundant of Buffalo deer elk & antelope— Went out and ran the line to the Madison River which we reached at 253.m lks [sic]. It is a beautiful stream, averaging about one foot in depth and   chains wide. We entered the Basin proper at 253.10. It is undulating covered with thick growing young pine timber, with numerous opening of glades interspersed. No water but in the river— an old blazed wagon trail runs along the S. bank of the river, and a light wagon or buggy has been along it very recently. It seems good to see a wagon track— Laid up on the river all day to mend and wash up. It has been two weeks since we camped on good water and we improve this [sic] Lots of hunting but nothing killed. Took an E. Elongation of Polaris and went to bed at 10 P.M. leaving Roney & Wheaton to take some time observations.

Monday, Aug. 17.

Roney worked all night and got nothing of any value— On the line at 6:15 leaving those two in camp. Made 2-1/2 miles before dinner, and ran 4 more in the afternoon working until dark. There is no water or grass between the Madison and its East Fork, and intended going as far as we could towards the latter, & then walk to it to camp, which had preceded us there. We happened however to strike pretty open timber and ran into the creek bottom & to within 30 chs. of camp. Making 6-1/2 miles today and leaving but 15-1/2. We reached this stream at 260. It is about 40 links wide, a muddy bottom & banks in places—but clear cold water— An open bottom on the S. 40 chs. wide on the N. timbered to the waters edge.

Tuesday, Aug. 18.

A light rain last night— Left camp at 7:20. Made two (2) miles by noon— Crossed a bad marsh about 261.70— and a nice little stream 15 lks. wide at 262.65— where we leave the Madison Basin— Quit work at 3:30 on account of a severe rain storm, at the 264. M.P. 12 miles more—

Wednesday, Aug. 19.

Rained all last night & until after day light this morning— Left Camp about 7:30. crossed a nice stream 10 links wide at 264.10 reached the summit of the Red rock Mts. at 265.30. Thick timber all day, and occasional showers of rain. Made 2-3/4 miles and camped on a little stream running N. Raining at dark. 9-1/4 miles more to run—

Thursday, Aug. 20.

Quite a heavy rain last night and cloudy & foggy this morning. Left camp at 7 o'clock. Made 3m. 20chs., camping on a small stream running North, camp at 270 mile post—six miles to go. Today we expected to be in Bozeman or at least at the corner, but we are two days only from the latter place, and with fair weather will make it Saturday night. Had a severe hail storm while at supper but it cleared up so that we took an azimuth at the E. elongation.

Friday Aug 21.

Rained all night and was raining at breakfast. Started to work at 7 o'clock got one sight & came into camp on account of the rain. Played cards till 11 o'clock when we ate dinner & went to work— Ran 1-1/2 miles and quit again in the rain at 3:30 P.M. Camped on a lake 12 chs. by 30. in a nice little open glade— Shot a large wild goose with my rifle, on the lake— Wheaton who proves a No 1 scout came in at dark and reports that if we strike the country ahead as he thinks we will we will finish tomorrow. We have 4-1/2 miles yet to run—

Saturday, Aug. 22nd, 1874.

Breakfast at 5 A.M. on the line at 5:30. in a fog so dense that I could not set a flag at a greater distance than three chains. About 7 o'clock it rained and the sun came out giving promise of a fair day. Ran 1-1/2 miles through heavy timber by 10:30 but at 273.10 struck an open sage brush valley running along the line, which gave us open running to 274.70 when we entered heavy timber again— Crossed two streams of 40 links each in the valley running west and half a mile west of the 275. post they unite and enter a narrow deep cañon— Had heavy chopping to The End which we reached at sundown. Stopped at 276.27.71 in a small opening giving a good view almost to the horizon in every direction, with a good camping place within 30 chs. to the west. From that point The Tetons can be plainly seen though 85 miles back on the line. C[illegible] S. 9° 19' E. It doesn't seem possible that we have finished our work, but such is the fact, and we are but two (2) days behind time. We have made a big run this week, 22 miles mostly through timber and rain on four days delaying us more or less each day. If Lon is at Bozeman I expect he is a little anxious about us but his anxiety will be short lived now, for we start for that town direct tomorrow. Our provisions have lasted well, and we now have suffi-cient coffee flour & beans to last two weeks & pork for a week, while sugar & dried coffee gave out today. It is now 10 P.M. We have celebrated in a mild way, by sitting around the camp fire, recalling some of the incidents of the trip, telling stories, congratulating ourselves on our success, all the time smoking and playing Pitch   I am alone by the fire now, the boys are abed and snoring beautifully, and I'll close the records of the West-ern boundary on the line with a Hurrah and add one more to the sleepers of our tent—

Sunday Aug 23

Broke camp for Bozeman at 8 A.M. Travelled about 16 miles and camped near the top of the divide between the Gallatin & Yellowstone— the altitude of which is 10200 ft. Do not know just where we can get down to the Y. but we will get down somewhere— Found some fine specimens today.

Monday 24th

With Billie left camp at day light to find a trail down the mountain. Tried several cañons but came back to camp at 10 A.M. unsuccessful. While out saw a herd of cattle and a hay stack in the valley below. Was undecided for a while whether to go west down a cañon which evidently runs into the Gallatin, or try and find a pass to the East— Finally decided upon the latter course. Reached a low point in the divide to the S. E. of our camp at 4 P.M. & camped in a rain storm. Grasshoppers numerous. Feeling somewhat tired sent Dick & Billie out in one direction and Frank and Tom Barry in another. The latter succeeded in finding a passable cañon as we think.

Tuesday Aug. 25th

Started down the Mt at 7 A.M. at 12 were almost to the valley, and camped at night on the banks of the Yellowstone near Tom Miner's ranche— Another heavy rain & wind storm. Learned that Lon & Mac [astronomer Augustus MacConnel] are in Bozeman awaiting us—

Wednesday, 26.

With Frank started out ahead of the pack train at 8 A.M. for Bozeman—supposed to be 40 miles away. Was taken with sick headache very bad about 10 a m and lay for two hours on the bank of the Yellowstone. Got a cold dinner at Tim Cotter's a ditto supper at Spragues at 5:30 P.M. 20 miles from Bozeman & drove on. Reached the latter place at 10:30 P.M. Lon & Mac abed, glad to see me. Found lots of mail. Four letters from Alice. Everybody well at home, no plat news.—

Thursday, 27.

Looked around town a little, signed & sent off to Aut a contract of $4800.00 subdivisions in Nebraska— [p. 248] Wrote home & to Alice—

Friday, 28.

With Lon & Mac went to breakfast with Mr. Bogest, spent a pleasant morning. He has a fine house well furnished, a nice sister and all the adjuncts of a home in America. Pack train came in at noon. Took them all to the hotel to dinner. In the evening Lon, Mac & I went out riding with Gen. Willson.* Wrote Alice a long letter—

Saturday, 29

Rode out to the Fort in the morning to see about getting some provisions there. Succeeded in doing so— Have had the mules reshod and are getting ready to start back to the corner Monday next.

---

*Brevet General Lester S. Willson, officer in the Union Army, merchant and politician in Bozeman.—Wikipedia

Sunday, Aug. 30
> Arose late. Wrote to Mr. Xeroes S. F.

November 18th, 1874 [from the 1873 diary]
> Lon reached Omaha, the same day of the month that we came in upon last year. He went in to Galena and wrote up the [field] notes. I employed competent draughtsmen and had the maps well made and about first of January, Lon went to Washington with the returns. In eight days after the accounts were taken up they were paid, Lon getting the draft through the U.S. Treasury Department and the hands of 72 men in two hours and fifteen minutes.

WHEN THE TIME came to do the final astronomical calculations for the northwest corner, at the 45th parallel of latitude, Professor Truman Safford, the eminent astronomer who established the southern boundary terminus, pleaded ill health in early August, so MacConnel went in his place. From Bozeman, Lon, Will, and Mac trekked back to the mountains to confirm the astronomy and set the western boundary's northern terminus. As they had discovered earlier, the only available stone was so hard that "tools made expressly for the purpose would hardly make an impression upon them," as Lon wrote in his official field notes.[7] "It was with the greatest difficulty that we succeeded in marking the boulders placed in the mound... ." They made the terminal monument out of wood.*

Lon also stated, "It is my opinion that this line runs entirely West of the Western boundary of the National Park," Yellowstone.

He and Will returned to Evanston, visiting Yellowstone on the way. No record of the trip apparently survives except a hunting story of Will's (p. 223; excerpt on back cover). At this time the National Park had a

---

*Lon gave detailed descriptions in his field notes:[8]

> I set a pine post 10 ft. long by 30 in. dia. ...3 ft. in the ground, with corners to cardinal points of the compass and marked as follows: viz: South East face "Wyoming," North west face "Montana," North east face "34° W. L." and "45° N.L. 1874," South west face "277 m. 72 chs. 66 lks." Deposit[ed] stone marked "34° W.L." and charred block—raise[d] conical mound of stone 5 ft. high by 9 ft. in dia. with pits 3 ft. square 2 ft. deep North, South, East, and West of post and 6 ft. distant as per instructions. Placed a boulder on S. E. side of mound marked as follows, in letters 3 in. square deeply graven... "Wyo. 277 m. 72 chs. 66 lks." Placed another on North west side...marked with same kind of letters "Montana," "W. L. 34°,—N. L. 45° 1874" Another on South side... marked "R."

They also marked 20 pine trees as witnesses, recording their diameters and locations.

supervisor, but no budget and no way to protect its treasures. In his field notes Lon reported,[9]

> Quite an extensive traffic is carried on by irresponsible parties in specimens and natural curiosities gathered in the National Park. They haul them by wagon loads to Bozeman, Helena, Virginia City and other points. They invariably claim they get them outside of the Park and until the boundaries are established and marked, it will be impossible to check the spoliation of this truly wonderful region by these vandals that infest the neighboring region.

Lon named a number of Park features. Cascade Creek, Pass Creek, and Sinking Water Canyon still bear the names he gave them, but four others were changed later. His own name was given to Richards Creek in 1958.[10]

High Praise for the Richardses' Work

As noted earlier, the 1873 survey found that the southern boundary of Wyoming ended about a half mile farther west than had previously been determined. The discrepancy was seven-tenths of a mile when the western survey reached the Idaho-Utah line. The General Land Office decided in Lon's favor, and on February 1, 1875, he announced to Will,

> our determination...has been tested by a Prof. Davidson & pronounced correct, & Hayden's map & Major's corner both wrong — one more feather for us —

In his field notes Lon allowed that Major was working under difficult conditions and that the spider silk in his transit may have shifted.*

The "feather" did little to ease Lon's concern about his ongoing unemployment, so he returned to Washington in April to lobby for more boundary contracts. One for Arizona went to someone better connected politically, yet there was still hope for Colorado and others. Before he left, Lon wrote Will on April 4, 1875,

> U.S.G. [President Grant] has without doubt been making some calculations and maneuvers for a 3rd term and is consequently looking more to the interests of new friends than old ones. If we get the work I shall certainly be surprised. If we do not, as I think we will not, I am at sea without chart or compass.

---

*Spider silk was used for the lines on transits (see p. 8). The ring holding it may have become misaligned. Major had also been working with a field chronometer, which was less accurate than an astronomical observatory in determining time and thus longitude.[11] However, Major's work elsewhere, such as the California-Oregon boundary, has also been considered problematic.

He must have been bucked up by praise from the new commissioner of the General Land Office, Samuel S. Burdett, and from Major John Wesley Powell. Six years earlier, Powell had led the geographic and ethnological expedition that included the first known boat trip through the Grand Canyon. The major had lost his right forearm during the Civil War, but that did not stop him from embarking on this perilous journey. Now, as head of the United States Geographical and Geological Survey of the Rocky Mountain Region, he was midway through an eight-year study of the arid lands for the government.[12] On April 23, Lon exulted to Will,

> Had a compliment in the land office. Dallas [the chief survey clerk] introduced me to the new Com'r as the Surveyor of Southern & Western Bdy's of Wyoming & remarked that our work was the best ever returned to that office. I also met Maj. Powell the explorer, in the Interior Dept. & he remarked to Mr. Curtis, Chf. Clk. for Com'r of the Land Office, that it was a great pity we did not get the Arizona line as he had had occasion to test our work & found it remarkably well done—the best he had ever seen.

Lon asked for and received an affidavit from the Commissioner about the quality of the two boundary surveys, for what comfort that might have provided:

> August 2, 1875.
>
> I cheerfully bear witness to the excellence of the character and quality of the returns…involving 646 lineal miles of survey. Considering the distance of the lines determined, marked and sketched through a trackless country, and the many obstacles impeding the progress in your work, as evidenced by the field notes of your survey. I cannot withhold the expression of my opinion as to your said work, and have to say that it is not surpassed by any survey of the kind on file in this office, and that it reflects creditably upon this office and yourself.
>
> I am, very respectfully, etc.
> S. S. Burdett, Commissioner[13]

No other sizeable contracts came Lon's way, possibly because the patronage system favored those with better political connections. He remained in Illinois and became editor and publisher of the *Freeport Journal* in September 1875. His days as a surveyor came to a close but his troubles did not.

Will kept surveying, alternating it with other work. After a decade of dissatisfaction he returned to Wyoming to try homesteading.

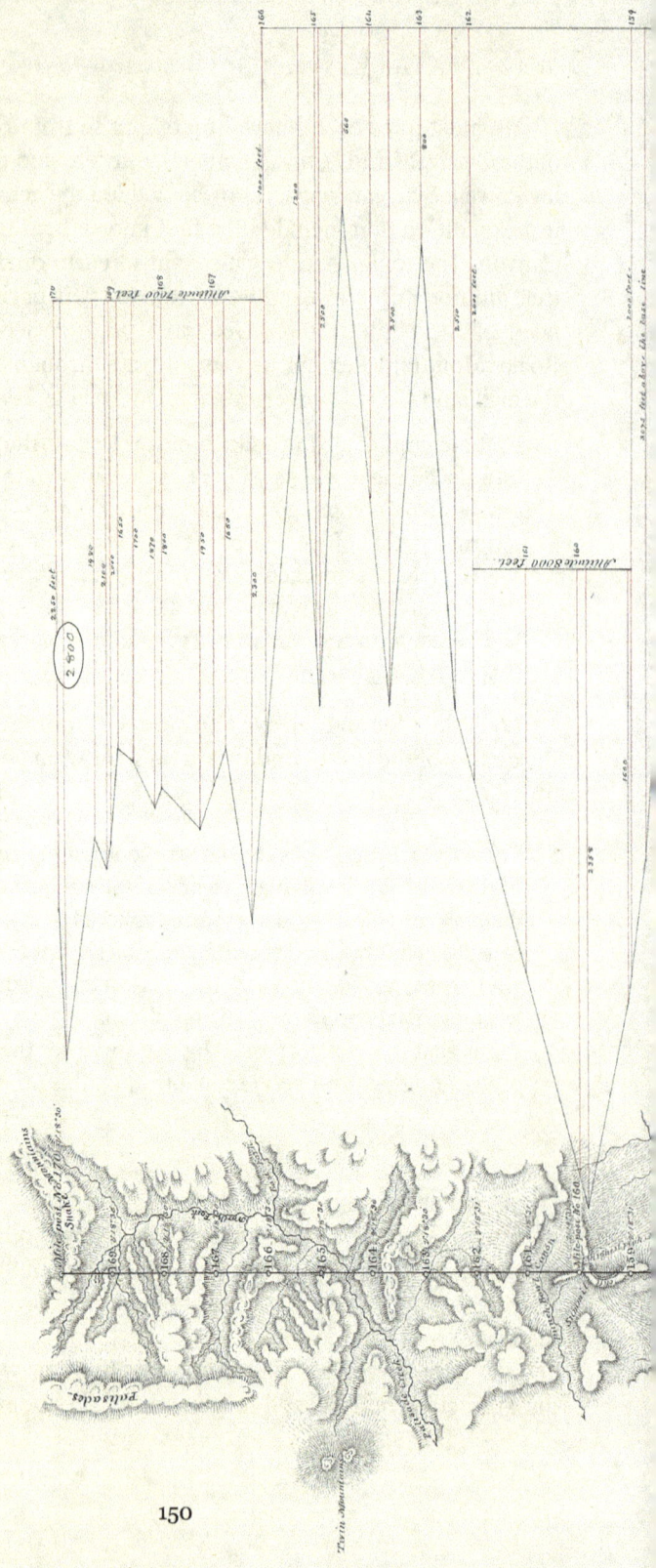

No. 6.

WEST BOUNDARY OF WYOMING

LONGITUDE 34 WEST

From mile-post No. 142, to mile-post No. 170.

Scale 2 miles to an inch.   Magnetic Variation East

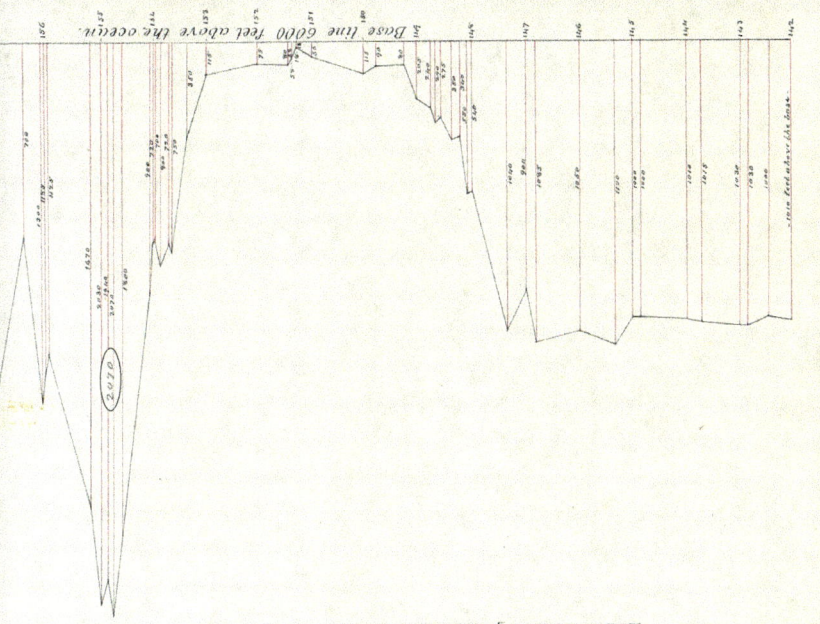

Barometrical profile. — Vertical scale 400 feet to an inch.

Section of plat from the 1874 field notes,[5] lightly Photoshopped for clarity. Original size is 25.33″ x 30″. Near Mile-Post No. 160, the writing heading southeast says "Highest Point Alt. 10512′."

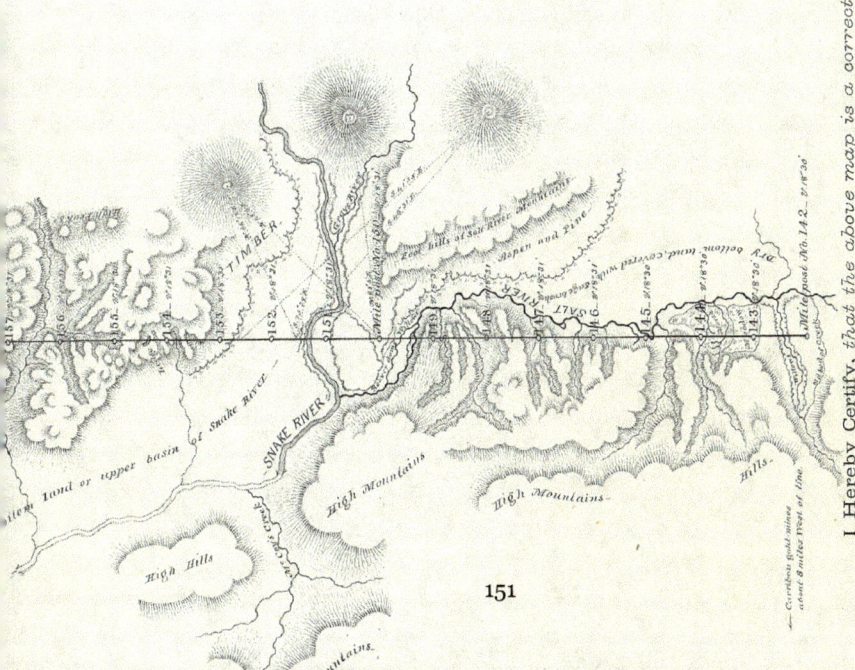

I Hereby Certify, that the above map is a correct representation of so much of the survey of the West Boundary of Wyoming, as extends from mile-post No. 142 to mile-post No. 170—, as surveyed and marked by me, under Contract from the Commissioner of the General Land Office, dated May 29ᵗʰ 1875.

M. Richardt.

U. S. Astronomer and Surveyor.

151

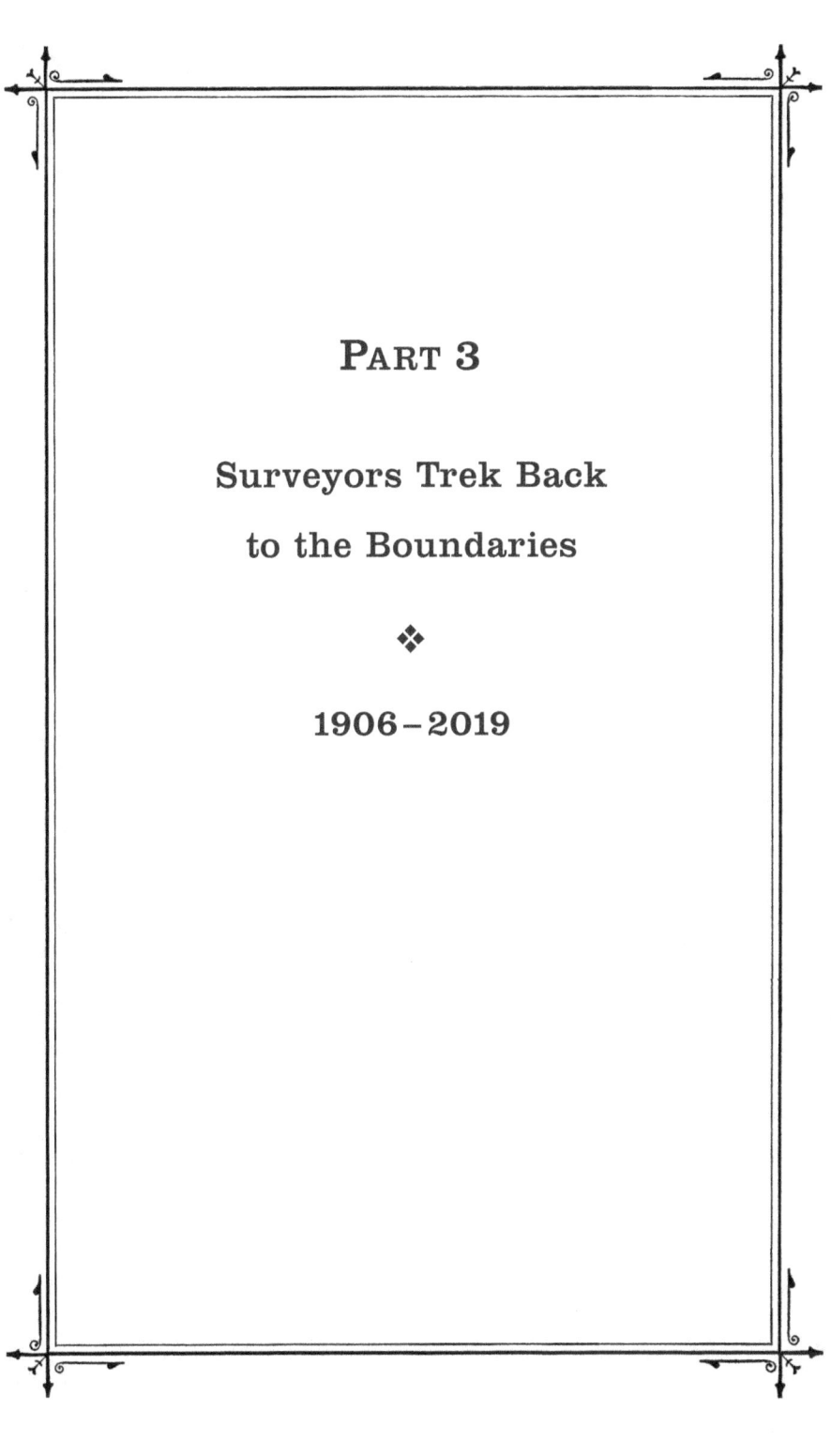

PART 3

Surveyors Trek Back
to the Boundaries

❖

1906–2019

Surveyors Trek Back to the Boundaries

M ANY POINTS along Wyoming's boundaries are remote and hard to reach, but surveyors have gone back to them for various reasons, including setting replacement monuments and historical markers.

In early September 1906, after three summers' work, the party surveying the Montana-Idaho boundary was closing in on the finish line: the western border of Wyoming. But no sign of it could be found, thanks to bad maps and a snowstorm. The contractor had to complete the survey the following summer, and snow still covered about a third of the ground.[1]

When Colorado challenged its border with Wyoming, a 1911 resurvey found no problem with the original one.[2] A century later, after pine beetles had destroyed 90% of one section of forest including some of the "bearing" trees showing the location of five of the mile posts, replacements were chosen from survivors. The original wooden posts had been replaced in 2001 with iron ones with brass information caps.[3]

Wyoming's other boundary markers were checked again over the years. On the northern reaches of the western border, mountainous terrain, fallen timber, or fire damage posed a particular challenge. Nevertheless, surveyors—many of them volunteers—located the state corner markers and restored or remonumented most of them.

A Surprise at Wyoming's Northwest Corner, 1958

In the mid-20th century, the U.S. Geological Survey (USGS) decided to "recover" (find) the Wyoming State line inside Yellowstone National Park. Since no private lands were affected by the line, there was no record of any attempt to locate it since the Richardses established it in 1874, according to an article by Raymond Hill, leader of the 1958 recovery expedition.[4] The USGS planned to find enough markers to confirm the line's position. "[T]he recovery of the terminal monument at the supposed intersection of the 34th meridian west of Washington and the 45th degree of north latitude was of particular importance," wrote Hill.

A decade earlier, field operations and subsequent research indicated that the Corner monument was either north or south of the 45th parallel, and the later research indicated that surveyors might be able to go in and find it. In preparation for the search, Hill combed A. V. Richards's field notes and plats for clues. He was so impressed with how "extremely detailed" they were that he included an excerpt in his article.

Some of the mile posts south of the Corner, or what was left of them, had been found on earlier expeditions. Tree blazes or the stumps left from clearing the line in 1874 led to most of the recoveries. Hill wrote,

> The last previous monument on the line was recovered 2.908 miles to the South. It required a pack trip of 2-1/2 hours to reach the vicinity of the terminal monument.... Upon searching for evidence of the line, we recovered two of the old line stumps on the south side of the ridge and blazed a true north line from the northernmost of these two stumps to the top of the ridge by means of a compass. Projecting this line northward, we measured with a tape from the ridge line to the theoretical location of the corner. This procedure of using tape, compass, and blazed line to search for a corner after finding evidence of the line has proved more satisfactory than continuing the search with the traverse [transit?]. We were able to proceed rapidly through the timber, unencumbered by equipment and packs, and range farther in searching for additional evidence of the line.

> ...After locating the terminal monument, we proceeded to take several pictures of the post, cairn, and bearing trees. As I was moving to another vantage point, I noticed a piece of finished lumber almost covered by dead branches and pine needles. On dislodging it, I uncovered another beside it—they were the stadia rods used on the original line. The side of each rod which had been against the ground was well preserved. The front of one rod and the back of the other had been laid downward. They were complete except for the level bubbles.

The Richards party must have decided to abandon the cumbersome rods, but they removed the vials with the level bubbles, which Dr. Stoughton said were quite expensive and somewhat difficult to procure. He added that Lon may have hoped to use the rods again if he received a contract to survey the Montana-Wyoming boundary in the near future.[5]

After giving a description of the rods from the 1874 field notes (see p. 250), Hill concluded,

Stadia rods from the 1874 survey found in 1958. For this photo they were propped up against the original corner monument.
Photo courtesy of John P. Lee, BLM, Cheyenne

As my rodman and I put on our packs and started down the mountainside in the lengthening shadows, bearing these rods, I could not help but feel that we held an almost-century-old link with a colorful era of our young Nation's expansion. We were aware, too, of the romance and history that is ever present though seldom perceived in our work. Surveyors and engineers in the future, as in the past, will always be an integral part of our country's development.

If the rods had not been carried out, they would have been consumed by the 1988 conflagration along with the wooden terminal monument and bearing trees. The Cheyenne BLM sometimes lends them out for exhibits. It was Hill who named Richards Creek after A. V. Richards.[6]

Attending to Wyoming's Boundary Markers, 1990s

As a rectangle, Wyoming has four corners in the usual sense. But along its boundary are other official "corners" where other state boundaries end. The idea of checking on them all was inspired by a surveyor's visit to the Sixth Principal Meridian. The 6th PM is a North-South line established in 1855 as the basis for surveying that part of the Louisiana Purchase that became Nebraska, Kansas, most of Wyoming and Colorado, and a bit of South Dakota.[7] The surveyor was Paul N. Scherbel of Big Piney, Wyoming. His son Scott A. Scherbel wrote,[8]

[T]he remonumentation efforts for him began with the finding of the initial point of the 6th PM on the Kansas/Nebraska border. He was traveling in the area and decided to drive over and look at that corner since most of the surveys in Wyoming are based on that position.

To his surprise, there was nothing visible. So he contacted the land surveyor societies in the associated states about recovering the monument. They showed interest, set a date, went to the site and found part of the original stone in place. The group decided that it needed something better, made a plan, obtained donations, enlisted the BLM and put it all together.

After that, several state surveyor societies began to be interested in recovering and re-monumenting state and other historically significant corners. Dad continued his interest and just continued the process with the northwest corner of Wyoming and other corners. I don't recall him mentioning any problem in

Paul N. Scherbel in 2012. He kept surveying till the day he died—aged 98.
Lines & Points[9]

157

getting interest and support from any of the groups involved. Perhaps the timing was just right. Monumenting corners is something most surveyors are interested in just by virtue of their vocation. The idea of doing something a little more historical apparently appealed to all involved.

The group is the Professional Surveyors of the Sixth Principal Meridian. The story and photos of the impressive monument they erected in 1987 may be found on various Web pages about the 6th PM.

The meridian's northern terminus, on the south bank of the Missouri River, was marked with a new "witness monument" in April 2007, about 150 years after the original survey by Charles A. Manners. The wooden post he planted was probably lost in the ever-shifting stream, and the same fate may eventually befall the concrete one made by Nebraska deputy surveyor Gene A. Thomsen and installed with the help of three fellow surveyors. The legal northern terminus is literally in a fluid state.[10]

The southern terminus, at the Kansas-Oklahoma border, has not been remonumented.

As noted, the 6th PM project led to the checking, preservation, or remonumenting of the eight boundary markers on Wyoming's borders, four of them on the lines surveyed by the Richards brothers. All are far enough away from any town to be easily lost to time, and all required varying degrees of trouble and expense.

Reestablishing the Corner for Wyoming, Utah, and Idaho

The point where Wyoming's boundary intersects those of Utah and Idaho seems to be a sort of Bermuda Triangle for surveyors. As noted, in 1871 Daniel G. Major placed the Utah-Idaho line on the 42nd parallel of latitude, but a few years later A. V. Richards determined that the Wyoming line was about 7/10 of a mile west of where Major had placed it. Richards was validated when the line was retraced in 1880, 1907, and 1914–15, but the red sandstone marker that made his corner official in 1915 came loose and gravity pulled it down the hill. Nearby mileposts were missing or had the wrong information.[9] This was the first point that the remonumenters dealt with on the western line, and they had their work cut out for them. The new markers are designed to stay put and are supplemented by others placed where more people might see them.

In Cokeville, Wyoming, about seven miles east, prominent arrows lead to the monument. A plaque in town tells the story of Major's marker,

The new monument and plaque in 2011
Jimmy S. Emerson, DVM, flickr.com

Richards' survey, and the remonumentation. At the ceremony held in August 1992 in Cokeville, when it was State Capital for a Day, the governor and other state officers were present. The U.S. director of cadastral (land) surveys, Francis D. Eickbush, gave a talk on the public land survey system.[12] He once worked for Scherbel, according to a participating surveyor.[13]

All this was the culmination of the "dependent resurvey" executed in July 1992 by the Wyoming office of the BLM with Scherbel as volunteer. With the 1915 marker dislodged and no others in sight, the surveyors had to take an "embedded mound of stone as the best available evidence of the original corner." They installed a new monument of hard red sandstone, pentagonal, inscribed with the three state names (photo above). On top is a brass disc with standard BLM wording, the position of the three states, and the dates 1874 and 1992. The marker was set in concrete 25″ in the ground[14] with the 1915 post immured in the concrete.[15] The fate of the 1874 marker is unknown.

The surveyors also restored the boundary's nearby markers. Only a stone mound remained to indicate the 68th mile post, so a new stainless steel one was set in its center. Its shaft extended 22″ to bedrock and was capped by a disc marked 68 MP 1992 along with the position of Utah and Wyoming. Moving north, nothing was found where the 69th mile post should have been, but a red sandstone marker was found wired to a fence downhill. A new stainless steel post was set in place, 26″ of it in the ground, with the information disk on top and a magnetic marker buried at its base. At the 70th mile, a sandstone marker was found that had UTAH instead of the correct IDAHO on its west face and W on its east face. This must have been from one of the intermediate resurveys, since Lon's field notes[16] say his sandstone post was inscribed with Wyoming | Idaho, along with 34TH W. L. 1874. The new brass disk was set in a concrete collar with a three-foot base, and the old stone was deposited alongside it. This disk was marked 70 MP 1992 Idaho | Wyoming.

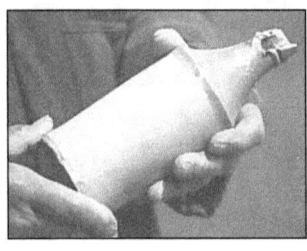

The ceramic bottle
Lines & Points[17]

Also remonumented was Major's "Initial Point," which established the boundary between Idaho and Utah on the 42nd parallel of latitude. The year before the 1992 resurvey, Scherbel and others from Wyoming and Idaho recovered the remains of Major's monument: a rotted wooden post with a ceramic bottle buried three feet below it. Scattered around were pieces of broken sandstone bearing the names of each state. In the remonumentation, a stainless-steel post was set with a brass cap marked 1871 INITIAL POINT 42ND PARALLEL NORTH 1992. The remains of the original wooden post were placed next to it. Three new stones mark the states, the year 1871, and the latitude and longitude. Mile Post 1 west of this Initial Point was monumented with the remains of a wooden post inscribed with now-illegible marks.[18]

The original marked stones and the bottle are on exhibit today at the Fossil Country Museum in Kemmerer, Wyoming.[19]

Scherbel was delighted with the project. "This is the acme of being a surveyor. It is the highlight of a career."[20]

The plaque next to the new tri-state monument says,[21]

IDAHO, UTAH, AND WYOMING INTERSECT POINT

THIS STONE MARKS THE INTERSECT POINT ESTABLISHED JUNE 15, 1874, BY A. V. RICHARDS, U.S. ASTRONOMER AND SURVEYOR, ON THE 34TH MERIDIAN WEST FROM THE CENTER OF THE OLD NAVAL OBSERVATORY DOME IN WASHINGTON, D.C. WITH THE STATE BOUNDARY OF IDAHO AND UTAH (THE 42ND PARALLEL NORTH), SURVEYED BY DANIEL G. MAJOR, U.S. ASTRONOMER, ON AUGUST 29, 1871.

THE INITIAL POINT MONUMENT OF D. G. MAJOR FOR THE 42ND PARALLEL NORTH IS LOCATED 7/10 OF A MILE EAST.

CONTRIBUTIONS FOR THIS REMONUMENTATION WERE OBTAINED FROM THE FEDERAL GOVERNMENT, STATES, COUNTIES, AND THE PRIVATE SECTOR.

Remonumenting the Northwest Corner

After a reconnaissance mission by Scherbel and others in 1993, surveyors returned in August 1994 to remonument the Northwest Corner. Though the original wooden marker post had burned away, the Corner was identified by the large mound of stones the post had been set in and by the stone markers placed in 1874. In charge of the remonumentation were two BLM surveyors and volunteer surveyors Paul N. Scherbel and Ronald W. Allen. Also represented that day were the U.S. Forest Service, the National Park Service (NPS), surveyors' associations in Wyoming and Montana, plus interested parties and family members—about 55 in all.[22]

The Corner is 1,700 feet above U.S. Highway 191. The NPS transported the materials to the site by helicopter, but the humans (including children) had to hike up there, about 1.5 miles.[23] The altitude (about 8,500 feet) and view were breathtaking.

Once arrived, the party reconfirmed the official Corner and set several markers intended to defy time and catastrophe.

Above: Looking west from the Corner, into Montana
Cody Schatz, 2019

Right: The new markers. The replica of the original monument stands at left. At lower right is the concrete slab holding the plaque and the brass disk indicating the Corner. The tree with the yellow sign is a "bearing tree," another aid to locating an obscured corner.
Cody Schatz

Top photo, 1994: While the slab sets, the Corner's GPS coordinates are taken. Scott Scherbel helps his son Alan, 7, use an SLR camera while his son Ben, 15, stands behind them.
From Paul N. Scherbel's scrapbook, photographer unknown

Middle photo, 2019: The slab with the official Corner marker disk and plaque
Cody Schatz

Bottom photo: Diagram of the marker disc shows the position of the states, with the Corner precisely in the center.[24]

The slab was placed in the same spot as the original monument. Deposited in the concrete is a marker erected by the Lupton and Roadifer families in 1990 in honor of the centennial of Wyoming statehood. Its disk and steel shaft had been placed in a stone mound about a half-mile northwest of the official Corner.[25]

Marker stones from the 1874 survey[26] were installed about eight feet from the new mound. If these markers become hidden again, two other disks with arrows will inform searchers that the Corner is 12 feet away.

The 2019 photos of the Corner were provided by Cody Schatz and Glenn Borkenhagen of Cody, Wyoming. At the time of this writing, Mr. Schatz, a land surveyor and civil engineer, was president of the northwestern chapter of the Professional Land Surveyors of Wyoming and a member of the Montana Association of Registered Land Surveyors. Mr. Borkenhagen, a retired dealer in surveying equipment, was a sustaining member of both organizations. He took part in the 1993 recovery, the 1994 remonumentation, and the search for the Wyoming-Montana-Idaho Corner.[27]

When the two returned to the Northwest Corner in September 2019 with Schatz's son Beau, aged 12, they hiked up the steep slope on the Montana side. Slippery from recent rain, the route became easier once they got past a tangle of fallen timber and found an elk trail.[28]

Top photo: The treated-wood replacement monument is set in a mound of stones like the original. Its four sides indicate Wyoming and Montana and state the boundary length (277 M 72 CHS 66 LKS), latitude and longitude, and the original survey date (1874).

On the bases of the sides are the initials of the entities that took part in the remonumentation: the Professional Surveyors of the Sixth Principal Meridian, the Professional Land Surveyors of Wyoming, the Montana Association of Registered Land Surveyors, the U.S. National Park Service, and the U.S. Bureau of Land Management, along with RESET '94.[29]

Glenn Borkenhagen, 2019

On the plaque, the logos of the the participating surveyors' associations of Wyoming and Montana bracket those of the National Park Service and the U.S. Department of the Interior.

Glenn Borkenhagen

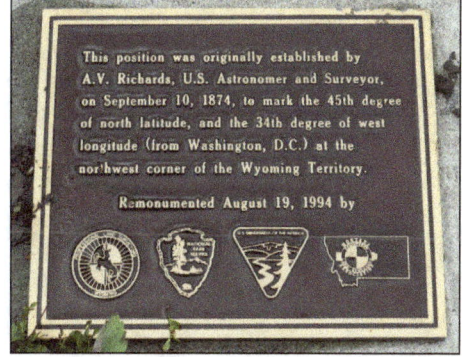

Recovering the Wyoming-Montana-Idaho Corner

The day after remonumenting the Northwest Corner, Scherbel and about 25 officials and surveyors went in search of the tri-state monument established in 1907 by Howard B. Carpenter. It was on a high rolling plateau 3.5 miles from a parking lot, and to reach it the party had to walk through ankle-deep ash and burned timber from the Yellowstone conflagration six years earlier. Like Carpenter, they were misled by inaccurate maps, but finally located their quarry. The marker, a pipe with a brass cap, was intact. They took GPS readings but did not place a plaque.[30]

Restoring the Southwest Corner Monument

The only boundary corner marker set by A. V. Richards that remained in place was the one for Wyoming's Southwest Corner. A century after its installation in 1873, it stood in a sea of sagebrush with no roads or other landmarks nearby to help surveyors locate it. One day in 1956, surveyors in a helicopter landed at a sheep ranch in the area to get directions. Home alone was a 13-year-old boy, Kim Aagard, who eagerly climbed aboard the copter to guide them to the marker.[31]

Roads were not built until years later, making access easier for vandals. In early 1996, Paul Scherbel and the Professional Surveyors of the Sixth Principal Meridian appealed to the Utah and Wyoming counties abutting the monument. (He reportedly said he saved it for last because he could walk to it.[32]) Permission was granted for restoration and the placement of an information plaque. The small plot of land it stood on was purchased from the Aagard family for $25.[33]

In the restoration, graffiti and vandals' carved initials were removed and a new stone mound built around the monument. A Commemoration Ceremony was held in September 1996, with Scherbel, representatives of Uinta County, Wyoming, and Summit County, Utah, and others in attendance. The president-elect of the Utah Council of Land Surveyors, Randall J. Williford, served as master of ceremonies. Deeds to the plot were presented to county commissioners by Kim Aagard.[34]

BLM surveyor James Clauflin closed with remarks about the survey

The monument in 1996, before its restoration

From Paul N. Scherbel's scrapbook, photographer unknown

The same side in 2022

Kim Aagard

system's protection of landowners. "The general public needs to become more knowledgeable about the monuments because they control the land."[35] The remonumentations in Wyoming and elsewhere, along with websites about markers, have boosted awareness. Aagard says that the development of sport vehicles like UTVs has significantly increased traffic past the Corner, and visitors often stop and read the plaque.

The south side of the monument in 2019 and 2022.
The damage, most of it apparently from bullets, occurred before
the restoration. The west side originally read UTAH 41° N. L.
and 1873; the east side WYO- 367 Ms. 48 Chs. 81 Lks.
The north side concludes with MING. 34° W.L.[36]
The disk on top had been placed in 1898 by the USGS.[37]

Photo at top left by Andrew Johnson, hmdb.org, top right by Kim Aagard. Plaque photo courtesy of Sonja Sparks, chief cadastral surveyor for the Wyoming State office of the BLM.

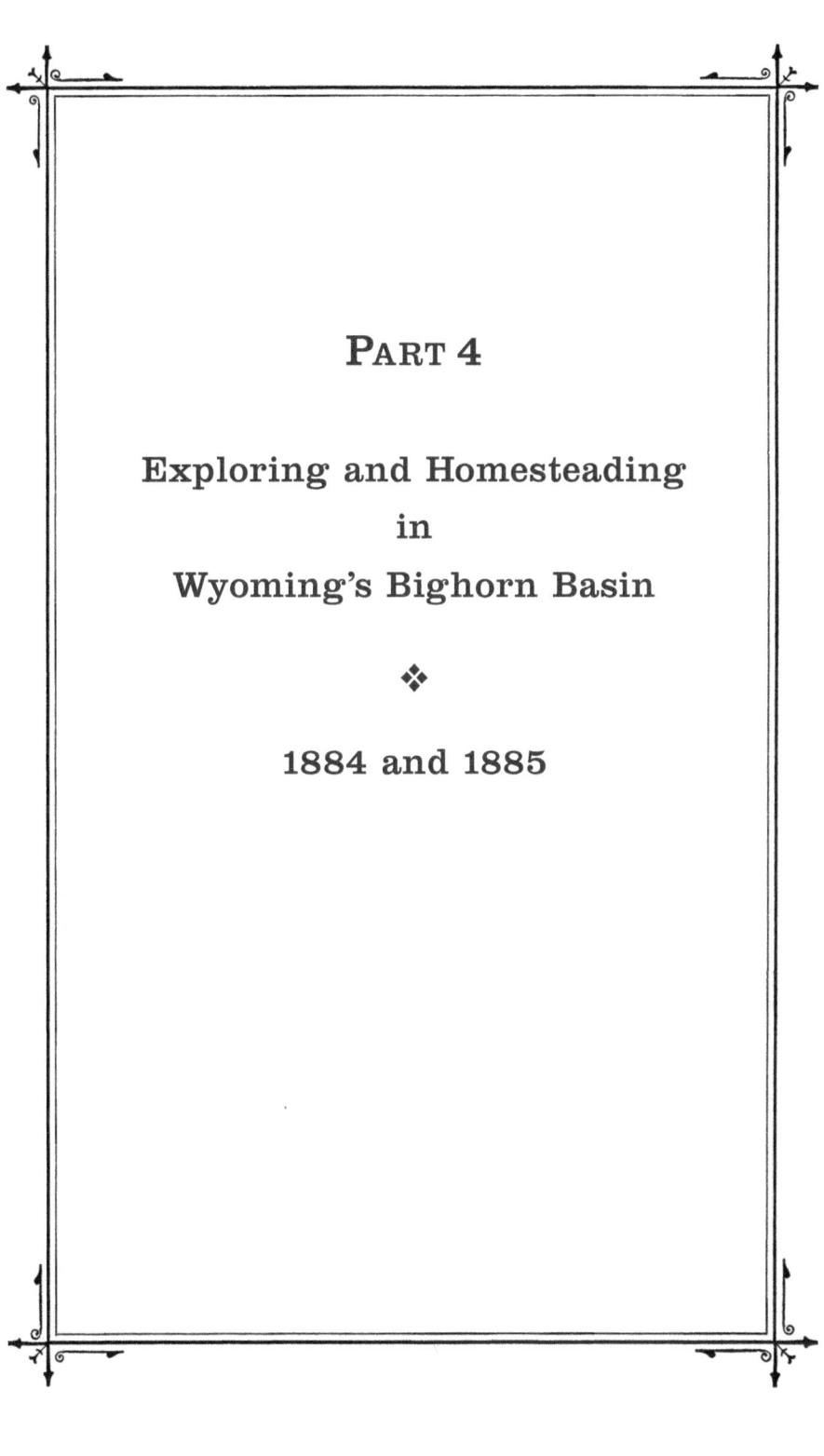

PART 4

Exploring and Homesteading
in
Wyoming's Bighorn Basin

❖

1884 and 1885

Exploring and Homesteading in Wyoming's Bighorn Basin

Background

AFTER TEN YEARS of struggle in Nebraska, California, Colorado, and Kansas, William A. Richards—a son of pioneers—decided to pioneer in Wyoming. His fortunes and those of his brother Lon had not been improved by the successful survey of Wyoming's western boundary, and in the next decade they (and many others) found hope in visions of a ranch in the West.

Late in 1874, they realized that expenses would consume most or all of what the survey was to pay. Will felt he had to postpone—yet again—his marriage to Harriet Alice Hunt (known as Alice). But after she and her elder sister wrote him about their distress over the postponement, a friend gave him a railroad pass from Omaha, Nebraska, to Oakland, California, and Will and Alice were wed on December 28, her 20th birthday.

The newlyweds lived in Omaha in 1875, then returned to Oakland. Will considered employment in his father-in-law's livery-stable business, but instead kept surveying and even delivered newspapers. After their first child was born, in 1876, they moved to a San Jose farm owned by Alice's relatives. Will alternated farm work with surveying, and in 1879 was elected county surveyor.

Like so many in that damp climate, Will developed lung trouble. To save his life, he left for the Colorado mountains in early 1881, forfeiting

Harriet Alice Hunt and William Alford Richards
at the time of their wedding, 1874[1]

169

Members of C.T. & Co.: Richards's friend Edwin S. Crocker is on the stool and Harvey Booth in the doorway. William Crawford and William Thompson may be the men at right. Crocker would later be tried for the murder of Booth and suspected in the disappearance of Crawford. The man at left is Frank Moore.

Uinta County Museum, Wyoming

property whose mortgages he could no longer pay. His wife sold off most of their furniture to raise funds, which largely went to creditors, but she kept her treasured Chickering portable piano. She and their four-year-old daughter, Eleanor Alice (Allie), joined him in Colorado Springs that fall.

Richards was healthy enough to haul coal, harvest ice for railroad refrigerator cars, and work as a surveyor. When their second daughter, Elta Belle, was born in 1882, he took a steady job as foreman of a Kansas stone-crushing plant. Mrs. Richards, nearly crippled by rheumatism, had to make this arduous move in sub-zero weather.

Evidently dissatisfied with this position, Will looked into a Colorado ranch claim. Then Elta Belle died of infant cholera, and the family returned in sorrow to Colorado Springs. The ranch claim did not pan out and neither did other ventures.

CRAWFORD, THOMPSON & CO.

P. O. address, Evanston, Wyo.
Range, twenty miles north of
Evanston, Bear River; also,
on No Wood River, Johnson
county, Wyo.
Brand, both sides; also, **I** on
both sides.
All horses branded **II** on left
shoulder.

BOOTH & CROCKER.

P. O. address, Evanston, Wyo.
Range, twenty miles north of
Evanston, Bear River.

Brand, both sides; also **I** on
both sides, **(ㅍ ㅍ)** left
side, with wattle on nose.

O on right thigh with **O O**
on right side. Earmark, overslope each ear, and wattle
on nose.
Horse brands **II** left shoulder, **O O O** left thigh.

From the brand books of the Wyoming Stock Growers' Association, 1884 and 1885 respectively. Crawford, Thompson & Co.'s 2 bar was in the first book, published in 1882.[2] Johnson County was spelled correctly in later editions.

Will's brothers were also frustrated. Lon had been unable to obtain other state boundary contracts despite the high quality of his Wyoming surveys. He tried other businesses in Illinois, including publishing and editing the *Freeport Journal.* Ever a firebrand, he fought what he saw as local corruption, to no avail. He continued talking up a western ranch to Will and their younger brother, Aut. Aut did move to Oakland, but he exchanged steady employment in the Omaha Post Office for sporadic work as a surveyor and as a clerk in the tax collector's office.

For Will, a ranch became a real possibility in 1884. He had been elected county surveyor of El Paso County and city engineer of Colorado Springs the year before, but he felt those positions were inadequate support for his family when another child, Ruth, was born. Edwin S. Crocker, an Evanston merchant and banker whom he had met sometime during the boundary surveys and who had offered to help him in various ways over the years, recommended trying a homestead in the Bighorn Basin. Cut off from the rest of the world by a ring of mountains open only in the

North and two passes in the South, the basin contained about the last unclaimed grassland in the country. Crocker's firm, Crawford, Thompson & Co. (C.T. & Co.) ranged cattle on the east side of the basin in what is known as the Nowood country, after the stream known then as No Wood Creek and today as the No Wood (or Nowood) River.

In October 1884, Will stayed at the C.T. home ranch while he explored the country. Along with a homestead site, he located a large, unclaimed tract of land on the Bighorn River that had potential for agriculture or cattle grazing. The widest and flattest tract along the river, it was ideal for irrigation by canal. He apparently had already discussed the possibility of forming a company with others in Colorado Springs and elsewhere, since his diary mentions "our" scheme. The Bighorn was untapped by small farmers because its waters normally ran too far below its banks for small-scale canal cuts to work.

After he returned to Colorado Springs, the Big Horn Ditch Co. was formed in February 1885 by 26 investors.[3] Each could claim 640 acres (a section, or square mile) under the Desert Land Act, which required only that the land be irrigated. The claimants need not have lived on the land. Will would survey and supervise construction of the ditch, and his salary would finance his move.

When he struck out for Wyoming, Will was 35 years old, middle-aged for the era. He spent the summer and early fall of 1885, 1886, and 1887 in the Bighorn Basin while his family lived in Oakland or Colorado Springs. At last, in the fall of 1887, they all moved into the cabin at Red Bank Ranch, traveling by wagon from Rawlins. Once the railroad reached Casper, in 1888, Will hauled his wife's piano from Casper to the ranch, a round trip by wagon of some 250 miles over rough "roads."

Annotated relief map of the Bighorn Basin. The lake at the southern end is today's Boysen Reservoir, where the north-flowing Wind River becomes the Bighorn River. The circled gap on the right is Birdseye Pass, used by Richards and others traveling to the Nowood country.

Shadedrelief.com[4]

Once the Big Horn Ditch was finished and most of its investors obtained title to their parcels, the tract was never used—except by political opponents who charged Richards with land-grabbing when he ran for governor in 1894. Even if the Colorado men had wanted to resettle there, though, the lack of a railroad would have discouraged agricultural development. Most of the claimants kept their parcels until the Hanover Land and Irrigation Company began buying them up in 1903. (Richards kept his.) Today, this tract is irrigated by the Lower Hanover Canal: 22 miles long, it largely follows the original ditch line and irrigates 13,685 acres.[5]*

These diaries cover Will's 1884 exploration and his return in 1885, when he started digging the Big Horn Ditch, filed his own homestead claim, and built a log house. Two members of his crew would also settle in the Nowood country and attain a degree of prominence.

When Richards was elected the first full-term governor of the State of Wyoming, he honored the man who helped him get a foothold there. Mr. and Mrs. Edwin Crocker were invited to join the Richardses and a few others in receiving well-wishers at the inaugural ball. Not long afterward, Crocker was arrested for the murder of his partner Harvey Booth and suspected in the disappearance two years earlier of another partner, William Crawford. Found guilty of Booth's murder by an Evanston jury on the first ballot, Crocker was acquitted in a Cheyenne retrial. Richards always believed he was innocent.[6]

Diary, Exploration of the Basin, 1884

Oct. 2, Thursday

Left Colo. Spgs. 2.15 P.M. Reached Denver 6 P.M. Spent evening with [friends] Jules & Manda.**

Friday Oct. 3rd.

Left Denver 1.25 P.M. Reached Cheyenne 6 P.M. Met Crocker there. Left at 7.30 P.M. reached Carbon 2 A.M.***

---

*With the Big Horn Ditch tract tied up, the Hanover Canal Company in 1903 surveyed what became the Upper Hanover Canal on ground higher above the river.

**Jules Hammond was a surveyor friend and Richards's partner in an ice-harvesting business during Richards's early days in Colorado Springs.[7]

***Carbon was a Union Pacific coal- and cow-town northwest of Laramie. The depot was said to have been moved down the tracks a half mile east of town because trigger-happy cowboys at the saloon across the street would take potshots at its furniture and at any posted notices. To get to the hotel, Richards would have had to haul his gear over a bad road riddled with sinkholes from mine cave-ins. Carbon became a ghost town after the mines closed and the U.P. moved away.[8]

*Detail of an 1883 map of Wyoming Territory annotated with some locations
mentioned in the diaries plus others. Place names in parentheses did not yet
exist. The dotted line roughly indicates Richards's route from Carbon to
C.T. & Co.'s home ranch. This map does not show all the high ridges east and
south of Red Bank ranch that partly enclose the Bighorn Basin.*

George F. Cram, Chicago[9]

174

BECKWITH, QUINN & CO.

P. O. address, Evanston, Wyo.
Range, fifty miles north of
Evanston, on No Wood and
Bear Rivers, Wyoming.

A. C. Beckwith's individual brand.
P. O. address and range same as that
of Beckwith, Quinn & Co.

*Like Crawford Thompson & Co., Beckwith, Quinn & Co. were Evanston
merchants with ranches in Uinta County and the Nowood country. Their
brand was a shield. The No Wood range was not listed in 1883.*

Brand Book, 1884

Saturday. Oct. 4th.

Stayed in Depot till morning. Stopped at Scranto[n] House. Conners
prop. Dibble keeps B.Q. & Co.'s Store.* Stone Jas. foreman for C.T. & Co.
got in at noon with two saddle horses. Stormy. Sick all night.

Sunday Oct. 5, 1884.

Mailed letters to Alice, Lon, Aut, & [Agt RCK?] Left Carbon 9 A.M.
with Stone, saddle horses & pack horses. Dinner at Missouri John's (Jno.
Mussingale) 15 miles from Carbon. His partner "old Jno Ross." Passed
two Ranches of Qualey** in Shirley Basin in P.M. Also Reed's sheep ranch
and reached camp in W [might be an N but is closer to a W] edge Shirley
basin at dark. 35 miles from Carbon. Crossed Medicine Bow 14m from C.

Monday, Oct. 6.

Broke camp about 8 A.M. Drove about 10 mi NW & camped for dinner. Sage Crk. In P.M. drove 10 m's, camped on small crk

---

*Scranton House was reported to be the best hotel in town, and John O'Conner was
its proprietor. Lewis Dibble managed Beckwith, Quinn & Co.'s store.[10]

**Michael Quealy and Patrick J. Quealy each had entries in the 1887 *Cattle Brands*,
with ranges in the Shirley Basin and P.O. boxes in Carbon. They also had interests in
coal mining.[11]

Tuesday, Oct. 7.

Cloudy & cold. Drove to N. Platte and crossed same, camping at cabin in enclosed pasture on Dewees Creek. Snowing at noon. Two horses left the band last night & we can not go on till found. Three men out hunting in P.M. Unsuccessful. Man from Tom Sun's Ranch camped with us. Sig went to Sand Creek.

Wednesday, Oct. 8.

Jim & Henry went back on trail beyond last camp. Clear with high wind. 6 P.M. Men all got in without finding horses. Remained in camp all day. i. e. the outfit did. I went out hunting in P.M. & killed one sage hen.

Thurs. Oct. 9.

Sig went back to Indian Grove to Claib Young's with 3 horses to hunt the strays. Young killed a man in Texas & was arrested in Rawlins last year. Five miles from our camp over on [long?] creek Jack Cooper killed Chico—Cooper now lives at Ferris. We moved over to Sand Ck. & stopped for dinner at 10 A.M. I killed a big buck Antelope on way over & carried the horns in on my saddle. He was old & strong & poor eating. In P.M. drove to Sweetwater & camped. Made about 25 miles & camped on S. side S. Water. 4 miles East of Independence Rock. Fair, warm & windy. Rode Indian in morning & Eagle in P.M.

Friday, Oct. 10, 1884

Drove across Sweetwater & up same 4 m's. passing S. of Soda Lake & N. W. of Independence Rock, the former a small Soda Lake the latter a large round-topped isolated rock. Camped for dinner on Dry Creek—a running stream— I rode Whitey & killed 3 antelope. A buck, a doe & a young buck. Brought the horns of the two last in behind me on the saddle. In the P.M. drove on up Dry Crk & camped on same. Sig overtook us with the horses, having found them tied up at Claib Young's & paid him $10.00* for them. Drove about 20 miles today. Clear & fair & windy.

Saturday, Oct. 11.

Fair day but high cold wind. Drove up Dry Creek about 10 ms & camped for dinner. In P.M. drove over divide on Rattle Snake Range at Fred French's & drove down Deer Creek about 17 m's & camped. Rode Ben again in A.M. & The Little Bay in P.M. Rode a grey "Dobbin" yesterday P.M. Three men bound to the Oil camp camped with us. [It] is about ten m's. from here at the N. E. foot of Mt. Garfield.

---

*About $308 in 2022, per measuringworth.com purchasing-power calculator

Today's map annotated with some places mentioned in the diaries. (Ranch locations are approximate.) topozone.com/wyoming[12]

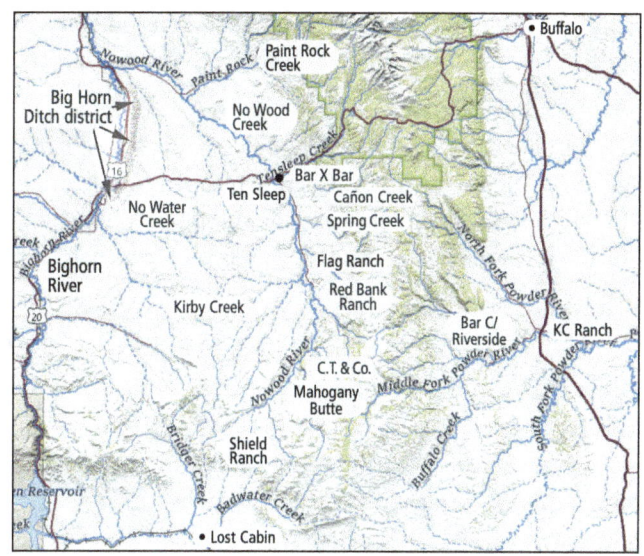

Sunday, Oct. 12.

Rode Indian again in A.M. & went hunting. Saw five fine black tail deer. Dinner on Deer Creek at 11 A.M. In P.M. drove to Mustang Spgs & camped at sundown at the 71 horse ranch.* 3 men there.

Monday Oct. 13.

Cloudy & windy. Broke camp early. Drove past old 71 Ranch on Poison Ck. 5 m's from Mustang Spgs & nooned on Bad Water 15 m's from M. Spgs. A nice stream of good water. The water at last camp gave me diarrhea. Rode "Calico" & Prick Ear. In P.M. drove 5 mi up Bad Water & camped on same. Rode Buck Skin. Cloudy & threatening rain.

Tuesday, Oct. 14.

No storm last night but it was warm & this morning is clear & pleasant. Sterling, a sheep man, camped with us. Rode Dobbin again & with Sig went ahead to Cottonwood. Sig went to the Home Ranch & I waited at crossing for the teams. Drove up Cottonwood 3-1/2 m's & camped for noon. Just North of camp & on W. side of road stands a stone mkd 5 on E, 1 on W, 6 on S, & on N, S.C-R.89.W. Drove on down the head waters of the No Wood over a rolling open country—some sage brush & no timber. Rode Dempsey. Camped 1/4 m. below Beckwith Quinn Co.'s. ranch about

---

*Probably the Wyoming Cattle Ranch Co. of Chicago, managed by John Clay, Jr., with a ranch office in Rongis.[13]

9 m's from noon camp. Weather clear & barometer steady. Ten m's more to C.T. & Co.'s home ranch and the end of our trip.

Wednesday, Oct. 15.

Left camp at 8 A.M. Reached C.T. & Co.'s ranch at mouth of Box Elder at 12 M. [noon] Weather warm & pleasant. After dinner Jim & I rode up to Smith's, a new settler near the [Mahogany] Bute. [Jordan] Smith comes from Holt Co. Neb., has a wife & 6 boys & one baby girl.

Thursday, Oct. 16.

Fine weather. Worked on the survey of C.T. & Co.'s claim at mouth of Box Elder.

Friday Oct. 17, 1884.

Clear & warm. Worked on survey for Chas. Wells.* Made $10.00. Agreed to make survey for Ritchie.

Saturday, Oct. 18.

Rode up to Ritchie's camp on Indian. He [illegible] up a corner [illegible] "The Dirty Woman." [illegible] in the camp. Snowed in P.M.

Sunday, Oct. 19.

Surveyed in forenoon for Ritchie. Rained. Came back to C.T. & Co.'s to dinner at 1-1/2 P.M. Jim & Kid [went to timber?] and are not back at 9 P.M. [Snowing?]

Monday, Oct. 20.

Rainy. Sig. went out to find Jim & Kid. Jim came in at 3 P.M. They camped last night with old Pucket's outfit on the mountain. The old man laid out & is not yet found & Sig & Kid are hunting for him. It has been a stormy cloudy day & I remained at the ranch all day.

Tuesday, Oct. 21.

Rode Indian to Ritchie's. Surveyed for them all day & finished. No dinner. [illegible] from —C ranch** on Powder River. Saw large herd of Elk near C.T. & Co.'s. Fair day.

---

*Charles Wells was born in 1854 in Germany and came to the U.S. in 1867. Employed about 1882 as a cowboy at the Frewens' 76 ranch, the first of the big English cattle outfits on Powder River, Wells was sent into the Nowood country as a representative for two of the outfits for the spring roundup at the W.P. ranch. By 1883, one of them had taken over the W.P. ranch and Wells went to work for them.[14]

**Owned by Thomas W. Peters and Walter C. Alston;[15] some Bar C cattle in the basin were owned by Geoffroy W. Millais, son of the famous painter John Everett Millais.[16]

Wednesday, Oct. 22, 1884

Breakfast at Ritchie's. Dinner at 2 bar [C.T. & Co.]. Rode Whitey out hunting for Elk which were seen near here. Saw nothing. Rec'd 15.00 from Ritchie. Good weather.

Thursday, Oct. 23, 1884

Clear. Jim went on round up. Sig & Charlie Wells started for Landers. Kid, whose name is E. [Robinson?], left with W. P. outfit* for [illegible] Creek. Henry & I surveyed in P.M. & found one section corner but failed to find one sec & two 1/4 cor's. They were never set. Jim came in from the Round Up at dark. He killed a big silver tip bear with a "45" pistol. [illegible] 1/4 beef disposed of.

Friday, Oct. 24.

W. P. wagon & Kid here. Surveyed Red Bank claim with Stone in P.M. Found 1/4 beef 200 yards from house where a bear had taken it.

Saturday, Oct. 25

Killed a bear last night & skinned him today. A very large Silver Tip [grizzly]. Surveyed the [illegible] claim for C.T. & Co. I shot the bear at the corner of the house & I stood just outside the door in my night-clothes—having been awakened by the bear trying to get at some meat hanging outside. [illegible line] He ran only 200 yards & we found him dead in the morning. He roared most terribly when I shot—more like the bellow of a mad bull.**

Sunday, Oct. 26, 1884

Cloudy & Cold. Surveyed at intervals all day. Started for mouth of Cañon Creek & came back on account of storm. [Cañon Creek is shown on an 1892 map, but he sometimes seems to be talking about Little Cañon creek.] With Jim rode down to the Booth*** corral above Ritchie's & showed Jim the claim he wants & he laid a foundation. Returning killed a large Golden Eagle with white feathers in tail i.e. a part white. As he rose

---

*WP was the brand of Worden P. Noble, said to have founded the first large cattle ranch on the upper No Wood, in 1880. He sold his stock interests to Horace Plunkett in 1883.[17]

During the next couple of years Wells worked for various outfits up and down the No Wood, building corrals, barns, and houses with a partner, Charles Bremmer. He got his own place on Box Elder creek, lived in the area the rest of his life,[18] and in 1911 would be one of the three members of the coroners' jury when Richards's daughter Edna and her husband, Tom Jenkins, were found shot to death at their cabin on Little Canyon Creek.

**See p. 219 for the full published story.

***He must mean Harvey Booth, since Jim was connected with C.T. & Co.[19]

BIG HORN CATTLE COMPANY.
A. J. WINN. Manager.

P. O. address, Powder River, Wyo.

Foreman, D. H. Reynolds.

Range, No Wood and its tributaries, Johnson county, Wyo.

Also own the following brands:

part of animal, with  and ⤫ on left jaw.

Range, Brigder Creek, Badwater and Poison Creek, Wyo.

Foreman, T. J. Turner.

Brand, same as cut. Also, own other brands **HA** left side. **△** left thigh, **JJ** left side.

Horses branded **L** on right shoulder and **U** on left, and **D** on left.

*The Big Horn Cattle Co., which began operations
in the Nowood country in 1883, was one of the many British
companies that invested in the western cattle industry
and failed after the winter of 1886–87.*[20]

Brand Book, 1884

The Bar X Bar's well-appointed ranch house

Photo by Geoffroy Millais[21]

from the bear's carcass, shot him flying with a rifle. Henry tryid [*sic*] out the Bear's oil & got 50 pounds.

Monday, Oct. 27.

Rode the "Dude" down No Wood to Cañon Creek & across to Crooked Creek to Chas [blank space] with Jim looking for a corner.* Found none. Came back by road past the Bar X Home Ranch & the Flag Ranch [Harvey Booth's place]. Smith came in from Buffalo & brought me a letter from Alice dated Oct. 12 & one from Aut. Pucket's partner caught a beaver. He mudded the roof of the new house.

Tuesday Oct. 28, 1884

In forenoon worked & took a bath. In P.M. rode to Flag Ranch, when it began snowing & I came back. Snowed all P.M. & cleared up after dark. Jno. Booth passed from Lander but brought no mail.

Wednesday Oct. 29

Clear & cold. We expected to go out on the calf round up today but the horses were strayed. In P.M. Jim & I rode after them. Was gone six hours & I rode Dobbin—the roughest horse I ever rode.

Thursday, Oct. 30

Packed up and started for the round up. Rode Silver Tail. Jim & I surveyed the Flag Ranche claim. It is a good one & lies well & I will file on it if C.T. & Co. do not. Had dinner on Little Cañon Creek and in P.M. ran two miles of line from the S. W. cor Sec 9 T44 R. 87** shown us by Chas Bremmer. Camped at Bremmer's on Crooked Ck. Weather clear.

Friday, Oct. 31

Cloudy & threatening in A.M. Jim & I finished the survey of the claim on the No Wood at the Big Trails reaching to mouth of Little Cañon Ck. & rode to Spring Ck by 1 P.M. Jim & the boys went on circle. Saw 3 Indians. Cleared up in P.M.

Saturday, Nov. 1, 1884

The 2 bar outfit started back to the round up. I started down the No Wood trail with Grey Eagle & Indian. Mr. Waln*** helped me pack &

---

*For the claims of the Colorado investors, Richards needed to find township or section corners marked by previous surveyors.

**Means Southwest corner of Section 9 in Township 44 North, Range 87 West.

***He may be referring to Robert A. Waln, who seems to have been the senior member of the Waln clan on Spring Creek. He came to Wyoming in 1878 as a freighter and then to the basin in 1884. On a ditch claim he is named along with an Asbury (or Ashbury or Ashbery) F., Lorenzo D., and Lincoln Waln, known as "Link." "Dow" Waln may be Lorenzo.[22]

he & Ferguson rode down with me & I camped at their camp in Ten Sleep at Dave Reynolds* $\overline{\text{X}}$ ranch with Marshal Clark. In P.M. hunted white tail deer with Link Waln. Killed nothing. Spent evening at $\overline{\text{X}}$ ranch with Marshal Clark. Weather fine.

Sunday, Nov. 2

Packed up and started at [illegible] Reached J. H. Booth's horse ranch on Paint Rock cr at dark. Was well entertained & given much valuable information by Booth. Weather fine.

Monday, Nov. 3

Left Booth's at 10 A.M. Stopped on Paint Rock at a deserted cabin. Reached the Big Horn 2 [mi above mouth?] of No Wood after dark. Expected to find no cabin but saw a camp fire. Thought it might be Indians but [illegible] found two white men [illegible] from Ohio. Geo. Able & [blank space] Wendt.** They gave me a good supper [illegible] making my bed in a wagon. Weather fine.

Tuesday, Nov. 4

Presidential election day and I [many lines illegible] ...forded the Big Horn...on Indian & hunted but killed nothing.

Nov. 5

[Most of page illegible] Mercury 9° at 7 A.M. ... Every body in the [illegible] are anxious for their papers to learn the result of the election but I haven't seen a paper in 30 days & don't know when we will know the result of the election. Crossed Big Horn & spent the day looking over the country west of River. Killed a nice young buck antelope & brot to camp on pack horse which I had with me— A horse raiser by name McMillan who lives on Paint Rock near Jno Booth's & has a squaw camped with us on his way to Billings on N.P.R.R. for winter supply of grub.

Thursday, Nov. 6, '84

Hazy. Piloted McMillan across Big Horn. Packed up & started up the river with Abel & Weintz. Crossing here. Drove about 8 m's & camped on River. Killed an Antelope just as we camped.

---

*Dave Reynolds was foreman of the Bar X Bar until sometime in the fall of 1884.[23]

**John Weintz. Born in Ohio to German parents in March 1863, Weintz came to the Nowood country in 1884. By 1903 he lived near Bonanza on a farm with 240 acres and 200 head of cattle. In 1888 his friend George Abel sold out to Weintz and said he was going to Alaska, according to a letter of Richards's.[24]

Friday, Nov. 7, '84

Was on road at 8 A.M. Very cold but clear. Drove 10 m's. & camped for noon on river. Camped for night on River. Late camp.

Saturday, Nov. 8

Moved at 8 A.M. Hazy. Passed Cottonwood & Luman's* at 10 A.M. Saw calf round up boys at 11 & camped for noon on Big Horn 8 m's from Kirby Creek. In P.M. drove to Kirby Creek & crossed Big Horn just above mouth of creek & camped at Kirby cabin.

Sunday, Nov. 9

Left Kirby cabin at 9 a.m. & drove about 9 m's up Kirby Creek & camped at 1 P.M. A dry country & not what we are looking for. In P.M. Abel & I walked up stream 5 m's & back. A Mr. McCulloch** a cattle man from Owl Creek, camped with us. Going up Kirby Creek.

Monday, Nov. 10

McCulloch went up & we came down stream to Kirby cabin when we camped for noon. In P.M. Abel & I surveyed around Kirby cabin—camped at water's edge. A large flock of sage hens came to river to drink at dusk. Killed one.

Tuesday, Nov. 11

In A.M. Abel & I surveyed below mouth of Owl Ck on W. side Big Horn. Dinner on Owl Creek. Clear & warm. In P.M. we all went across hills toward a Butte where there are some extinct geysers. Went as far as Stagner's*** who lives 3 m's S. of mouth of Owl Crk on Reservation, when we found the distance too great to go afoot and returned to camp. Killed two rabbits with pistol.

Wednesday Nov. 12

Started on trail homeward. Bkft. before daylight. Abel & I surveyed some & camped for night on B Horn opp. mouth of No Water. A beautiful

---

*John Luman of Lander trailed cattle into the Bighorn Basin in 1881, and owned around 7,000 head. He lived at Paint Rock with his half-Oglala Sioux wife.[25] Brand books of 1883 and later show a Tinnin & Luman ad with a Lander post office, but it is uncertain that the Luman is John Luman.

**J. D. McCulloch of Owl Creek had an ad in the 1885 Brand Book. Nothing else about him could be found.

***Speed ("Pete") Richmond Stagner established a cattle ranch in 1878 and lived on the Shoshone reservation with his half-Shoshone wife and their large family. In 1894 he was elected into the Eastern Band of Shoshone.[26]

day without a cloud. Drove within 2 m's of as far as we made in day & a half going up.

Thursday, Nov. 13

Abel & I found a corner on W. side Big Horn & ran line across river & ran 4 m's line on E side before dinner. I ran 2 m's in P.M. alone. Crossed team to E. side & camped 1 m. below mouth of Dry Cottonwood.

[Locates site for the Big Horn Ditch project.]

Friday, Nov. 14, '84

Bkft at daylight. Abel & I chained 14 m's in Tp 47 & 48 Rs 92 & 93. Camped at night on Big Horn about 4 m's above the [boys camp?]. The land we passed over today suits me for the location of <u>our</u> scheme. [emphasis added]

Saturday, Nov. 15

Abel's horse went up the river and we didn't move camp until noon. I finished my examination of land in A.M. Reached our old camp in P.M. About time as our grub was exhausted.

Sunday, Nov. 16

Cloudy & threatening a storm. Started homeward at 8 A.M. Reached Jno. Guerrero's two cabins on Paint Rock at one P.M. & stopped to make dinner. Heard that Cleveland was elected. Began snowing in evening.

Monday, Nov. 17

Snowing. After breakfast packed up & moved up to Jno. Booth's for dinner. In P.M. found a Tp [township] corner & got ready for work tomorrow. Stayed at Booth's all night.

Tuesday, Nov. 18

Clear & cold. Worked on survey for Guerrero in P.M. And stayed all night at his cabin without my bedding. Weather good but cold. Chained 6-1/4 m's.

Wednesday, Nov. 19

Slept tolerably well last night in front of a fire place with my overcoat on and my saddle blankets for a bed. Mem— ask Crocker about Booth's claim. Jno. H. Booth, Lander, Wyo. Finished survey & rode to W.P. where stayed all night.

Thursday, Nov. 20

In A.M. surveyed for W.P. In P.M. rode to Otter Creek, arriving after dark. Saw Burke* and agreed to make survey for him.

Friday, Nov. 21

Surveyed on Otter Creek for Pearce.** In evening rode a "W.P." horse to Spring Creek where I stopped all night. A cold cloudy day.

Saturday, Nov. 22, 1884

Slept at Dow Waln's last. Saw Charlie Gunn there. Was up before daylight intending to go to Bar X but as it was snowing I rode to the camp on Otter Creek 5 m's for breakfast then packed up and came to Two Bar Ranche. Snowed nearly all the way & is cloudy at night. Found no mail.

Sunday, Nov. 23, 1884

Coldest morning yet. Slept well in the new house. Started at 10.30 A.M. for Ten Sleep riding Bute, a pinto. Met Burke near — X home ranch and stopped there for dinner. As Burke was going out to Lander, that loses his survey for me. In P.M. rode to Spring Creek to survey for Dow Waln and found that he had gone to Ten Sleep. Stayed all night with Charley Gunn.

Monday, Nov. 24

On road early. Not very cold. Reached Ten Sleep 10 a.m. and found Waln had returned to Spg. Ck by another route and I had missed him. Mem. Camps on the Rockies, Wm. A. Baillie – Grohman – Chas. Scribner's Sons. In P.M. rode to Spg Ck. & found Waln had not arrived. Gone somewhere else. Stayed all night with Gunn.

Tuesday, Nov. 25

Clear once more & not cold. Left Spg. Ck. 8 A.M. Stopped 2 hrs on Otter Ck. looking at the land. Met Peirce there & he rode back to $\overline{\text{X}}$ home ranch & gave me check $50.00. Rode on to 2 bar ranch arriving at dark. Spent evening at old [Dan's?] & played Casino. Traded fish pole for pocket compass. Have finished my business here & tomorrow start homeward going to Shield ranch. B.Q. & Co.

Wednesday, Nov. 26

In A.M. packed up to start home. In P.M. rode to B.Q. & Co.'s ranch on head of No Wood & stayed all night. Threatening to snow.

---

*Milo Burke succeeded Dave Reynolds as foreman of the Bar X Bar. He was a member of M. Burke & Sons, an Omaha livestock commission firm.[27] He would establish his own ranch homestead in Ten Sleep and become one of its leading citizens.

**John Peirce was foreman of Plunkett's WP herd.[28]

Thursday, Nov. 27

Clear. Walked down stream 3 m's & made a survey for B.Q. & Co. Dinner at the old Crawford cabin. Supper at B.Q. & Co. Thanksgiving, & the cook made us a good dinner. Stone came in at dark. Earned $25.00

Friday, Nov. 28, 1884

Jim & I rode to Bates Spring in the forenoon. In P.M. chained from Cornell's claim up past the Crawford cabin. Cloudy & threatening snow. Very tired. Stay with Cornell tonight. Harvey [blank space] and Ben Shannon here returning from Rock Creek.

Saturday, Nov. 29

Jim & I looked for Twp corner. Dinner at B.Q. & Co. Clear & cold. Rode to D Ranch* in P.M. 18 mi. Stayed all night

Sunday, Nov. 30, 1884

Rode from D Ranch to Wind River—32 m's. Lunched on Bad Water 18 m's from D. Camped with sheep herders. Noble's men. 7000 sheep. Fair and pleasant.

Dec. 1st, 1884

Slept warm and well last night out of doors. Left with sheep men. On road at 8 a.m. Reached Lander at 4.30, a ride of 43 m's without dinner or unsaddling. Am tired tonight. Will stay here tomorrow. Letter from Crocker dated Oct. 19.

Dec 2. Tuesday

In A.M. packed up blankets & wrote some postal cards. In P.M. Jim got drunk and raised a row & tried to run a horse race. Put him to bed in a stall in the stable. Weather beautiful. Attended I.O.O.F Lodge in Evening. Saw 3 degrees conferred. Fremont Lodge #11 [International Order of Odd Fellows]

Dec. 3 Wednesday

Slept in dining room last night as Jim was so drunk I wouldn't sleep with him. Up at 6 a.m. Took stage for Rawlins. Dinner at Beaver Crossing, 30 m's. Supper at Ronges** 30 m's from Beaver. Team stalled on Beaver Hill. Reached 10 P.M. Left at 2 a.m. in snow storm. Stage Route Lander – Little Popo Agie – Beaver – Sweetwater Bridge – Rongis – Crooks Creek – Lost Soldier – Bull Springs – Bell Springs – Rawlins

---

*Part of the Big Horn Cattle Co. See p. 180.

**Rongis was a ranch, stagecoach station, and post office. It became a post office in 1883, with John J. Signor as postmaster.[29]

Beaver Hill about 1901
Riverton (Wyoming) Museum

Thursday, Dec. 4

Left Rongis or Signor's at 2 a.m. Snowing. Breakfast at Lost Soldier Ck. 30 m's and drove on from there to Rawlins. 45 m's which we reached at 4 P.M. 75 m's in 14 hrs. using 5 - 4 horse teams. Waited till 6 P.M. for supper. Rec'd 3 letters from Alice. Very wintry & colder than any place I have been in two mo's.

Friday, Dec. 5, 1884

Left Rawlins at 1 A.M. Bft. at Laramie. Reached Cheyenne at 10.30 A.M. Saw Hay at Stock Growers Bank. Met Nellie Wakeley [a friend from Nebraska] Bot suit of clothes. Saw Hobart in P.M. Harvey Booth came in from East. Spent evening with him.

Saturday, Dec. 6, 1884

In A.M. fixed up Booth in Land Office & took 10:30 train. Reached 2.30 [station name left blank] Left for C. Spgs 3:40. Reached home 7:30 P.M. Snowing. So endeth this chapter.

Diary, Return to the Basin, 1885

[Two members of the Big Horn Ditch crew would settle near Richards; Coleman would become a state senator and Gebhart a newspaperman.*]

Wednesday, May 6, 1885.

Left Colo. Springs at 8.30 A.M. with 2 wagons, 1 buck board, 8 horses, 3 men & camping outfit, for Big Horn. Men's names Chas. E. Black, Gus. Coleman, Will [blank space]. Drove to Pring's Ranch 15 miles. Fairley** horse balked. Camped in rain. Slept in Pring's barn.

Thursday, May 7.

Horses nearly all balky. Traded a bay mare to Pring for an old sorrel horse and $10. Drove to monument 5 m's in hard snow storm. Put horses in stable. Had dinner at hotel. Pitched the tent and went to bed after a good supper of our own.

Friday, May 8.

Still snowing. Drove to Sedalia 27 m's. Camped. Horses in stable.

Saturday, May 9.

Drove to Denver 25 m's. Worked Fairley horse by pulling him around by the neck. Put horses in stable. Slept with Jules Hammond.

Sunday, May 10.

Laid over in Denver. Raining all day. Tom Gebhardt [*sic*]. joined the party. Slept with Jules.

Monday, May 11.

Boys pulled out for Rawlins at 7 A.M. I took train for Evanston at 1.25. Supper in Cheyenne. Took a sleeper.

Tuesday, May 12.

Reached Evanston at 2.30 P.M. Dinner at Depot Hotel. Crocker met me & we drove down to Ranch 25 m's

Wednesday, M. 13.

Surveying all day. Rainy.

---

*Augustus C. "Gus" Coleman was a teacher and surveyor who had come to Colorado Springs from New York for his health. Owen Thomas "Tom" Gebhart was a friend of Charles Black, a fellow printer. Gebhart, Coleman, and possibly Black would return to toil on the ditch for several seasons. Richards would turn over the supervision of its construction to Gebhart, and the work was completed in 1889. Gebhart would found the *Paint Rock Record* in 1893, and edit or manage other basin papers for years to come.[30] The fourth man was Will Gamble, about whom nothing could be found.[31]

**David B. Fairley was a member of the Big Horn Ditch Company.[32]

Thursday, May 14.
Surveying all day.

Friday, May 15. ditto
Saturday, May 16. ditto

Sunday, May 17.
Surveyed around Booth's place & drove to E-n [Evanston]. by 2 P.M. Dinner at Crockers. Snowing.

Monday, May 18.
Snowing, hailing, thunder, lightning. Two men injured by lightning.

Tuesday, May 19, 1885.
Writing letters in A.M. Wrote to Father, Mother & Lon, Draper*— Barlow, A. C. Wakeley. Crocker & Ed. Rivenberg returned from Salt Lake. Euchre [a popular card game] in evening. Mrs. C. & I against Booth & Miss Anderson the school ma'am.

Wednesday, May 20.
Crocker & Booth went to Ranch. Booth gave me box & cigars & one for Jim, also knife for him. Booth told me I could have two cows to milk and also a work team if I wanted it. Told me to survey & plow out a ditch for the Flag ranch and to tell Jim that if he had enough fat cattle for an early drive to let him know & make it. Left Evanston at 1.30 P.M. for Rawlins. Waited 50 minutes at Granger for the Oregon Short Line. Reached Rawlins at 1 A.M.

Thursday May 21st.
Spent the day in writing letters & loafing. Bo't hat. Teams did not arrive nor have the plow & scrapers.

Friday, May 22nd. 1885.
Teams got in at 4 P.M. Camped at Govt. corral. Everything O.K.

Saturday, May 23.
Spent day loading up. Supper at Hotel.

Sunday May 24.
Left town at 7.30 A.M. Drove about 15 m's to a creek and had dinner. Drove 2 m's more & camped.

Monday May 25.
Passed Separation creek in 5 m's. Alkali lake at [8 with 9 written over

---

*Edwin F. and Arthur G. Draper were members of the Big Horn Ditch Co.; Arthur was on the Board of Directors.[33]

it, or vice versa] m's and took dinner at Sand Spring 16 m's. In P.M. drove 8 m's to Camp Creek. Killed antelope.

Tuesday, M. 26.

Dinner on Muddy 10 ms. over the mts. In P.M. drove about 12 ms to Sweetwater, just below Cottonwood.

Wednesday, May 27.

Drove up Sweetwater past the 71 Ranche & 10 ms above to Signor's or Rongis. Learned that we did not save any distance by going through Whiskey Gap. Wrote to Alice.

Thursday, May 28th.

Drove North from Signors to the road from 71 to D. Ranche. About 12 ms without a road. Then 3 m's on road. Camped on some water holes.

Friday, May 29.

Laid in camp all day as 2 horses had very sore shoulders. Killed an antelope in evening. Doe with two young.

Saturday, May 30.

Worked the grey mare & Crazy on lead & put Frank & Dick on buckboard. Drove 9 m's & camped for dinner at cabin on Muskrat. In P.M. drove 6 ms. & camped on Muskrat.

Sunday, May 31.

Drove to Poison Creek about 18 miles. Killed a big buck antelope. Every body has diarrhea from drinking bad water.

Monday, June 1st.

Horses strayed & did not get them till late. Found 2 two bar horses with them. Dinner on Badwater 10 ms. Camped at D Ranch on Bridger Creek 15 miles from Badwater. Cracked tongue on Buckboard.

Tuesday, June 2nd, 1885.

Crossed over Rattlesnake Range to head of Kirby Creek and drove down [ditto marks under Kirby Creek] about 12 ms. Very rough road. Joe Jones, a young chap who is the discoverer of the Lost Cabin Mine,* took supper with us & said round up was 5 m's down stream.

Wednesday, June 3.

Up at 3.30 A.M. Rode down to catch Round up & found them gone.

---

*Numerous Lost Cabin mines were "discovered" and lost again. One was just south of the Bighorn Basin. A Joseph Jones is not connected with any known story available today.

Crossed Kirby Creek & followed trail of Round up to the Muddy. A very hard day. Susan gave out & we left one wagon on the mountain. Saw Jim Stone & Henry.

Thursday, June 4th.

Round up left. Skinned 3 bears that a herder killed yesterday. Lay in camp all day on the Muddy looking up a road to the mouth of No Water. Bad water and diarrhea again.

Friday, June 5th.

Rode down near mouth of Muddy. Rode back & moved camp down.

Saturday, June 6, 1885.

Moved down to fork of No Water. 5 miles from Big Horn. Dry camp.

Sunday, June 7, 1885.

Reached our destination "the Big Horn["] at the mouth of No Water at 10 A.M. Am glad to get here. It is a month yesterday since we left home & two weeks today since we left Rawlins. Our great difficulty lay in getting from Kirby Creek across here 25 mi's & it took 4 days through very rough mountains with no water. The season is a dry one & water is unusually scarce. The Big Horn is very high. We have a pleasant camp, have unloaded our wagons & find nothing broken. It has been a hard disagreeable trip but a firm purpose & a good deal of energy brought us through.

Monday, June 8.

Surveyed all day. Found all the corners. Dick, the horse, got stuck in quick sand. Rained near night. Fish for supper.

Tuesday, June 9, 1885.

Cloudy & rainy. Worked with the level on preliminary survey of ditch, looking for location for head. Rode out in P.M. on grey mare.

Wednesday, June 10.

Levelling to find head of ditch. Ran 1-1/2 miles. Cool & cloudy. River has fallen 2 feet since our arrival Sunday.

Thursday, June 11.

Ran level in A.M. Transit in P.M. Heavy wind toward night.

Friday, June 12.

Ran 2-1/2 m's of ditch. Saw deer near camp.

Saturday, June 13.

Reran the 2-1/2 miles run yesterday, throwing the line further up

2 feet. Killed an antelope [running?] at 5 P.M. & got into a hard rainstorm coming in. A heavy storm of rain, hail, thunder & lightning raged all night.

Sunday, June 14, 1885.

Storming all day. Read "Geoffrey's Wife" by "The Duchess." A very good story.

Monday, June 15.

Rainy. Wrote to Alice & will mail the letter when I can. [Letter begins on p. 211.]

Tuesday, June 16.

Worked with Transit in A.M. Very muddy. Packed up camp but did not move it. In P.M. worked with Level. Clear and warm.

Wednesday, June 17.

Moved camp 4 miles down stream. Very muddy. Ran 1-1/2 miles level line.

Thursday, June 18.

Ran 1-1/2 m's ditch in A.M. Ran section* lines in P.M. Boys caught fine mess of white fish in evening.

Friday, June 19.

Ran Sec[tion] lines in A.M. Level in P.M. Saw 8 horses across river. 1 white, 1 sorrel white face, 1 sorrel, 1 mouse colored [roan?], 1 black mule

Saturday, June 20, 1885.

Ran 1 mi. ditch line in A.M. Dinner on line. Ran 1-1/2 mi's in P.M.

Sunday, June 21.

In camp all day. Had an attack of inflammation of bowels. 3 men from Luman & Lovell's** round up on W. side of Big Horn camped with us. Rained at night.

June 22, Monday.

Rained until 8 A.M. Moved camp. The cowboys killed a yearling and gave us plenty meat. Surveyed in P.M. Rained at night.

---

*A section is a square mile, 640 acres. A township is 6 miles square, or 36 sections.

**Henry Clay Lovell established a home ranch on the No Wood after placing two large herds on the west side of the Bighorn River in 1880–81. His financial backer was a fellow Kansan, Anthony Mason, and Mason-Lovell eventually had the largest herd in the basin by far, at least 20,000 head.[34]

June 23, Tuesday.

Rained nearly all night. The three cowboys left at noon. My bowels are out of order. Ran sec. lines in P.M. Cleared up near night. River rising rapidly.

Wednesday, June 24.

Ran ditch line. Rained in P.M.

Thursday, June 25.

Round up came in. Worked till 1.30 before dinner. Horse racing in P.M.

Friday, June 26.

Worked till noon. Rode up to Round up camp. Mouth of No Water. Saw good horse race. Got cow. Tom Hoskins stayed all night with us.

Saturday, June 27.

Ran level line. Part of Round up went back.

Sunday, June 28.

Ran 2 m's ditch. Dinner on line. About 20 Crow Indians in camp at sundown. Passed on up the river.

Monday, June 29.

Ran level line. Very hot, so hot that couldn't run in P.M. as the level swelled.

Tuesday, June 30.

Ran 3 mi. level line. Two teams passed down the river from Kirby Creek following our trail. One Indian went down coming back from the party that passed us

Wednesday, July 1, 1885.

Moved camp & ran Sec[tion] lines. Rained in evening a little.

Thursday, July 2, 1885.

Left camp at 5 A.M. Dinner at 11 on line. Ran 3 miles. Luman's round up outfit went back up the river going to Kirby. Killed two young antelopes.

Friday, July 3.

Ran 3 mi line. Killed a doe antelope.

Saturday, July 4.

Gus went back after plow & scrapers. Ran ditch line in A.M. Rained & thunder storm. Have another attack of bowel complaint.

Sunday, July 5.

A fair day. In camp. Better but not very well.

Monday, July 6.

Plowed and scraped some. Don't feel well.

Tuesday, July 7.

Started with team (12 horses) for Buffalo. Stayed all night at Jno. Booth's.

Wednesday, July 8.

Drove from Booth's to 10 Sleep & stopped at W.P. Ranche with Dunham. Booth passed going home. Met Abel on road coming in from Buffalo. 3 squaws came to house in P.M. Expected Booth to bring my mail but he didn't.

Thursday, July 9.

Left 10 Sleep at 6.30 A.M. Dinner at a "pole camp" on the mt. – 15 miles – In P.M. drove 4-1/2 hours crossing the North Fork of Powder River. Am now camped in an opening in the pine timber, on top of the Big Horn Mts. Altitude here about 8300. Have a good camp but being all alone it seems a little dull. Lots of mosquitoes.

Friday, July 10.

On the road at 6 A.M. Reached Buffalo 6 P.M. Found lots of letters.

Saturday, July 11.

Busy writing letters, loading up &c.

Sunday, July 12.

Left town at 8 A.M. Saw Keays at ╫ Ranch* Lunch on N. fk Crazy Woman. Supper at 76 Ranch** on Middle frk. Crazy Woman. Saw fellow who had been struck by lightning. Distance from Buffalo 24 m's.

Monday, July 13.

On road at 6.30. Reached K. C. Ranche*** at 4 P.M. distance 28 ms. No Water from S. Fk. Crazy Woman to N. Fk. Powder River 19 m's. Have another attack of diarrhea, but the prescription of the Buffalo Dr. helps me.

---

*Cross H, formerly the brand of Hackney, Williams & Co., was by 1884 owned by the Wyoming Land & Cattle Co.[35] By 1888 a W. P. Keays owned a restaurant in Buffalo and was active in Johnson County Republican politics. He was Johnson County clerk in 1891 and treasurer in 1895.[36]

**Founded in 1879 by Moreton and Richard Frewen, English aristocrats famous for blowing through money. The 76 was the first and one of the largest cattle outfits on Powder River.[37]

***KC Ranch, today's Kaycee. KC was the brand of earliest homesteader, John Nolen.[38] The inclusion of a KC brand in the Peters & Alston ad is interesting.

Tuesday, July 14.

Drove to N. H. Ranche.* 20 long miles. At noon wrote some letters.

Wednesday, July 15.

On road at 6.35. Reached top of Big Horn Mts at 2 P.M. Got stuck once by getting off the road & packed 500 pds. up a long steep hill on my back. Camped at night on Cañon Ck. near Flag Ranch. Came 20 m's & am very tired

Thursday, July 16.

Left wagon in Cañon Creek & rode a horse up to 2 Bar Ranch 5 m's to see Stone. Went fishing with Stone in P.M.

Friday, July 17.

On road at 5.45. Drove to 10 Sleep 30 m's. Supper at W.P. Ranche.

Saturday, July 18.

On road at 7. Reached George Abel's Ranch at 3 P.M. Very hot.

Sunday, July 19.

On road at 6.30. Reached camp at 4 P.M. Camp had been moved 1-1/2 m's up stream.

Monday, July 20.

Cooked & worked 4 teams on line.

Tuesday, July 21.

Took two mares & buck board & drove to Geo. Abel's where stayed all night.

Wednesday, July 22.

Drove up Paint Rock. Dinner at Kansas [Lovell's ranch]: fished in P.M. Supper & lodging at Frank Sykes.**

Thursday, July 23.

Bred Susl to Sykes' stallion. Caught 24 trout. Supper at Abel's.

Friday, July 24.

Returned to camp in time for dinner, bringing in some fine fish.

---

*One of the ranches of Horace C. Plunkett, an Irish aristocrat, and Alexis Roche, younger son of a Lord Femroy.[39] By 1885 N and H were among many shown in the Frontier Land and Cattle Co.'s ad in the brand book.

**Sykes came to the Paint Rock country well before 1881, and had a cabin on Medicine Lodge Creek. He has been described as "irascible."[40]

Saturday, July 25.

Rode out & found a place to move camp to, and was on the ditch till noon. Heavy wind in P.M. Killed 3 sage hens.

Sunday, July 26.

Moved camp. Bathed.

Monday, July 27.

Had Jno. & Dick shod & with them & the little wagon left camp at 10.30 for the 2 Bar Ranch. Reached Geo. Abel's at 6.30

Tuesday, July 28.

Drove to 10 Sleep & stopped at Bar X Bar Ranch.

Wednesday, July 29.

Drove to Otter Creek. Met man named Richards. Saw Dow Waln. Family named Goldsby camped on Otter. Caught 15 trout in P.M.

Thursday, July 30.

Dinner with Frank Bull* at —X home Ranche. Reached "||" [2 bar] Ranche 5 P.M. Geo. Baker there. Jim & the men gone with cattle to R. R.

Friday, July 31.

Rested up at the Ranche

Saturday, Aug. 1st. 1885.

Surveying on ditch to be taken from Little Cañon Creek to irrigate the claims of A.C.R. [brother Aut] and Booth

Sunday, Aug 2nd.

Ran some lines to determine the location of the ditch.

Monday, Aug. 3rd.

Surveying Flag Ranch Ditch.

Tuesday, Aug. 4th.

Stayed a 2 bar Ranche all day. Dick lame. Wrote letters & read The Captain's Room.

Wednesday, Aug. 5th.

Finished surveying the ditch.

---

*Bull was the "so-called ranch keeper." He brought his bride, Martha, there in the fall of 1883;[41] she was one of the first white women to live in the Bighorn Basin.[42]

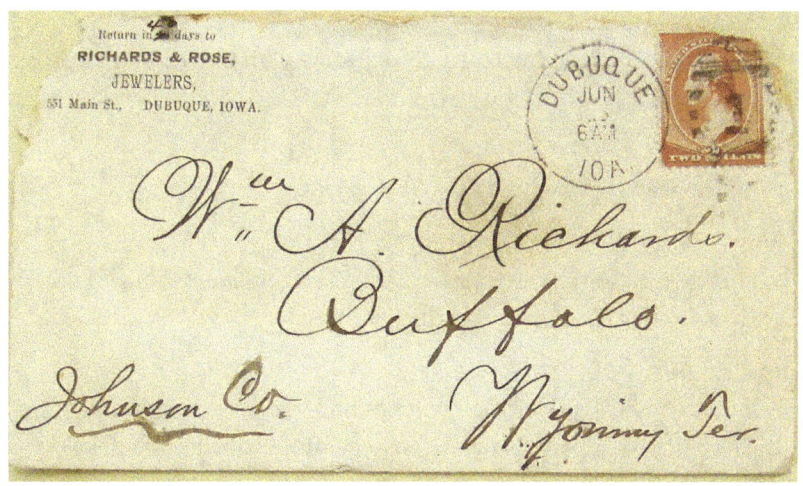

Envelope from Lon. Will usually received mail at the Riverside Post Office, at the Bar C Ranch over the hills east of Red Bank. After August 1886 he began using the more convenient new post office at Lost Cabin, just south of the basin. Delivery difficulties inspired Lon to ask for return after 40 days, not 15.

William A. Richards collection, WSA

Thursday, Aug. 6, 1885.

At 2 Bar Ranche, resting up the horses, writing & mending

Friday, Aug. 7, 1885.

Started for Buffalo. Drove to Spring Creek & stayed all night.

Saturday, Aug. 8.

Drove onto the Mt. & camped. A man named Schofield & two hunters one Geo. [Hobson?] & the other Billy - - travelling with me.

Sunday, Aug. 9.

Heavy frost last night. Dinner at saw mill. Reached Buffalo at 6 P.M. Heard of Gen. Grant's death July 23rd.

Monday, Aug. 10.

Met Sykes. I took him to a Dr. to have his eye treated.* Wrote letters &c.

Tuesday, Aug. 11.

Same as yesterday.

---

*Sykes had injured his eye on a juniper snag.[43]

Wednesday, Aug. 12.

Started back for the Big Horn. Sykes going with me. Dinner at Cross H Ranch Camp on N. Fork Crazy Woman.

Thursday, Aug. 13.

Dinner near 76 Ranche. Camped at Dick Carr's.

Friday, Aug. 14.

Dinner on N. Fork Powder River. Killed an antelope. Camped on Powder River 1 mile above K. C. Ranche

Saturday, Aug. 15.

Dinner at Red Bank crossing. Sykes had a good night's rest last night — the first one. Camped near N. H. Ranche. Rode to Bar C 6 miles for mail.

Sunday, Aug. 16.

Crossed over the mountain and camped at Flag Ranche.

Monday, Aug. 17.

Dinner on Otter Creek. Stopped at the Swede's on Cañon Creek.

Tuesday, Aug. 18.

Dinner on Broken Back [creek]. Reached Sykes' at sundown.

Wednesday, Aug. 19.

Laid over to rest horses. Killed a cow elk before breakfast. In P.M. caught 10 pounds of trout in two hours.

Thursday, Aug. 20.

Left Sykes' after dinner and camped at Geo. Abel's.

Friday, Aug. 21, 1885.

Drove to Big Horn. Supposing the boys had moved camp when they had not. I drove 5 miles past camp and laid out.

Saturday, Aug. 22.

Pulled into camp at 11 A.M. Found every thing all right. Boys had a 1/4 of beef given them by Luman. As I bro't potatoes, turnips, beets & peas we will live high for a few days.

Sunday, Aug. 23.

Laid in camp resting. Took one load 6 miles up River to a fenced pasture & was caught in a heavy rain.

Monday, Aug. 24.

Moved camp to Sec. 13 T. 47 NR 93. Corum's* claim. A fine camp in timber. Plenty of grass & water.

Tuesday, Aug. 25.

Surveying. Found a big error of 23 chs [1,518 ft] in line bet. Secs 7 & 18, T. 47. NR 92W. Rained at night.

Wednesday, Aug. 26, 1885.

Surveying & brought plow & scrapers up from below 5 mile dry ditch. Dinner at 4 P.M. Rained hard.

Thursday, Aug. 27.

Tom, Will, & I surveying. Gus & Charlie cutting hay. Killed an antelope #9. River rising & very muddy.

Friday Aug. 28.

Working on ditch above the side hill. Killed 3 antelope making 12.

Saturday, Aug. 29.

Worked on ditch. Smith the Montana man here.

Sunday, Aug. 30.

Smith went to Kirby Creek. No work today.

Monday, Aug. 31.

Charlie went after the scraper down the river. Working on ditch.

Sept. 1. Tuesday.

4 teams on ditch. I cooked and worked on map of ditch line.

Wednesday, Sept. 2nd.

Boys all on ditch. Stranger here for breakfast. 3 horses one brown 1 bay both branded one bar on left shoulder—and one dark colored pony— branded [V, like a square-root symbol] on left hip.

Thursday, Sept. 3, 1885.

Finished map & wrote some letters as follows. To B. H. D. [Big Horn Ditch] Co., Alice, Father, Lon & Aut.

Friday, Sept. 4.

Charlie for the settlements for potatoes & plow points, with a saddle horse & pack horse. Worked on ditch.

---

*John J. Corum was a member of Big Horn Ditch Co. and on its board of directors.[44]

Saturday, Sept. 5.

Worked on ditch. Cowboy named Avant* stayed all night.

Sunday, Sept. 6.

No work. Resting. Large band of Indians went down.

Monday, Sept. 7.

Avant crossed & went up River. Saw & fired at a supposed Mt. Sheep across River. Killed a buck Antelope going out to work. No. 13.

Tuesday, Sept. 8.

Working on ditch.

Wednesday, Sept. 9.

Working on ditch. Charlie returned bringing mail but nothing else as his pack horse bucked and broke the saddle.

Thursday, Sept. 10.

Working on ditch. Tom went after old plow points. Terrific wind in afternoon.

Friday, Sept. 11, 1885.

Boys on ditch. Killed a buck antelope on line No. 14. Selected a place to move camp to. Rained a little at sundown.

Saturday, Sept. 12.

Boys on ditch. Worked in camp. Beef Round up on W. side Big Horn.

Sunday, Sept. 13.

No work. Fire at corral on W. side. Gus killed 2 antelope making 4. Bill killed 3 sage hens & 3 rabbits.

Monday, Sept. 14.

Moved camp about a mile up stream to the vicinity of our 2nd camp.

Tuesday, Sept. 15.

In camp. Mending wagon tongue.

---

*Cicero (Roe) Avent lived in the Bighorn Basin for most of his long life. In 1885 he was foreman of George W. Baxter's LU ranch on Grass Creek, on the west side of the basin. He left the LU for Otto Franc's Pitchfork ranch in 1888, and in 1893 he was foreman of the Bay State Cattle Co.'s home ranch at Ten Sleep. He got his own place somewhere in the Greybull valley in 1889 and settled there in 1896. Avent served as deputy sheriff of Fremont County in 1889–90, and was a Big Horn County commissioner from 1915–17. Census records place him in Cody City in 1940, aged 80. He is said to have died on May 3, 1942, in Billings, Montana, and is buried in Laramie, Wyoming.[45]

Wednesday, Sept. 16.

In camp. Jackson* with band of horses came to dinner & stayed all night.

Thursday, Sept. 17, 1885.

Started for Paint Rock with buckboard at 8 A.M. Stayed all night at Abel's.

Friday, Sept. 18.

Ed Korman [or Karman] & I drove up to Sykes. Caught 12 pounds of fish. Dinner with Sykes. Supper at [Lucie?] Williams. Got 250 pounds potatoes of Sykes. Reached Abel's at 11 P.M.

Saturday, Sept. 19.

Wrote letters until 11 A.M. Then Geo, Ed & I went hunting on No Wood. Geo killed a deer, I a wolfe. Saw a band of Elk & one lone bull.

Sunday, Sept. 20.

Drove to our camp on Big Horn.

Monday, Sept. 21.

On line with the men. Killed 3 antelope making 17

Tuesday, Sept. 22.

In camp cleaning up.

Wednesday, Sept. 23.

Plowed one furrow on ditch line between the pts. where Ditch is made from [#?] 650 to 985.

[Then follows a log of dates, locations, weather, and barometer readings, not transcribed.]

Thursday, Sept. 24, 1885

Moved camp to mouth of No Water. Very windy. Killed five doe antelope last night. #18

Friday, Sept. 25.

Very windy. Working in camp. Rained a little at night.

Saturday, Sept. 26.

No wind. Very smoky. Put horses in pasture over Sunday.

Sunday, Sept. 27.

Gus & I rode ten miles up Dry Cottonwood. Saw only antelope.

---

*This may have been Teton Jackson, the famous outlaw and horse thief.[46]

Monday, Sept. 28.
   Horses stampeded last night. Spratt stopped with us.

Tuesday, Sept. 29.
   Spratt moved on

Wednesday, Sept. 30.
   Surveying upper end ditch

Thursday, Oct. 1.
   Same as yesterday.

Friday, Oct. 2nd.
   Spratt passed going back & left me McGrath's horse.

Saturday, Oct. 3 '85.
   Finished work on ditch

Sunday, Oct. 4.
   Surveying for head gate

Monday, Oct. 5.
   With Tom, Charley & Gus & a four horse team drove up to mouth of Kirby Creek. Arriving after dark.

Monday, Oct. 6.
   Froze water in a bucket last night. Crossed Big Horn & camped near party of 6 from Denver. Gus killed antelope — 5 for him

Wednesday, Oct. 7.
   Located 1-1/2 miles ditch. Moon & [man?] wife & two children camped here.

Thursday, Oct. 8.
   Working on ditch. Very windy.

Friday, Oct. 9.
   Randolph & family & 4 Denver men went down river. Working on ditch.

Saturday, Oct. 10.
   Plowed the line of Big Horn Ditch and located head of Kirby Creek.*

Sunday, Oct. 11, 1885.
   Ran Transit line over upper end B.H.D. & started down River at

---

*The Big Horn Ditch was well north of Kirby Creek. This survey may actually have been for his brother Lon's dream of a colony on Kirby Creek.

10.30 A.M. Drove 14 miles & camped just above mouth of Gooseberry.

Monday, Oct. 12.

Reached camp at the pasture just above mouth of Dry Cottonwood at 3 P.M. Wounded two black tail bucks & trailed one up and found him.

Tuesday, Oct. 13.

Moved camp down stream 12 miles. Killed 3 doe antelope making 22. Surveyed some in P.M.

Wednesday, Oct. 14.

3 saddle horses went back to pasture. Will went after antelope. Wolves had eaten two. Finished surveying & closed up work.

Thursday, Oct. 15.

Moved up to Abel's on Paint Rock. Killed 2 antelope making 24. Gus killed one making 6.

Friday, Oct. 16.

Moved up to Forks of Paint Rock. 6 miles. Visited Sykes—where I got more mail.

Saturday, Oct. 17.

Drove to 10 Sleep. 20 miles

Sunday, Oct. 18, 1885.

Nooned at Spring Creek. Camped on Otter Creek. Surveyed for C. C. Goldsby on latter place. Chg. $5.00

Monday, Oct. 19.

Reached the Flag Ranch at 1 P.M. Spent P.M. in packing up the boys. Settled up in evening, agreeing to have their checks sent to them at Fort Collins.

Tuesday, Oct. 20.

Charlie, Tom & Will with one team & wagon started for Colo. Spgs. accompanied by David Loban, an invalid. Gus went up to Ritchie's where I have mail. Am making up statement for Company & writing letters. Have a peculiar pain over my heart. Sometimes think I may have a serious attack of heart disease. [He would die of a heart attack years later.]

Wednesday, Oct. 21.

Rode to Riverside P.O. with Jim Westfall, a —C boy.

Thursday, Oct. 22.

At Riverside P.O. writing letters

Red Bank Ranch in 1907 and 2007

The ranch is nestled near the bluffs that snake around central Wyoming, the "red banks."

A visitor wrote, "The governor's ranch is remarkable for its elevation. It is nearer heaven (in more ways than one) than any ranch in the Big Horn basin." [47]

Photo is a composite of two taken by Richards's daughter Edna about 1907. [48]

Ranch house and bluffs in 2007
Author photo

Friday, Oct. 23.
Rode back to Flag Ranch

Saturday, Oct. 24, 1885.
Drove Susl & Blanco in buckboard to Smith's. Met Tom Gill* and worked on survey of Smith's place. Slept at Ritchie's & nearly froze.

The house and its window frames
Author photo

Sunday, Oct. 25.
Finished survey & drove to Flag Ranch. Got some coffee, sugar of Smith & let him have some powder & Quinine pills. Nearly sick with a cold.

Monday, Oct. 26.
Gus & I making a door & windows

Tuesday, Oct. 27.
Made Gill's plats & wrote him. Rained last night.

Wednesday, Oct. 28.
Sold Frank Bull buckboard & harness. Mexican Joe here. [Guerrero?]

Thursday, Oct. 29.
Ran 2-1/2 miles line last night. Bot saddle of Bull.

Friday, Oct. 30.
On Mt. surveying saw Hanks [or Hauks]. Caught in storm & got wet.

Saturday, Oct. 31.
On Mt. surveying & hunting. Got nothing.

Sunday, Nov. 1.
Rode up to Smiths & back.

Monday, Nov. 2, 1885.
Luman's outfit passed. Jim Stone here in P.M.

Tuesday, Nov. 3.
Wrote Alice & went up to 2 Bar Ranch. Round up camped on Box Elder. Quite a hard storm of rain, hail, & snow last night. Some thunder.

*Tom Gill had a ranch at Mahogany Butte.[49]

Wednesday, Nov. 4.

Gus went to Spring Creek for oats. Smith boys camped here en route to Buffalo.

Thursday, Nov. 5.

Snowy. Arapahoe Indians passed. Mollie with them.*

Gus got back with 590 lbs. [oats?] @ 3c	[$]17.70
Owed Waln before	5.00
	22.70
Paid Waln by Gus	10.00
Owe Waln Co.	12.70

Friday, Nov. 6.

About 4 inches snow this morning. Gus & I went hunting. Saw no tracks even.

Saturday, Nov. 7.

Round up passed. Albert also[.?] Surveying on Mt.

Sunday, Nov. 8, 1885.

Rode up to 2 Bar to dinner. Got some beef, sugar & dried fruit. The [Captains?] from T. D. Ranche stopped at night returning from Riverside & brot. me mail. Gus sick.

Monday, Nov. 9.

Fair, clear morning. Wrote letters & took them to —X ranch.

Tuesday, Nov. 10.

Moved up on Mountain. [Tuck?] from 2 Bar Ranch camping with us.

Wednesday, Nov. 11.

Began snowing last night & continued until 3 P.M. today.

Thursday, Nov. 12.

Started for top of Mt. but found snow too deep. Followed some deer in P.M.

Friday, Nov. 13.

Moved down to Flag Ranche

Saturday, Nov. 14.

Rode down to 2 Bar Ranche. Fair Day. — X outfit passed.

---

*Mollie might be the English-speaking woman in a band of "Indians" that came to the cabin when Coleman was away, according to a latter-day account.⁵⁰ The men demanded breakfast and thought Richards was strange for serving the women first.

Sunday, Nov. 15.
At cabin washing, mending &c. [Two?] boys passed. Smith boys too.

Monday, Nov. 16, 1885.
Gus & I went to 2 Bar. Gus to school election at T.D.* Smith boys
stayed with us.

Tuesday, Nov. 17.
Rode Fairley over to Bar C Ranche. Good deal of snow on mountains.

Wednesday, Nov. 18.
Fair. Rode back to Flag Ranche

Thursday, Nov. 19.
Gus went to Spg. Ck. Smith & son here.

Friday, Nov. 20.
Smith here. Gus returned. Also men from Burke's here.

Saturday, Nov. 21.
Raining. In camp all day.

Sunday, Nov. 22.
Smith & Gus started for Buffalo. [Bayne?] passed. Packing up.

Monday, Nov. 23.
Moved down to 2 Bar.

Tuesday, Nov. 24.
Surveyed & got horses

Wednesday, Nov. 25.
Moved up to Shield Ranche.

Thursday, Nov. 26, 1885.
With Briggs rode over to 71 Horse Ranch 38 miles. No dinner today.

Friday, Nov. 27.
With Cornell, Arthur [illegible; & Biggs?] of the Shield & Okey** the

---

*The particulars of this election are unknown. The Smiths, whose place might have
been the T. D. ranch, engaged Gus to teach their children. We are told that he taught
for two years at this school, said to have been the first in the Bighorn Basin. Gus later
taught at Hyattville.[51]

**John B. Okie's place was just outside the south rim of the Bighorn Basin. He had been
in Wyoming only three years, having arrived in Rawlins at age 17. He would get rich
through sheep, the mercantile business, and money-lending. His mansion, aviary-
greenhouse, airstrip, roller rink, parties, wives and children are described on WyoHis-
tory.org. Named Lost Cabin at some point, it became a post office in 1886.[52]

A monument honoring Richards as the first person to divert water from the Bighorn River for irrigation was dedicated in 1969. Sponsored by the South Flat Women's Club and basin historian Paul Frison, the monument stands near the original headgate of Richards's canal.[53]

Author photo, 2006

sheep man & Charley Rinearson moved to old cabin on Muskrat.

Saturday, Nov. 28.
    Moved on to 71 Home Ranch on Sweetwater.

Sunday, Nov. 29.
    Moved up to Rongis

Monday Nov. 30.
    Rode in stage to Rawlins

Tuesday, Dec. 1.
    Left Rawlins at 12.30 A.M. Reached Cheyenne at 10 A.M., Reached Denver at 3 P.M. Stopped at Grand Central.

Dec. 2.
    Reached home at 11:30 A.M. All well.

Dec. 9.
    Went to Franceville

Dec. 10.
    Returned.

Dec. 11.
    Sent off Gus' preemption filing dated Nov. 24. Settlement Nov. 4. Made Tree claim* for E 1/2 NE 1/4 Sec. 10 T. 43 N. R. 87 W

---

*May mean a claim under the Timber Culture Act of 1873, a failed attempt to promote tree planting in the West. Homesteaders could obtain an additional 160 acres if they planted trees on one half of them; Gus's claim was for 80 acres total.

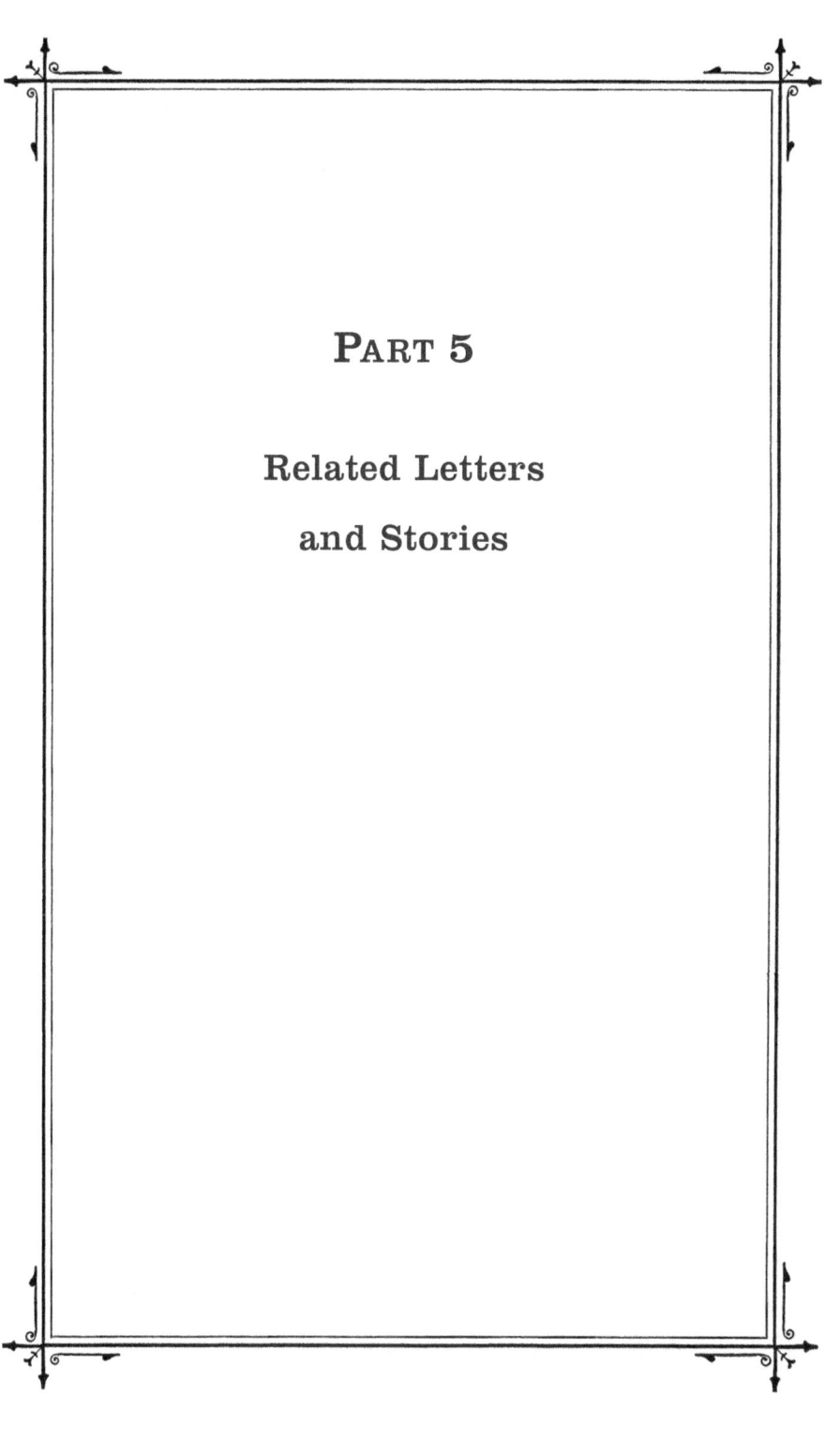

PART 5

Related Letters

and Stories

Richards's Letter to His Wife

Monday, June 15, 1885[1]
In Camp on Big Horn

My Darling Alice,

It will be at least two weeks before I can go out to Buffalo and mail this letter but I am kept in the tent this afternoon by rain and feel like talking to you awhile although it must be through the unfeeling medium of the pencil. Perhaps the most interesting thing I can say will be to give you an account of our trip from the "D" Ranch where I last wrote you. The country from there here is very rough and difficult to traverse with heavy loads and was unknown to me, but I heard that the Round up would be on the No Water near where we wanted to go, so we endeavored to catch them.

June 2nd we left the "D" Ranch and drove 25 miles crossing the Rattlesnake Range of Mts. where in places we had to put six horses on our big wagon. [The next day was hard going as well:] About 5 P.M. Susie the pretty mare gave out & we had to leave one wagon. About 3 miles from where we left it we overtook the Round up, in the most [un]imaginable place for a camp of any kind. The Round up consists of representatives from every Company, Ranch, or party owning cattle in this vicinity, or district which includes a tract nearly 80 miles square. It was composed of about 12 separate camps, consisting of wagons & tents, scattered along a small muddy stream of alkali water, with hardly enough level land on its side to camp upon & no trees. There were over 50 men in the outfit and 400 horses. Each outfit kept its horses separate & a man herded them some distance from the camp. They had gathered several hundred head of cattle that they were taking with them, & all night mounted men rode around them & kept them in a body or "bunch." We had to take such a camp as was left and it was the worst we had on the trip. The boys were considerably downhearted and discouraged but I told them not to be alarmed[;] we would go through all right.

I hunted up Crocker's outfit and found that their Foreman, Jim Stone, was Foreman of the Round up, in charge of all that gang of men and horses. They seemed glad to see me, and having been out in camp a month were about out of tobacco, and as I had plenty I repaid them for some of their kindness to me last Fall. They informed me that it was 35 miles to the mouth of No Water, that there was no road leading there, that the Spring had been unusually dry and there was "no water" literally in the bed of the stream & could give me no assistance towards getting there &

that they were not going there, but were going over to the No Wood, so that our following them was in vain, & we were where we didn't want to be and no visible way of getting out. When I told the boys all this they <u>were</u> blue.

Next morning I had breakfast with Stone at 3.30 A.M. & rode out with some of his men who showed me a she bear and two cubs that they had killed the previous day. Gus & I skinned them, but their hides are worthless at this season as the hair all comes off. I will get $5.00 apiece bounty on them by taking the hides to Buffalo.

I sent Charlie & Tom out that afternoon looking up a road to go upon & they found water 4 miles from camp. Next morning we hitched up and started[,] intending to drive ten miles and send the horses back to the nearest water[,] taking enough for ourselves in the little keg & canteens. Just where we wanted to camp we found a tiny little spring which we dug out & from which we watched the horses that night & next morning. The next day was a hard drive, but we again found a standing pool at noon of good rain water & refilled our keg.

That night, Saturday, June 6th, we camped in sight of the Big Horn but [meaning "only"] five miles distant, but our horses were too tired to get there. Next morning at 10 o'clock we reached the end of our long tedious trip, and I never saw a better pleased lot of men. The Big Horn is too high to ford or we could have crossed it at the mouth of Kirby Creek & recrossed here and had a good road all the way. We could make the same trip again in a week's less time, as we now know all the country.

We arrived in good order, nothing broken or lost & the horses about as good as when we started. We had no accidents or unusually hard times but the constant moving & tearing up camp & repitching it & the anxiety about water were all wearing & we were glad when we found a resting place.

We have a beautiful camp under huge old cottonwood trees, in the angle between the No Water and the Big Horn, the former being about 50 feet South and the latter 100 feet west. The ground is covered with a rich growth of grass, which is pleasing to us & acceptable to the horses. There are quite a good many birds here, and several have nests in the trees. They are not the least bit afraid of us, and go on with their business as though we were only cattle or other harmless beasts. A couple of larks are the most familiar, and they perch on the wagon or corner of the tent and sing their short but sweet little song to us all the day long.

Monday morning we began surveying the ditch & worked hard all the week. I think as favorably of the land as I did last Fall & guess it will make splendid farming land. We had no fresh meat last week & the boys all but Will Gamble disliked bacon very much. Saturday afternoon I took my gun out and told Will to come out about 5 o'clock with a team to bring in an antelope. We quit work at 4:30 & the boys went to camp, 3 miles distant, & I went up on a hill looking for antelope. I could see but one, between me & the wagon which was coming toward me. I kept back out of sight and as I expected the old buck took fright at the wagon and came tearing over the hill past me as hard as he could run. My nerves were steady and we wanted meat and although he was going at a fearful rate of speed I fired, and had the satisfaction of seeing him turn a sommersault & land with his heels in the air— shot through the heart. I motioned Will to drive up; we threw him into the buckboard & started for camp.

Had proceeded but a little when a fearful rain and hail storm struck us & we got wet through. We reached camp almost as soon as the boys and they were surprised and overjoyed to see the antelope. The storm continued all night and all yesterday and at intervals today. We kept comfortable, and ate & read & smoked & slept alternately. I read a story called "Geoffrey's Wife" by "The Duchess." The heroine Mona is in many respects like you. Her truthfulness, candor & goodness fit you exactly, and the trials she had with her mother-in-law you can appreciate. Her beauty is of course over-rated and you are as handsome as Mona. To my mind you are the only one I know whom the character fits at all, and I am sure that I have all the love for you and trust in you that Geoff. had for Mona. It is no. 90 of the Lowell's Library and I hope you will get it as it is a good story and nothing sensational or vulgar in it. Some of [Nolly's?] sayings will surely make you laugh—your very heartiest and most musical laugh. It is nearly dark so I will kiss you good bye for today—

July 5th Sunday

I wonder how my girls spent the "Glorious 4th"? I will probably find out when I reach Buffalo. We spent the day tamely enough. The survey of the ditch has been more difficult than I anticipated and we had got so near the end that we could finish in one day, so we determined to work the 4th & finish it. But a heavy rain storm came up about noon and [we] couldn't work in the afternoon, and lay in the tent. It was just as well for me for I had an attack of Diarrhea, such as I had twice last summer & it was best for me to remain quiet. I lay abed all the afternoon and read "The Giant's Robe" by "F. Austey." No. 1845 of the Seaside Library. It is a good story & made the author's reputation & fortune. You can get it and it will be pleasant to know we have both read it, & admired and detested the same characters.

Since I wrote the first part of this letter we have worked steadily and hard. We have all been well, and no accidents have happened. The boys do well, and work well, and I think we will get along pleasantly. I am getting awfully tired of teaching "tenderfeet" how to live in camp, and often wish for some one who had had more experience. The boys are all willing enough & obedient, but I at last begin to feel that I am getting older than "the boys," and find them neglecting many small but important things, through thoughtlessness, which cause us serious trouble. I am getting to think that there are no unimportant things in life. The neglect of a trifle often causes the direst disaster. To be safe we must be careful about every detail. We are constantly employed and time flies rapidly. We are cheerful and apparently contented.

I get through the days all right, but I seldom go to sleep at once after going to bed. My mind leaves this wild & desolate region when I close my eyes and in an instant I see the little sitting room and bedroom, with my dear good wife at the table reading or writing to me–Allie & Laura writing or cutting out pictures, little Ruth watching them intently and sometimes saying a little easy word or two. I see it all very vividly and my heart sinks as I think how long it must before I can take the dear ones to my arms again. After that it takes me a long time to shut out the vision and get to sleep. [Allie and Ruth were their daughters and Laura their hired girl.]

You know I am not morbidly sentimental nor easily made homesick, but I feel as though I ought not to have come here to stay so long. I know the separation is as hard for you as for me, but life is not long enough for us to throw away half a year of each other's society. It will require a very grave necessity to cause me to do so again. I have always tried to put my own pleasure & desires [to] one side, at least partially, when duty seemed to call me. I foresaw the dreariness of this summer, for both you and me, but I could see no other way of earning money for our support. I can not yet content myself to sit down and live from hand to mouth. I can do that and stay with you where you are but the years are passing rapidly, and we must make some provision for our later years, and for our babies. I have no great ambition for myself. A little would satisfy me, but every day shows me more clearly that there is nothing in this world very dear to me but my faithful wife and loving babies. If I can provide for them & make them happy & retain their love and esteem I shall be satisfied, but I don't feel that I can sacrifice any more of their cheering companionship. My one great fear is that something may happen to some of you before I get home.

I know that there is no more likelihood of it now than if I were with you, but when I allow myself to think of what might transpire in a month or a day even it makes me turn faint. It is unnecessary to urge you to be careful of yourself and the children, for I know you are, but you are acting as both Mama & Papa now, & I hope & pray to find you well & happy when I get home.

I will now tell you a little of our life since the first pages were written. We have only two things to be anxious about. One is our horses which have to run loose, and the other is to keep a supply of game on hand. The horses have behaved admirably. We keep one picketed and the rest stay near camp, but if they were to run away or be stolen by the Indians you have had sufficient experience with lost horses to know where we would be. The Indians are all peaceable & we have seen but one band, but they will all steal horses if they think they can get away with them. We don't worry much about them, but the anxiety will be with us until we finish the work.

The meat question is an important one but more easily controlled. So far I have killed all the game, all antelope. We have not been out long at any time. Gus Coleman is the only one who hunts any. The others don't care to after working. Gus is out now, where he saw some elk the other evening. He didn't shoot at them then because he thought they were mules, & didn't discover his mistake until it was too late. Two weeks ago three cowboys passed through here & they were out of provisions. I invited them to stay all night which they did, two nights. Just then we were eating bacon and a cowboy detests bacon, so they caught a yearling calf nice and fat, & killed it, and left nearly all of it with us.

We kept it for a good 8 days when it spoiled & we gave it to the Indians I spoke of seeing. They like spoiled meat. They were a band of about 20 Crow Indians going on a visit to the Shoshones. There were two ugly old squaws and several children—no little babies or papooses though. The youngest was a little girl about 4 years and she was riding a pony all alone. She was dressed in calico & buckskin, had her black hair braided & ornamented with rings & brass fixings tied into it, and had her face painted with a red paint. The boys wore ordinary clothing but were painted & all wore moccasins. One of the men was an Indian Dandy, a regular Dude. He was tricked out with all the beads and finery he possessed, and had on a stove pipe hat with a piece of looking glass fastened on one side. He wore brass bracelets on his wrists & on his arms above his elbows and had rings in his ears and all over his fingers. He was the funniest looking creature I ever saw. Another one could talk English some, and I asked him who the Dude was but I couldn't understand his reply. He made us all laugh & he soon rode away. They wanted us to give them flour and coffee & sugar & matches & were the worst beggars I ever saw. I finally gave them a quarter of the beef that was spoiled & they left. We heard of another band of them about 30 miles from here, & one of the squaws stole a package of arsenic & thought it was baking powder and made biscuits with it, and it nearly killed all of them, but I haven't heard that any have died yet.

The Round Up reached here the 23rd June, and were near here two days. It was quite a treat to us to see a white man. They had horse racing two afternoons & we saw the races. They were very good races too. Jim Stone caught a cow & calf for us & we expected to have trouble in breaking the cow to milk but to our delight, we found she had been milked before & was very gentle. We have a pen built for the calf at every camp, & keep him in it during the day & the cow in it at night. She comes up regularly and we get about three quarts of milk twice a day. It comes very handy in making bread & we have some oatmeal too. We have some Farina & I am going to make a pudding for dinner. We live very plain. Will Gamble is cooking and he isn't a very good cook. After awhile I will [hole in paper] cooking. Bread. coffee, beans, and dried apples or peaches with meat is our regular diet. I have all the milk I want to drink, but am afraid it makes me bilious.

We have had good camps, & have found dozens of birds' nests. If the children were here I could show them a dove on a nest not ten steps from the tent. When I first went out near her, she flew off out of the tree down on the ground, and went fluttering along dragging her wings on the ground like she was wounded & it seemed that I could catch her easily, but every time I put out my hand she fluttered off, and when she had led me quite a distance from her nest, she suddenly became all right, and flew away out of sight. Wasn't that a cute trick for a bird to do, Allie! I have seen lots of them do it. I found her nest and now I can go quite near it and she won't fly at all. There were lots of young antelope now too, but we can't catch any of them. Today is Sunday, and Tuesday I expect to start for Buffalo and if the P.M. there has sent my mail to Booth's as I wrote him I will hear from my little family Tuesday night. I can hardly wait till then. [Then a discussion of family matters after he received mail at Buffalo.]

Do you like long letters? You have all my love & I send you lots of kisses.   Your loving husband, Will

A Close Call as Wyoming Surveyor General

On an inspection tour of surveys in July 1891, a flash flood burst upon Surveyor General Richards and his party near Fort Washakie, on the Shoshone Reservation. Five years later, when he was governor, Richards described the close call to Col. John W. Clark of the Shoshone Agency.[2]

> I am in receipt of your letter of a recent date relating to the finding of a surveyor's chain by an Indian near the scene of my experience with a cloud burst, some years since. As a souvenir of a very interesting occasion, not devoid of hardship and danger, I would like to again possess this chain. It is the only thing that has been found of more than two hundred dollars worth of property carried away by the water rushing down a gulch thirty feet wide that was dry fifteen minutes before the accident and contained not a drop of water fifteen minutes after it occurred. During the half hour, however, while the torrent raged, one horse was drowned, another saved by being roped from the bank and its head thus held above water, a buck board demolished and its contents carried away while the driver barely escaped with his life. I will be greatly obliged if you will leave it for me with the Express Agent at the depot in Cheyenne and will repay whatever expense attended its recovery.

Richards must have been reminded of what this "interesting occasion" cost him. Right after the cloudburst he had reimbursed others for their losses. The proprietor of the Lander Hotel, H. G. Nickerson, received $225 for his horse, wagon, and harness, and the two surveyors in Richards's crew received smaller amounts for their personal effects. His own lost personal effects, along with the gear and supplies, brought the total to $318[3]—about $10,600 in 2022 dollars.[4]

Though the losses had been sustained in the line of duty, the General Land Office could not cover them: The funds would have to come from a congressional appropriation.[5] Legislation was drafted in 1892 by Wyoming Senator Francis E. Warren and approved by the commissioner of the Land Office. Its passage was urged in a report submitted by Wyoming Senator Joseph M. Carey.[6] The report's detailed receipts and affidavits did not inspire Congress to pass the bill.

In 1900, Senator Warren presented the same information in a new bill, which passed.[7] Did it help that Richards was in Washington, serving as assistant commissioner of the General Land Office?

It's unknown if Clark sent him the chain, but it seems likely he did.

Richards's Letter to President Grant

From a typewritten copy with an incorrect date.[8] Location of original is unknown.

[July 1870]

Honored Sir;—

Presuming somewhat upon the kindness with which I was treated upon a former occasion by your Excellency, I respectfully solicit your attention for a short time to a matter of considerable moment to me.

Last May upon an application from my brother, A. V. Richards, you gave me an excellent letter of recommendation to R. K. [sic] Livingston, Surveyor General of this State. I immediately presented it and was promised a contract of surveying. Having had some experience with the Indians and being acquainted with the nature of the country throughout the state, I told the General I would prefer having my work on the Elk Horn river, immediately west of Madison County, that being the only safe territory of the state now unsurveyed. With as plain a verbal agreement as I could wish that my brother was to be associated with me on a full contract of six thousand dollars on the Elk Horn River, I returned to Omaha. I remained here perfecting my arrangements for doing the work and incurring pretty heavy expenses thereby while my brother was arranging his business with a view of going with me, until the 13th inst. when I received the enclosed letter from Genl Livingston which needs but little explanation. The work offered me amounts to three thousand eight hundred and sixty dollars and lies near the Republican River, comprising a part of the summer hunting grounds of hostile Indians and near the scene of the Massacre of Buck's surveying party last season when every one of a party of eleven men were killed. The expense of performing the work would not be less than two thousand dollars, leaving the sum of nine hundred and thirty dollars as my share of the summer's work for a fair start in the world.

••••[dots in typed copy, probably indicating a cut]

Before receiving the official notification of the amount allowed this State for surveys, Genl. Livingston assigned to other parties the work promised me. He assigned all other work except that offered me in his letter and had started the deputies into the field, notwithstanding his assertion to me that it was not the practice of the office to promise work ahead of the appropriation. From the fact that I have seen Genl. Livingston several times since our first meeting when he might have made known to me the intended change in the location of my work and from other circumstances not necessary to be mentioned here, it is evident that he wanted to keep me in ignorance of his real intentions until the last moment—and then force me into taking a contract of little or no value and in an Indian country. On the 16th inst my brother reached Omaha and upon due consideration and a calculation of the cost and risk necessary to perform the work I respectfully declined to take the contract and my brother returned to Galena.

This is a plain statement of the facts in the case and I can corroborate every assertion I have made. Doubtless it is of little interest to you, but I make the statement that you may know with what degree of respect a recommendation from the Chief Magistrate of the United States is received by the Surveyor General of the State of Nebraska.

Your kindness in giving me the letter you did I fully appreciate and shall always retain in grateful remembrance of your goodwill. Hoping you will pardon the liberty I take in addressing you, I remain,

Very respectfully,
Your Obedient Servant.
[Signed] W. A. Richards

Hunting and Other Stories
of W. A. Richards

A Night Shot at Ephraim.

Forest and Stream, March 5, 1885

Last November, when on a surveying trip in Northwestern Wyoming at the foot of the Big Horn Mountains, I was stopping at a cattle ranch where we slept in a log house sixteen feet square. The logs for a similar house had been laid up adjoining this one, endwise, as nearly as the projecting logs of the roofs would allow. We killed a steer for beef, quartered it, and hung the quarters up between the two houses. One morning the cook discovered that a forequarter was gone. Bear tracks were discovered, and were followed 300 yards, where the remains of the quarter were found buried. Although we looked carefully over the bare ground, there was no

---

This encounter was mentioned in the diary, October 25, 1884. "Ephraim" was a general term for grizzly bears back then. Stories are given in chronological order of publication.

sign of the bear having allowed the beef to touch the ground while in transit.

The next night we put our dog outside the house for a guard and retired after the usual evening game of casino. Between 12 and 1 o'clock I was awakened by a slight noise between the houses. Of course I thought of the bear, arose very quietly, put on a pair of old slippers, took down my rifle from its hooks, took two cartridges from the belt hanging on one of the hooks, and gently opened the door. The wooden hinges creaked a little, and as I stepped outside I saw an unusually large bear backing out from between the houses just ten feet from me. My gun was unloaded—fortunately—and the bear deliberately ambled off to the further corner of the new house, just forty-five feet from where I stood; and as he turned to go around the corner stopped, with his left side toward me, and quartering a little from me, and turned his head to take a good look at me standing there in the chilly night air clad in my briefest costume.

By this time I was ready for him, quickly bringing my sights in line against the sky I dropped the gun upon him and blazed away. The roar of that old Sharps, in the perfect stillness of the night, was terrific, but the bawl that the old bear gave discounted it. For an instant I was "scared silly," but the next I saw the bear headed my way, and in about one second I was inside the house and had the door barred. Glancing out of the window, beside the door, I saw the bear go on around the house. By this time the boys were all up, and we cautiously went out, but could see no bear, and in fact we didn't go very [far] from the house. I was chaffed a little by the cowboys about shooting steers, and having nightmares, and so on, but I was content to wait for daylight for my vindication. I had used a .45-75 Sharps, the shells loaded by myself with 80 grains of powder and 420 grains of lead; and in a pretty lively experience of fifteen years on the plains and in the mountains I had never heard any animal make a noise such as the bear had made, except when mortally wounded.

At daylight we went out, and just 150 yards from the house found my game dead—a very large male grizzly, shot clean through, the ball having hit him center on the left side, and on account of his position, having passed out just behind the foreleg. His weight was not less than 1,000 pounds. His coat was perfect, and we carefully skinned him, leaving the claws on. I brought the skin home with me, and had it tanned and lined, and the head half-mounted, and it makes an unusually fine robe or mat, which, of course, is highly prized.

I will just add that if my gun had been loaded when I stepped out of the door, I would have fired at once, and being so close could not have re-treated inside nor anywhere else before the bear would have caught me, in which case I think it would have been my hide instead of his that orna-mented the fence. As it was I call it a lucky shot.

Our dog got back after daylight the next morning, and the bare sight of the bear skin sent him yelping into the sage brush again. W. A. R.

COLORADO SPRINGS, Col.

AUTHOR'S NOTE: W.A.R. sent the bearskin, preserved somehow, to his broth-er Aut in Oakland, California. After it was properly tanned and backed with black felt, Aut had it put on display in the window of a local carpet store. Once the tro-phy was retrieved, he enthused to Will in a letter, "You are in great luck if you ever get the skin, for it is mighty fine to step on with your bare feet on a cold morning when you first get up."

Shortly thereafter he added, "Your bear skin has been admired by thousands and I have told your adventure more than ten thousand times." When he finally had to ship it to Will, Aut lamented that he had "grown quite attached to it and will hardly be able to keep house without it....the room looks desolate without it. It is very 'swell' as a lounge cover, or as a rug to lie on, when it is spread in a bow win-dow in the sun, on the floor, when a fellow has had his Sunday morning breakfast, and bath,—has donned his slippers, cigar and morning paper,—has the windows open, (temperature 60 above) and the songs of birds, and the gentle breezes are

wafted into him, he can easily imagine himself a Turkish Sultan, or any Eastern Nabob he has a mind to. ... Si Swinnerton...was struck by the appearance of an immense bear in a window, and... was much surprised when he saw your name on the card. ... He was quite envious of you and your prowess as a bear slayer, said he had never killed a bear, but he was going to try for one this Fall."[9]

The grizzly's huge head made a "swell" seat for W. A. R.'s first grandchild, William Richards McCreery.
About 1905, author's collection

Richards was the first Johnson County commissioner from the Big-horn Basin. What that meant for him was spelled out in the April 7, 1888, issue of The Big Horn Sentinel, *published at Buffalo, Wyoming.*

Traveling Under Difficulties.

The Pleasure of Being a County Official in Some Parts of Wyoming.

To one who thinks there is pleasure in making the trip across the Big Horn mountains at this season of the year from the No Wood country, an experience such as that gone through by County Commissioner Richards a few days ago would certainly convince him to the contrary. Mr. Richards resides on the Big Horn river with his family, where he is engaged in ranching and stock growing. [He actually lived on the No Wood.]

The inconvenience of reaching the county seat in the winter season, Mr. Richards was fully aware of, but thinking his presence might be required on matters pertaining to the interest of the county he left his home on horseback last Tuesday morning, booked for Buffalo, accompanied by one of his men with a pack-horse loaded with the necessary provisions and bedding for camping out, if necessary. The party rapidly covered the distance to the mountains by the morning's ride, but about noon they encountered snow of a considerable depth, and the nearer they approached the top of the "divide" the more apparent did it become that the abandonment of the trip on horseback, at least, was necessary.

This being done, Mr. Richards sent his companion back to the ranch with the horses, after arming himself with a pair of snowshoes and a scanty supply of provisions (which consisted of a part of a loaf of bread), and made tracks Buffalo-ward. His progress on the trip was not as rapid as he anticipated, for no sooner had he lost sight of his companion than he found that he was to encounter a "chinook," and with the wind blowing at a terrific speed and the snow thawing traveling was almost impossible.

Night finally overtook the traveler before he had quite reached the top of the divide. Mr. Richards concluded to make the best of the situation, and finding the most suitable spot, he drove his stakes for the night at the side of a big pine stump, where he built a fire and rested his weary limbs on top of several feet of snow. The wind kept up at a furious rate all night and with his scant supply of food and a pipe and tobacco the traveler sat up all night, first warming on side and then the other, and reflecting over the bad deeds committed in his past life.

Day dawned and the Johnson county commissioner resumed his on-ward march, first over precipices and then down ravines and picturesque canyons. All day long he tramped faithfully, not knowing where night would again overtake him. About 6 o'clock in the evening a broad valley opened out before him and in looking over the country he discovered that he was on one of the tributaries of Powder river and within a few miles of the Frontier Cattle company's home ranch.*

Reaching the ranch Mr. Richards received a kindly welcome, and here he remained two days to rest up from a tiresome and what may be termed a very difficult journey. Being supplied with a saddle horse from the ranch Mr. Richards...resumed his journey, arriving in Buffalo Sunday without experiencing any further trouble.

RECREATION.

Volume IV.   MAY, 1896.   Number 5.

G. O. SHIELDS (COQUINA), Editor and Manager.

My Best Shot.

The best shot ever made by one who has successfully hunted large game for 25 years, over the country extending from the Mississippi river West to the Pacific Ocean, North to Montana, and South to Mexico, may be hard to determine. Every man who has hunted much has at least one story of an especially good shot, which, under favorable circumstances, he delights to tell about. This is mine:

In the latter part of September, 1874, with a party of 14, including a professional guide, I camped one day at the Great Falls of the Yellowstone, in the then newly opened National Park. We traveled with a pack train of mules, there being at that time no roads in the Park, but few trails, and these were little used. [The surveying party originally numbered 14.]

We laid over at the falls during a heavy fall of snow, and were ready to move on the morning of the 18th of September. As we had no meat in camp, I determined to go ahead of the outfit and try to kill something near the trail. I asked the guide what direction the trail followed, from the falls

---

*Frontier Land and Cattle Co. was owned by Sir Horace Plunkett, an Irish aristocrat. Plunkett did not spend winters at the ranch.[10]

to the Upper Geyser basin, and showed him where North was with a pocket compass. He replied that the trail ran Northwest, marked its course in the snow for me, and said I couldn't miss it, as it followed Alum creek—easily recognized by its taste—after crossing the divide.

Telling the rest of the party I would hunt on the North side of the trail and join them before noon, when they would stop for lunch, I started out in a Northwesterly direction. The country being mountainous, heavily timbered, with many windfalls and canyons, it was impossible to go on horseback off the trails, so I walked and sent my horse with the outfit.

As the first eminence was reached I looked back. The view was beautiful and impressive beyond description. Twenty years have not sufficed to erase it from my memory. At my feet the most picturesque waterfall in America—a vast volume of water taking a leap of 400 feet into space, to fall in a mass of spray on the rocks below. Thence it goes careering, at race-horse speed, down the grandest canyon on earth, whose almost perpendicular sides rise higher and higher until, before a change in its course shuts them from view, their tops are lost in the clouds a mile above the river.

Along the lower sides of the canyon innumerable hot springs were sending up jets of steam into the frosty air, while the earth about them, dismantled of its covering of snow by their heat, showed a variety of colors only equalled by those of the rainbow. Up the canyon's sides all inequalities of surface were hidden by the downy robe of snow, while crowning the heights were the magnificent forests, gorgeous in their autumn dress. Snow for a background everywhere. Yes, snow even over my feet, half way to my knees, and the sensation imparted thereby admonished me that I was hunting for game, not for scenery, and that this snow might be useful as well as beautiful, for any track seen in it must be a fresh one.

I pushed on Northwest, up the mountain side. Six consecutive months of this work had made me a good mountain climber, and I soon placed several miles between me and the falls without seeing a track in the virgin snow. Then my ear caught a sound not unknown but unexpected. If heard anywhere else one would say it was the exhaust of a steam engine. Heard here, it was recognized as the intermittent puffing of a small geyser. It was on my course, and when reached I found a number of geysers, some small and active, others larger, in good working order, only waiting for their time to come, which might be any moment. I looked for vandal signs of other visitors—the name carved on the cones built by the ceaseless waters, or the mutilated tree—but found none, so I passed on and left no record.

Ten years later I saw a telegram that had been rushed through, from Montana, stating that an eminent savant of the Smithsonian Institution had achieved undying fame by discovering this same group of geysers. He was rewarded and their glory increased by having his name attached to them. How near we sometimes come to glory and yet miss it!

But geysers will not fill the camp-kettle any more than scenery will, and I must keep ahead of the pack train. At 11 o'clock I had seen no sign of game, and was forcibly reminded that my digestive organs were out of a job. I turned Southwest, expecting to find the trail in half a mile. It was well worn, and would be easily distinguishable, even under the snow, should I still be ahead of the pack train. Noon came and still no sign of the trail. I tightened my belt and let out a link in my gait. The mountain range forming the divide between the Yellowstone and the Fire Hole rivers has a trend to the Southeast. Going Southwest I reached the summit, and began the descent. I tried all the streams I crossed in search of Alum creek. The water of all was disappointingly sweet.

At 2 o'clock I stopped, sat down on a log, and tried—although the idea did not then shape itself into these immortal words—to find out "where I was at." The guide said the trail ran Northwest, all the way, for 25 miles. By my pocket compass I had traveled Northwest 4 hours, or 10 miles, including stops. I had gone Southwest 3 hours, or at least 9 miles, and no sign of a trail. I might have crossed it on a rocky point, but did not believe I had. My faith in going Southwest was gone. Only one thing could be done with certainty—go back to the falls. I would surely find the trail before I got there. The hypotenuse of the triangle, around two sides of which I had traveled, was 13 miles long, with a mountain range to go over, snow a foot deep, fallen timber everywhere, and my appetite getting better every minute. I could make it by dark, so I started.

The proper course was turned off on the compass and the climb begun. I had gone but a short distance when my left foot slipped and something seemed to snap in my left knee. Only a little sprain, and no time to nurse it. But it grew worse. Soon the knee would not bend and the slightest motion caused the most intense pain. Again I sought a log, and I then knew where I was at.

I was in the midst of heavy timber, on a mountainside, the camp in some place to me unknown. There was no human being, aside from our party, within 50 miles, and I was unable to travel, under ordinary circumstances. If at home I surely couldn't walk without crutches, but if I stopped here it would be like taking up a permanent residence. No one could find me or help me out of the scrape I was in. I must go to the falls, but I would be compelled to sleep out on the mountain one night at least. That was certain.

I was dressed rather lightly, too, for camping out. My heaviest garment was a canvas hunting coat, mostly pockets. I had a pipe, a plug of good natural leaf smoking tobacco, and plenty of matches, but nothing to eat. My rifle was a 45-caliber needle gun, restocked and fitted with set triggers. I had a good revolver, a knife, and plenty of cartridges. I must kill something before night or go without both supper and bed. I had seen neither game nor sign of game all day. The prospect was not bright.

Determined that the refractory knee must either work or break, I again started up the mountain. The logs seemed more numerous and higher than ever. I put my right foot on each of them first; then drew up the left one and put it down on the other side. No stepping over any but the smallest. The knee grew stiff. I became anxious to shoot a grouse, a squirrel, or anything that could be eaten. A pine marten was the first living thing I saw. A ball from the pistol knocked his head off. He looked like a rat but he went into one of the pockets.

While working up through a little gulch to avoid logs, I heard a great crashing in the brush on one side. I looked for an elk and was ready to shoot, but the animals went out of the brush, into the timber, without my catching a glimpse of them. I went over to where they started from and found the tracks of 6 old and 4 young bears. I was content not to have seen them and was glad they went away from instead of coming toward me.

The sun was almost down, I had just reached the top of the range and must soon camp. I would then see how a pine marten could be made to serve for two meals, and his skin for a bed, for a winter night. The prospect was not cheering, and I fell to thinking of the home camp; the good warm supper and my generous roll of blankets. I forgot that I was hunting and looked only for easy places in which to walk.

Suddenly looking ahead my heart almost stops beating, for there, under a big pine tree, not more than a hundred yards away, stands a fine, sleek, plump black tail doe. She never saw a man before and shows no sign of fear. Here is meat, and plenty of it, waiting to be cooked and eaten. A front shot is a hard one, but I have no fear of missing. I know my gun and my sights. The elevation is right, I can hit her right in the sticking place. I carefully bring the gun around to my shoulder. It is already loaded. I cock it, set the trigger, lower it toward the game, and put my finger in front of the trigger. Cool? Perfectly. Meat for supper, *sure*. When

"THE DEER WAS RAPIDLY GOING OFF."

about 10 feet above the doe, bang! went the old needle gun, with a report like that of a cannon. I had forgotten that I had a thick glove on. It had touched the hair trigger. The gun had gone off and the deer was rapidly going off.

The language I used would not look well in print. I was mad enough for the hydrophobia. But under such circumstances a hungry hunter can think and act quickly. With my teeth I pull off the glove. In a second another cartridge is in. The timber is thick and the deer is flashing through it; but just ahead of her is a small opening, not over 30 feet wide. She will cross it quartering from me. As she comes into view I hold well ahead of her and high. I am mad enough to hit a silver dollar that distance. The old needle gun cracks. The stricken doe leaps 10 feet into the air. Her velocity is so great that she falls and rolls, over and over, endwise; but does not rise.

Exultation succeeds my anger. Here is meat in plenty and killed in a legitimate manner. I step the distance—230 good paces. The deer is dead before I reach her, the ball having gone in behind the knuckle of the right shoulder, passed through the heart and out at the point of the left shoulder.

That was my best shot.

Others have been equally difficult, still others more remarkable, but none that filled all the requirements of a good shot as did this one.

The first thing I did was to throw away the rat. Then the saddle of the deer was taken off. One quarter was not enough. I had recently seen two prospectors who had been lost in the mountains for 10 days, and their wild, hungry, famished appearance still haunted me. Game was not plentiful and there might be more of a hitch in my calculations than there was in my left leg.

Then a camping place was found, where fallen timber was abundant, and a fire was started against the side of an immense log. There was a convenient pine root, flat, shaped like a star fish, the trunk all rotted off. This was dragged near the fire and served for both seat and table. Then the fat, juicy venison steaks were spitted on the iron wiping stick, broiled over the coals, and eaten with a relish, although without salt or pepper. Pounds and pounds of meat were stored away. Then the pipe—and no hunter need be told what solid comfort that means. That lucky shot had materially changed the aspect of affairs.

Bedtime arrived, and though this story is already too long I want to give my fellow hunters the benefit of a new idea developed that night. The log against which the fire was built was soggy and would not burn readily. It had an upward bend in it, which left quite a space between its lower side and the ground opposite the fire. I moved the fire to the other side of the log and made my bed on the warm ground where the fire had been. I could lie close to the log and the heat from the fire would reach me without the greater heat from the blaze burning hands or face. I slept several hours and awoke covered with snow which was falling steadily.

No more sleep, so more venison was broiled, some to carry in my

"THE FAT, JUICY VENISON STEAKS WERE SPITTED UPON THE IRON WIPING STICK."

pocket for lunch. At daylight I moved on with the remaining quarter of venison—all that was left—slung to the gun over my shoulder. Within a mile of the falls I found the trail. It led Southwest instead of Northwest and I would never have reached it on the course I was following when I turned back to the falls.

In half an hour after reaching the trail I was met by a member of our party, leading my saddle horse. After discovering the true course of the trail he knew I would camp out and that I would have to come back to the falls. So he started back confident of meeting me on the trail. He had lain out himself, but had made the connection he had planned.

At 5 o'clock we reached camp, just in time to prevent a searching party from starting out. It was 2 weeks before I walked again, without crutches. As the guide had proposed to go out and find me for $50, we thought he had purposely misinformed me as to the course of the trail. After thoroughly frightening him by threatening to lynch him, we discharged him and never heard of him again.

AUTHOR'S NOTE: Yellowstone National Park historians Paul Schullery and Lee Whittlesey sent me this story and provided other assistance, particularly in regard to the geysers Richards came across. Alas, the geographical puzzlements of his story remain.

He seems to believe he came across the Norris Geyser Basin, named after Philetus W. Norris, second superintendent of the Park (1877–81). Norris first described the basin and opened it to tourists—and is said to have given it his own name about 1880. The Smithsonian connection comes from his having conducted ethnological research there until his death in 1885. Lee Whittlesey thinks that the Norris Basin was too far over rough country for Richards to have reached it; he favors the Violet or Alabaster Springs, southwest of the Falls. But Richards says he went northwest.

The story was written 20 years after the fact, so Richards may have misremembered some facts. He also seems to have used poetic license to craft a story pleasing to the legions of readers interested in Yellowstone. For instance, the idea of seeing the canyon and its mists from a nearby promontory is appealing, but the canyon is not visible from its rim unless you go much farther northwest than Richards said he did.

After considerable back and forth with the Yellowstone historians and other interested parties, I do not feel anything has been resolved. Richards was in excellent shape, 25 years of age and fresh from two months of surveying the rugged western boundary of Wyoming, so I think he could have gotten to Norris. But he either misremembered which direction he went or started from some other point, since Norris is due west of the Falls, not northwest.

Most frustrating is that this seems to be the only existing account of the visit to the Park by Will and Lon Richards on their way back to Evanston and the rail-road. In his western boundary survey field notes Lon lamented the pillaging of Park treasures, and he named some creeks (see p. 148), but neither he nor his brother—both copious chroniclers—wrote anything else about that trip that has come down to us.

A Remarkable Shot.
Recreation, December 1897

In 1873 I was hunting on Sheep Mountain, in Southern Wyoming. On its summit, near the Little Snake river, there is a well defined crater, now closed, at the bottom, and overgrown with grass.

Here I came on a small band of mountain sheep, which immediately disappeared over the farther rim of the crater. Crossing over after them and looking down the side of the mountain, which was a mass of broken rock, without any timber, I saw the sheep strung out, working their way around the mountain side, about 200 yards below me. The last in the line was a young buck, who stopped and gazed up the mountain with an evident desire to come back. Resting my gun across a large boulder I took deliberate aim, just behind the knuckle of the shoulder, and fired. To my great surprise he fell as though electrocuted. There was scarcely a struggle, and I could not imagine where I had hit him. If shot through the heart he would have darted forward a few yards, at least. With a broken back he could still struggle; but he lay perfectly still. It was no easy task to get down to him, for he lay on a slide of shale which was just about as steep as a man could travel on.

At last I reached him and took hold of a hind leg, when it seemed the whole side of the mountain had started for a lower altitude. Naturally I at once sat down. I retained my hold on the leg of the sheep, with my left hand, while I had the gun in my right hand, and was therefore unable to protect myself much. Some of the rocks were exceedingly sharp.

In the toboggan race the sheep was ahead, part of the time, and the other part I was ahead. The inevitable precipice lay before us, but the grade changed somewhat, in our favor, and we stopped, just in time to escape a plunge that would have been disastrous.

I was not hurt, to speak of, but some portions of my clothing were decidedly the worse for wear. The sheep was considerably skinned up, and had left quite a trail of hair down the mountain side.

My first thought was to see where he had been hit. He had stood with his left side toward me, and examination showed he had been struck just where I had aimed. The ball, from a 50 calibre needle gun, had not only gone through his heart but entirely through his body; yet that should not have killed him instantly. On examining his horns, which were not unusually large, the secret was revealed. The bullet had gone through his head, just above the eyes, but had entered at the right side and had gone out at the left.

It was evident that just as I fired he had thrown his head around, on his side, exactly in the line of sight, and the ball had first gone through his brain, then through his heart.

No wonder he dropped dead. Probably few animals have ever been shot sidewise, through the head and through the body at one shot, with one bullet.

Richards' stories about his encounters with Bison bison *years earlier appeared in newspapers around the country in 1903 and 1904, together or separately. The version of "Wild Fight For Life" given here is from an undated and incomplete clipping in the author's collection. It was chosen over the others for transcription because of its personal connection to Richards. It may come from* The Pioneer, Bemidji, Minnesota. *The second story is transcribed from* The Los Angeles Times *of February 20, 1903.*[11]

Wild Fight For Life.

The following article is from the pen of Hon. William A. Richards, Commissioner of the United States General Land Office, and a former governor of Wyoming.

Years ago the editor of THE PIONEER was foreman of the composing-room of the Freeport, Illinois, *Journal*, of which paper the late Alonzo V. Richards, a brother of William A., was editor and proprietor, and who was a leading and highly esteemed resident of northern Illinois and southern Wisconsin, and a warm and personal friend of the writer. At that time the present Mr. Richards was a young man and frequently visited at Freeport, and from that city left for the west to join a government surveying party, and was very anxious that we go with the outfit. Since that time the world has dealt kindly with our former friend, William, and he is now one of the most prominent politicians and leading public citizens in the country.

————

I have a very distinct recollection of my first experience with a herd of buffalo. I was one of a party of fourteen traveling south from Fort Kearney, Nebraska, on foot, with two two-mule teams to haul our camp equipment and supplies.

We had reached a point about forty miles from Fort Kearney when, about the middle of the afternoon, as we were driving along a ridge or high plateau, with a little valley to the west, there suddenly appeared on the summit of the opposite ridge to the west of the valley a huge black line about half a mile long, which the chief of the party, who had been on the plains before, informed us was a herd of buffalo. This ridge was about half a mile from us, and we were about opposite the center of the line. It was apparent that with our loaded teams it would be impossible to get beyond the line before the herd would be upon us. Our chief, who had had experience of this kind before, immediately called a halt, directed that the two wagons be brought up close together, one behind the other, and that the mules be unhitched and placed behind the wagons opposite the side from which the buffalo were coming, and securely fastened to the wheels. One man was detailed to each mule to keep it as quiet as possible. Then ten of us were instructed to take as many cartridges as we could put in our pockets, form a line, go out and meet the buffalo and try to split them and keep them divided until they had passed the wagons.

We were armed with Spencer carbines, which shot a 59-calibre bullet with a charge of powder much too light for that weight of lead and that kind of game. There was a magazine in the stock which would carry seven cartridges, and a lever which was used in the same manner in which the Winchester lever is used today. After the magazine was exhausted the gun could be used as a single shotgun, i.e., loaded from the breech by hand. We went out some 300 yards from the wagons and began to shoot. At that time the rear end of the herd had not come over the opposite ridge, so that we were facing a mass of buffalo half a mile long on the front and extending at least as far back, the animals packed as solidly together as it was possible for them to stand, and coming at what was only a fast walk until we began to shoot, when they broke into a gallop. It was impossible for us to stop them, as those in front were urged forward by those behind, and the crowding extended clear to the rear. The front of the line presented a terrifying appearance to a boy who had never fired a gun at anything larger than a rabbit. It seemed to be a solid mass of black heads, horns and humps, and extended as far as we could see in every direction in front of us.

I remember very distinctly that when I fired my first shot, the front of the line being about 100 yards from us, I thought I had certainly struck a horn. I did not then know that one could hear a bullet strike a body of flesh at that distance, but when I had fired several shots and heard them all strike I knew I was hitting something other than horns. At that particular moment there came into my mind a story I had read in the old fourth reader at school of an experience of this kind, in which old Leatherstocking, Cooper's hero in his story of "The Prairie," was the central figure. On that occasion the tide had been turned in favor of the few persons about to be overwhelmed by the onrushing herd by the donkey, which was used for a pack animal, lifting up his voice when his domain had been encroached upon. As it had been successful on that occasion I thought some more noise might be of benefit at this time, and, having pretty good lungs, I exerted them to the utmost, joined at once by the rest of the firing party. My theory worked out all right. At any rate, the noise of our guns and voices, with what execution our bullets were doing, caused the herd to divide and pass on either side of us, but we soon found ourselves in a very precarious situation.

When the herd was first split the buffalo could see as well as hear us and veered off either way, but those who were following created such a noise themselves and raised such a cloud of dust that they could hardly see or hear us, and soon began to crowd in on us in a manner exceedingly disquieting. We could see nothing except a black mass, which now almost surrounded us, and were being forced backward and in upon each other to such an extent that it became very doubtful whether we were going to be successful in our effort. Of course, if we failed in this, it meant that we would be trampled under foot, and the entire party as well as the outfit literally wiped off the face of the earth. What with our shouting and shooting and the terrific noise of the herd and the excitement of the occasion there was little time to figure on the probability. We only knew that we had been forced into a solid line, and were simply splitting the herd because we would not double up or give way on either end. We had been giving back, foot by foot, for what seemed to me a very long time, had very few cartridges left, and it was becoming evident we could not stand the strain much longer, when our backs came in contact with the wagon, and at almost the same instant we saw daylight ahead of us, and there was the end of the herd. Those at the wagon said that for more than half an hour they had been entirely surrounded by buffalo, as the herd had united as soon as the wagons were passed. The chief of our party declared that in ten years' work on the plains this was the closest shave he ever had had from being annihilated by buffalo. The most remarkable thing about the whole affair was that when the herd had passed and the dust had settled there were only two dead buffalo lying upon the plains, while more than 300 shots had been fired. With such guns as are used to-day for hunting purposes a large proportion of the shots would have killed. With the guns which we were using, a shot in the head from the front would not even knock a buffalo down.

Having a small supply of water in our wagons, we camped at this place, but got very little sleep, as the herd stopped within a short distance of us and spent the night there. On account, doubtless, of the wounded buffalo and the smell of fresh blood they were in a state of turmoil all night, while the wolves, both coyotes and the large gray wolves, kept up an incessant howling all night long. In addition to these unpleasant features there was the constant fear of a stampede of the herd in our direction again. This did not occur, however, and we moved on the next morning in good order with a plentiful supply of buffalo meat, the first we had obtained on the trip.

This was my introduction to buffalo hunting, of which I did a great deal during the next few years. In that time I saw herds of buffalo larger than this herd, but we were always so fortunate as not to get in their line of march.

Hunting a Buffalo Bull.

The buffalo is under ordinary circumstances a docile animal, neither aggressive nor combative, but I had some experiences with them which went to show that when aggravated they are exceedingly dangerous. I found that ordinarily a buffalo, like any other wild animal with which I have had experience, including the grizzly bear, would run from a hunter if given the opportunity, and when wounded it would not ordinarily charge a man from a greater distance than about fifty yards. Upon one occasion I met one which was an exception to this rule. I was hunting on foot with a Henry rifle, which was the first model of the Winchester. Buffaloes were not plentiful in that locality, but finally I sighted an old bull lying on the plain, with nothing to conceal a hunter within half a mile of him. Hunting on foot, I needed meat badly, and could not afford to let this old fellow get away. I worked around directly behind him and then advanced toward him. Buffaloes are not very wary when lying down, and I approached to within about 150 yards, when I concluded I was as close as I cared to be, and took a shot at him.

When lying down, a buffalo's back slopes considerably on account of its forequarters being so much the heavier, and my bullet struck this sloping surface on a rib, made a slit in the skin and did no further damage. The old fellow jumped up and started to run at right angles to the line I was following, giving me a good shot at his side. I fired, but having underestimated the distance the ball dropped and struck him just above the hoof of the foreleg. Although I found subsequently that this ball broke no bones, it had a very bad effect upon his temper, for, to my great surprise, he turned and came straight toward me.

THE BUFFALO'S CHARGE.

I would have liked to go somewhere, but the plain extended for a mile in every direction without a break, and I felt certain I could not outrun him for that distance. There was nothing for it but to hold my ground and shoot, which I proceeded to do, and I was much gratified to see that I retained my nerve, as I could hear every ball strike him. He came on without any hesitation, and I kept shooting as fast as possible, but after a few shots became very much alarmed respecting the number of cartridges remaining in the magazine. I had no time to look to see whether I was throwing in a cartridge every time I threw down the lever, and every time I pulled the trigger it was with a sickening feeling of uncertainty as to whether the gun was loaded or not. Aside from this I was getting a little doubtful of the propriety of holding the fort much longer, when, just as I was about to pull the trigger for another shot, he suddenly stopped. He was near enough so that I could have thrown my hat upon his horns. I had determined to fire that shot and then turn the fight into a foot race, and I was consequently very much pleased when he showed a disposition to call it a draw. I did not fire again because I felt morally certain I had the last cartridge in the gun; besides this, the shot was as apt to start him forward as to do him any injury, and I was very certain I [he?] had had enough of it, so I stood there holding the gun on him, but hoping that it would not be necessary to fire.

GAME TO THE LAST.

He certainly presented the most terrifying aspect of any animal I had ever faced. He was of immense size, had been shot several times where it brought the blood, was standing with his feet slightly apart, his head somewhat lowered as though he would like to charge me, with blood and foam running from his month and nostrils while he sent forth a low bellow of rage. This situation did not last long. He had come just as far as he could and had stopped, not because he was afraid of me, but because he could not come a step farther, and he stood there and glared and bellowed until he began to weave a little from one side to the other, and suddenly he went down. He was dead when I reached him.

I found two or three bullets in his foretop or flattened on his skull, while the ball which killed him had passed along the side of his neck and had entered his body between the neck and the shoulder blade. But for that one fortunate shot this story would probably have had an entirely different ending.

Pinchot Recalls One of Richards' Stories

Richards's talent as a raconteur was noted by Gifford Pinchot, founder and first chief of the U.S. Forest Service. Though Richards was commissioner of the General Land Office at the time of their acquaintance, Pinchot, like others then and afterward, called him "Governor." In his autobiography, Breaking New Ground,[12] *Pinchot recalled,*

Governor Richards was a plainsman turned politician whom it was easy to like and easy to get on with. As a companion he was delightful, and some of his stories were top notch. One, for example, told how Richards himself crept up on an antelope that was lying down with its legs crossed under it, and broke all four of them with a single bullet from his rifle. That is a tall tale, but I believed it when the Governor told it, and I believe it still.

Was it a tall tale? It's definitely a long shot, but impossible?

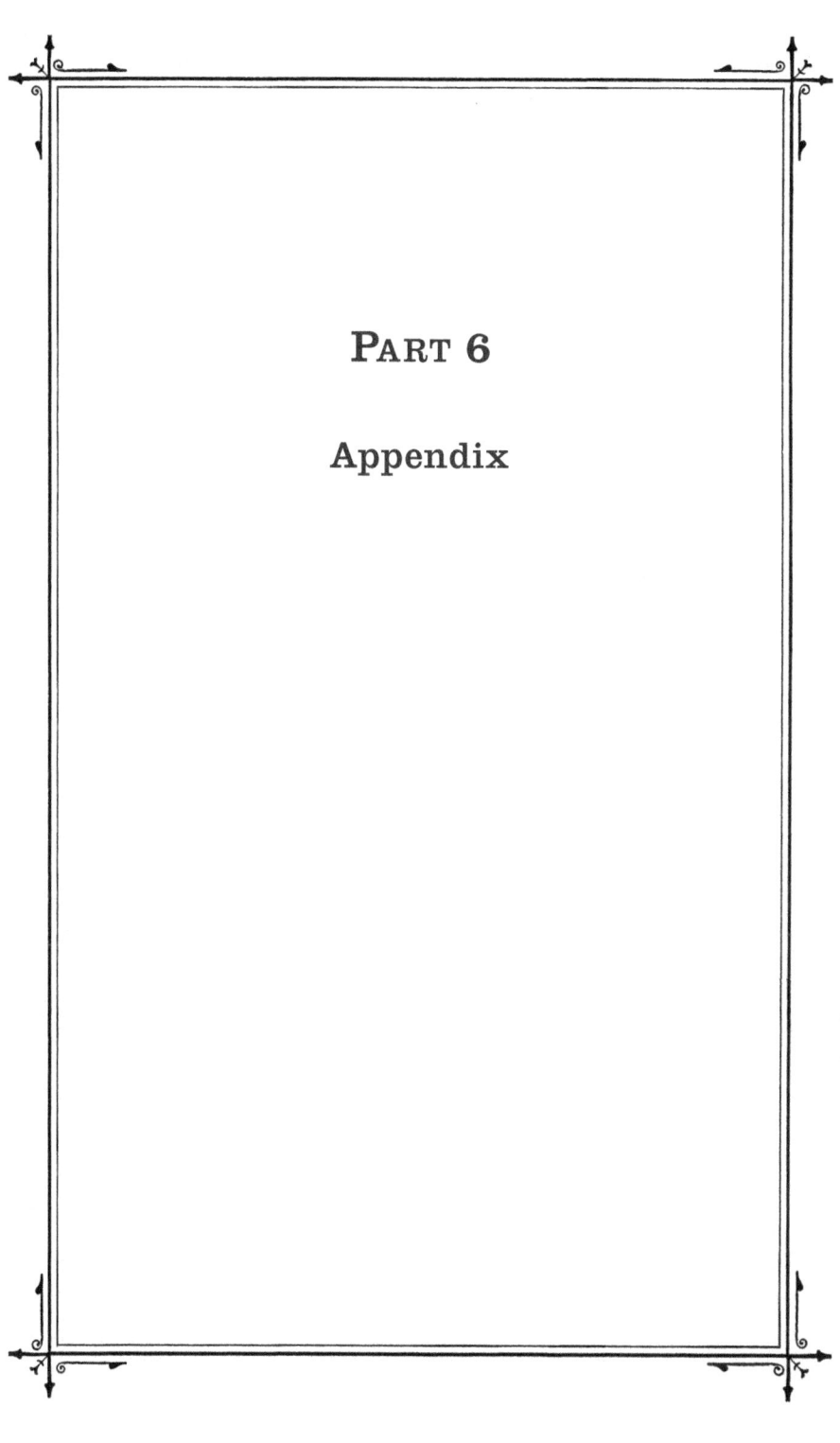

PART 6

Appendix

Richards' Surveys in Nebraska, 1869–1875

WILLIAM A. RICHARDS got his start in surveying in 1869, laying out townships for future settlement in the new State of Nebraska. The surveys, conducted by Chauncey Wiltse, were in the southeast corner of today's Lincoln County and the southwest corner of Dawson County.

After becoming a U.S. deputy surveyor, Richards executed surveys of his own from 1871 through 1875, most of them in joint contracts with others. One required marking the sections inside townships of 50,000 acres recently purchased from the Pawnee. This joint contract with his elder brother, Alonzo V. Richards, was completed in 1873 on the way to their survey of the southern boundary of Wyoming Territory. On his own, Will resurveyed the outer boundary of the reservation, finished the field notes, and filed them with the U.S. Surveyor General for Nebraska.

The point of reference for the Nebraska surveys is the Sixth Principal Meridian, a north-south line through Nebraska and Kansas established in 1855 that would be used for surveys in those states as well as in Wyoming and parts of Colorado and South Dakota. Its east-west baseline is on the 40th parallel of latitude (the Kansas-Nebraska border); its north-south line fell at what later would be 97° 22' 08" longitude west of Greenwich (passing through Columbus, Nebraska).

Most of the maps and the contract information were provided by Gene A. Thomsen, a Nebraska deputy surveyor and historian.

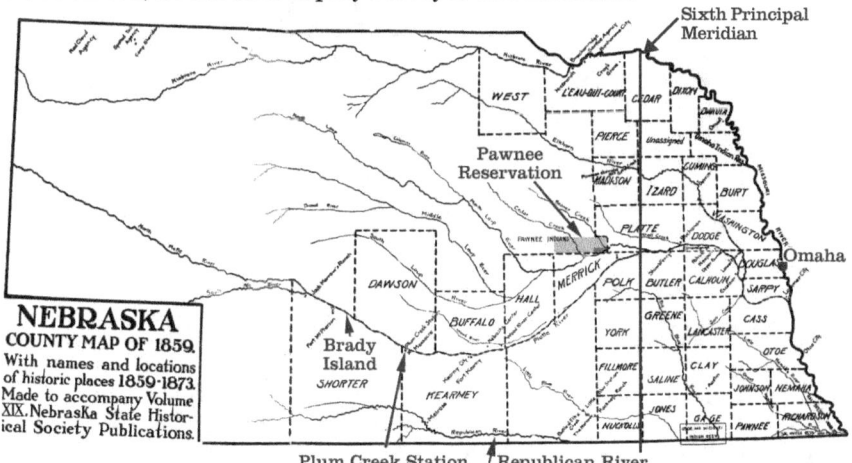

Map of Nebraska annotated in brown. The 50,000 acres are in the southeast corner of the Pawnee reservation. Some place names are mentioned in diary.

History Nebraska[1]

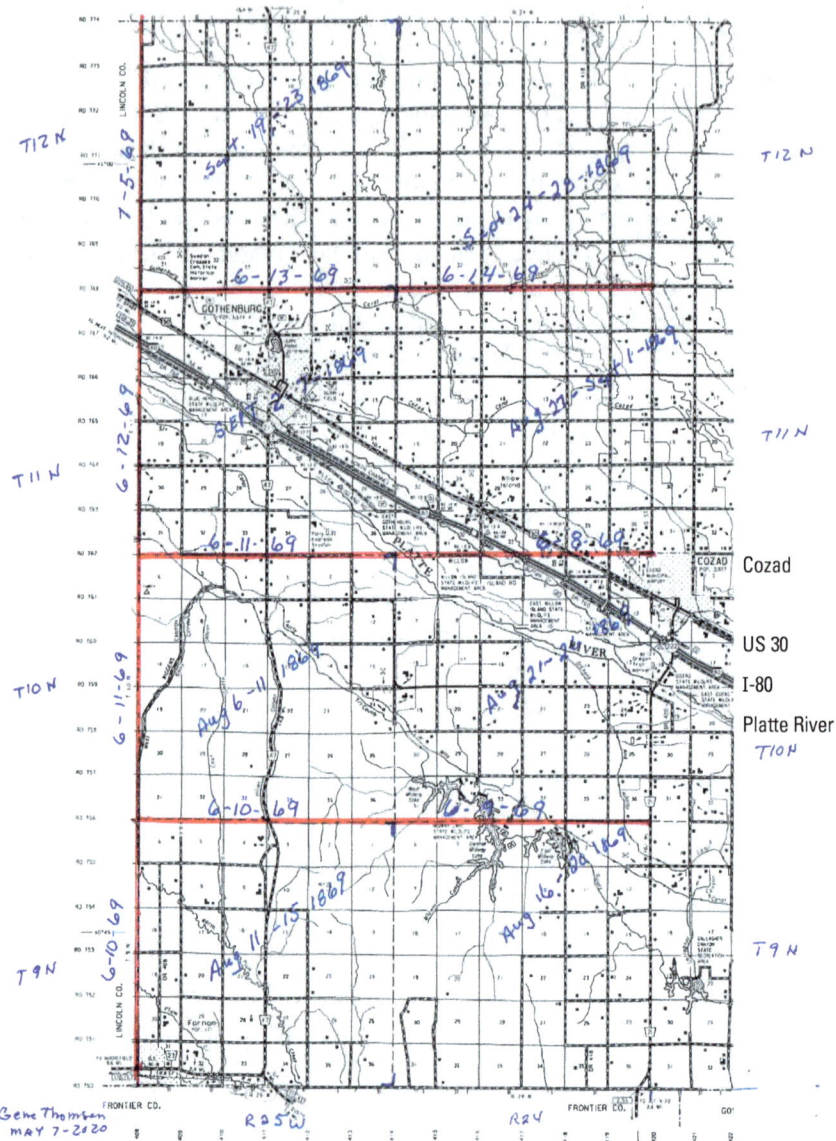

Map I of the 1869 surveys that Richards took part in, this one in the southwest corner of today's Dawson County, Nebraska. On both maps the lines in red are the township and range lines that were run, with the dates in blue. Dates written diagonally mean they surveyed all of the sections in that township. Map shows Townships 9-12 N, Ranges 24-25 W, north of the baseline and west of the Sixth Principal Meridian. Contract #16, dated April 27, 1869; Wiltse & Lonsdale were contractors for both surveys. Crew: George T. Kendall and Albert G. Kendall, chainmen; W. A. Richards and C. P. Moore, axemen & moundmen.

Map and contract details provided by Gene Thomsen.[2]

To North Platte & Buffalo Bill's Scout's Rest Ranch

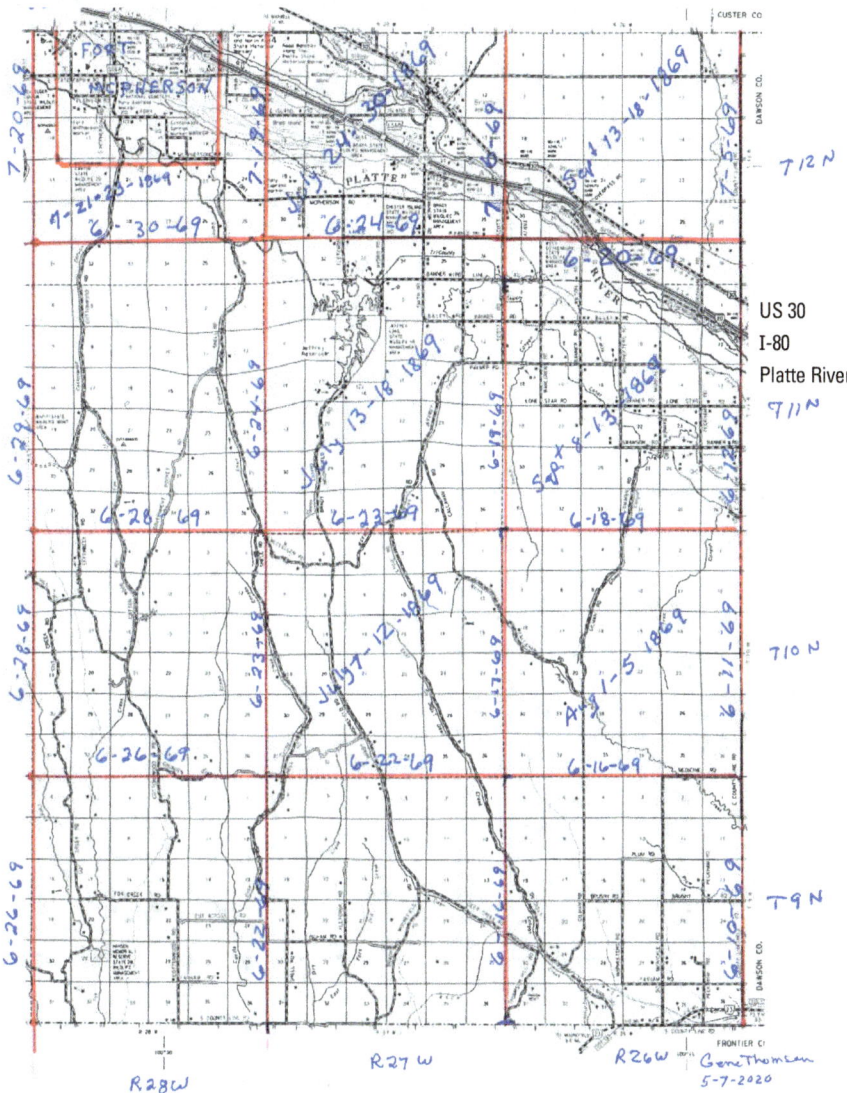

Map II of the 1869 Wiltse surveys (_west_ of Map I), in the southeast corner of today's Lincoln County. The party surveyed up to the boundary of Fort McPherson (upper left) but not inside it. The fort, about four miles south of Maxwell and about two miles south of Interstate 80, is still active as a national cemetery for military personnel.

This map shows Townships 9-12 N, Ranges 26-28 W, north of the baseline and west of the Sixth Principal Meridian.

Map and contract details provided by Gene Thomsen.

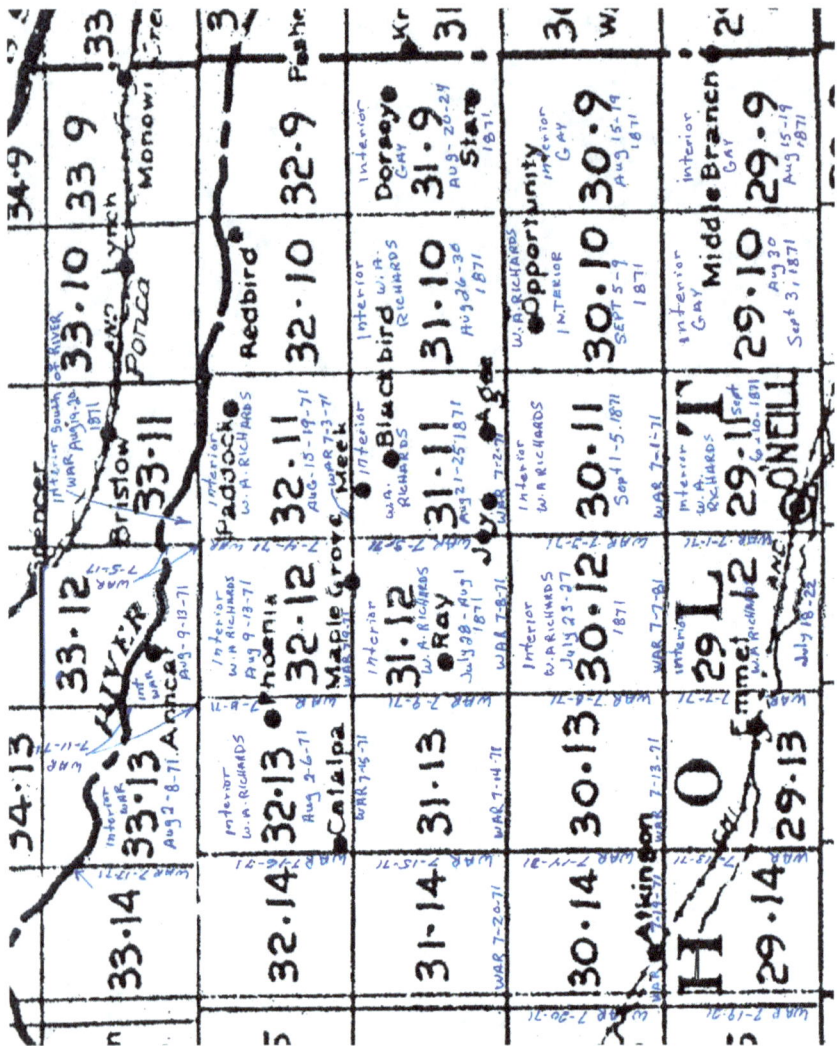

Richards's first surveying contract, a joint one with Joseph W. Gay (probably an associate on the 1869 Wiltse survey), was executed in the northeast corner of Nebraska, in today's Boyd County north of the Niobrara River and Holt County south of it. Contract #46, $5,900, dated June 15, 1871. They marked out section corners within the townships (36 sections to a township, in a square grid) as well as some township and range lines indicated by dates on the map. The large numerals indicate the township and range. Once the field notes were written up and approved, the request for payment was submitted on February 17, 1872.

Another contract, #45, was issued at the same time and for the same amount to Wiltse & Kendall (George T. Kendall). Richards's brother A. C. is listed as a chainman on both surveys.

Map and contract details provided by Gene Thomsen.

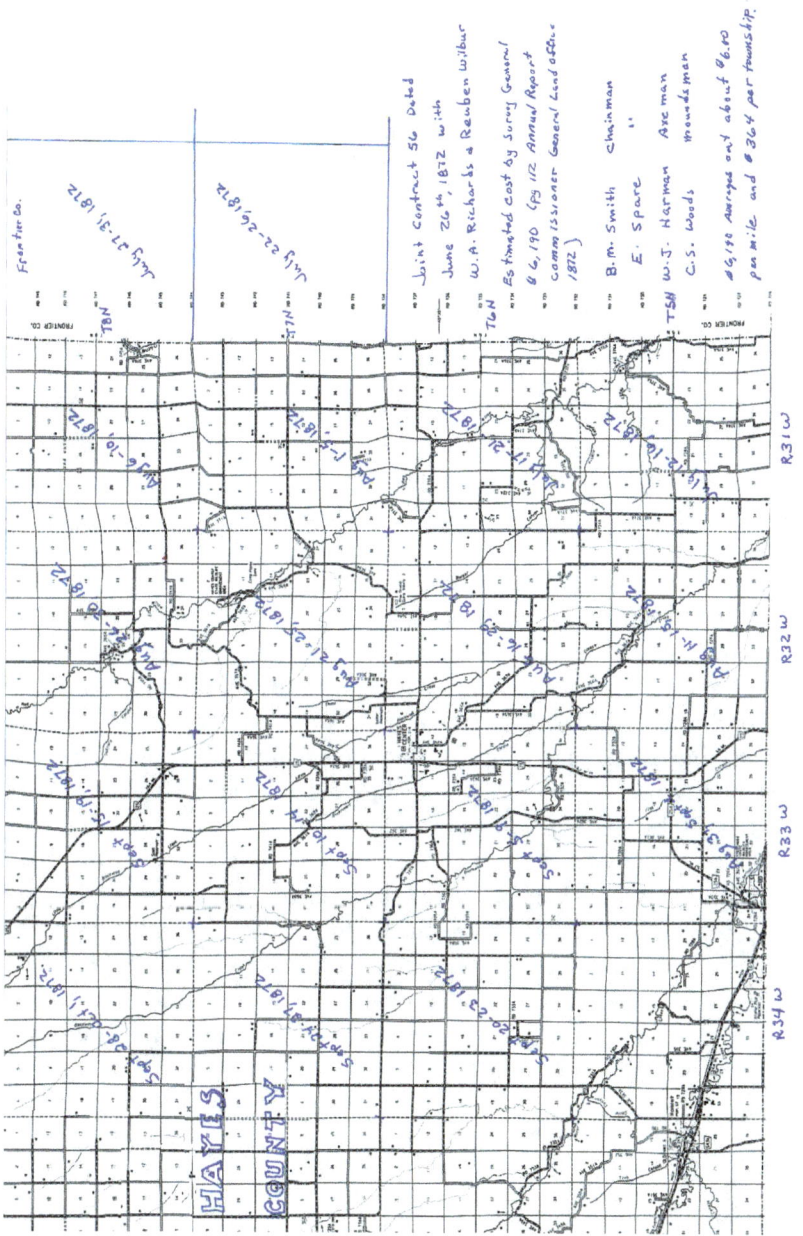

Richards's 1872 joint contract with Reuben H. Wilbur was executed in today's Hayes and Frontier counties, Nebraska. Contract #56, dated June 26, 1872, was for an estimated $6,190, which averaged out to about $6 per mile and $364 per township. Map shows Townships 5-8 N, Ranges 31-34 W.

Map and contract details provided by Gene Thomsen.

THE MAP on the next page shows the survey of 50,000 acres (78.125 sq. miles) below the Loup River that were purchased from the Pawnee, about 18% of their reservation. Contract #68, dated October 9, 1872, was awarded to A. V. and W. A. Richards. They worked that fall with a crew composed of Luther North, [Horace?] Zigler, chainmen; George C. Collins moundman, Charles S. [Farrer?] axeman.

Luther North was second in command of a group of Pawnee Scouts who chased the Cheyenne. The famous North brother was Frank, an interpreter between the white men and the Pawnee who was in charge of the Pawnee Scouts. Richards may have thought it wise to have one of the Norths on the survey crew in case they ran into any Indians.

The outer boundaries of the reservation, surveyed in 1859, had largely become obliterated by 1872. After W. A. Richards wrote Nebraska Surveyor General E. E. Cunningham about it, he received a contract to reestablish the boundary. Contract #69, dated December 14, 1872.[3]

The Richardses finished the survey of the 50,000 acres and Will reestablished the boundary in the spring of 1873, on their way to the Wyoming boundary survey. Chainmen were M. J. Lorraine, Arthur C. Wakeley, E. Spare, and S. C. Clark. Moundmen were Fred North (possibly related to Luther) and J. L. Pattison; axemen were W. S. Byers and L. B. Alexander. Four of them would take part in the Wyoming boundary survey.

The bond of $1,152 for contract #69 was put up by Chauncey Wiltse and Reuben H. Wilbur.[4] This was double the expected pay, as required by contracts issued by U.S. surveyors general.[5]

The Pawnee would soon cede the rest of their land and in 1875 move to a reservation in Oklahoma. When the land was put up for auction, with the proceeds going to the Pawnee, the lax terms and the hard times favored those with money—such as Chauncey Wiltse. He was one of the largest purchasers: 4,309 acres. And he probably knew where the best land was located. In future sales of reservation lands, the terms were tightened to favor settlers.

—Gene A. Thomsen[6]

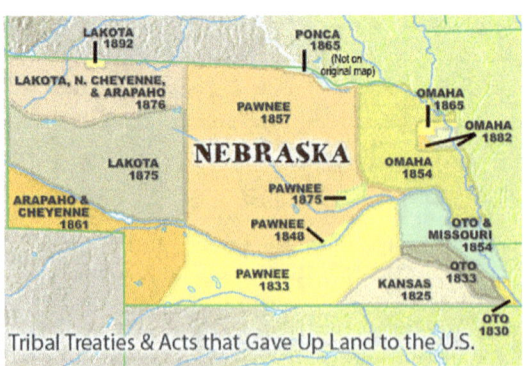

Tribal Treaties & Acts that Gave Up Land to the U.S.

Land ceded by the Pawnee and other tribes in Nebraska nebraskastudies.org[7]

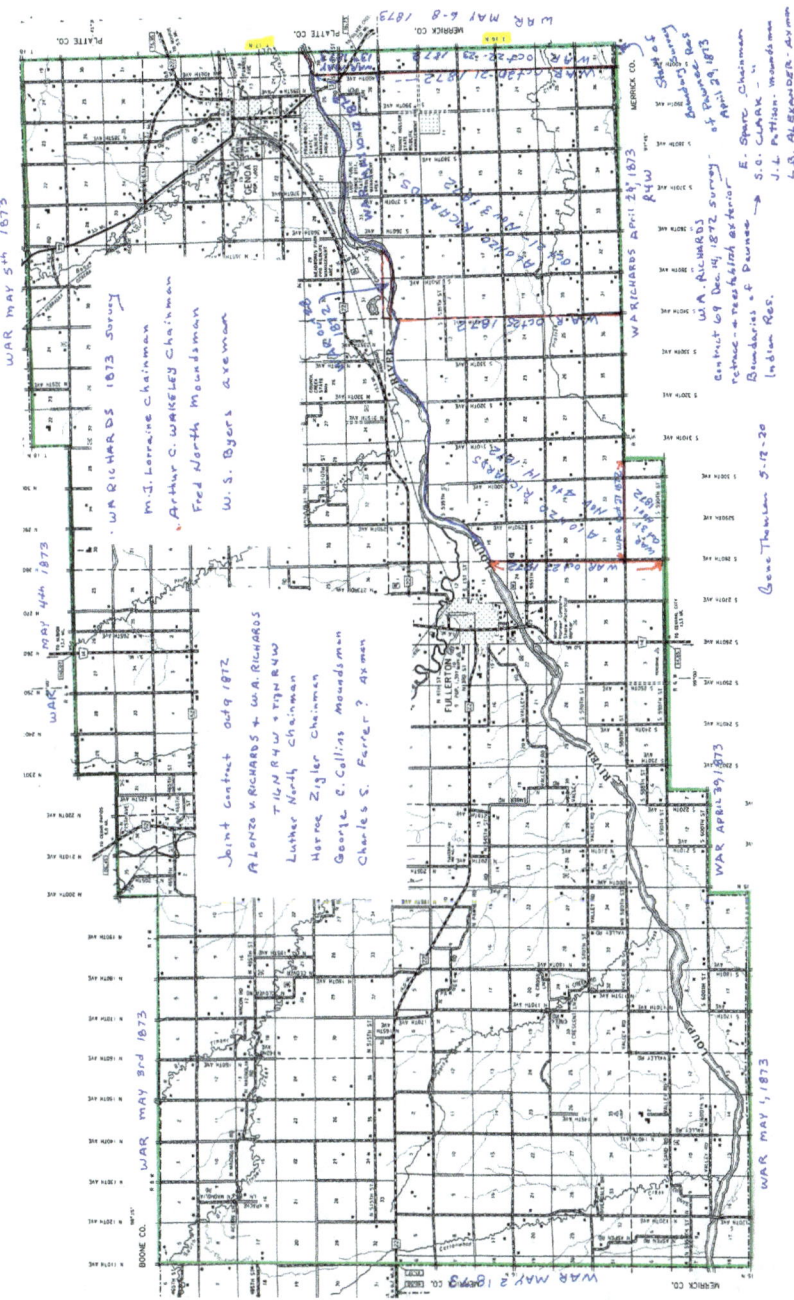

Richards's resurvey of the Pawnee reservation boundary in 1873, defined by the green line. Today's Nance County encompasses all of the reservation plus six sections.

Map and contract details provided by Gene Thomsen.

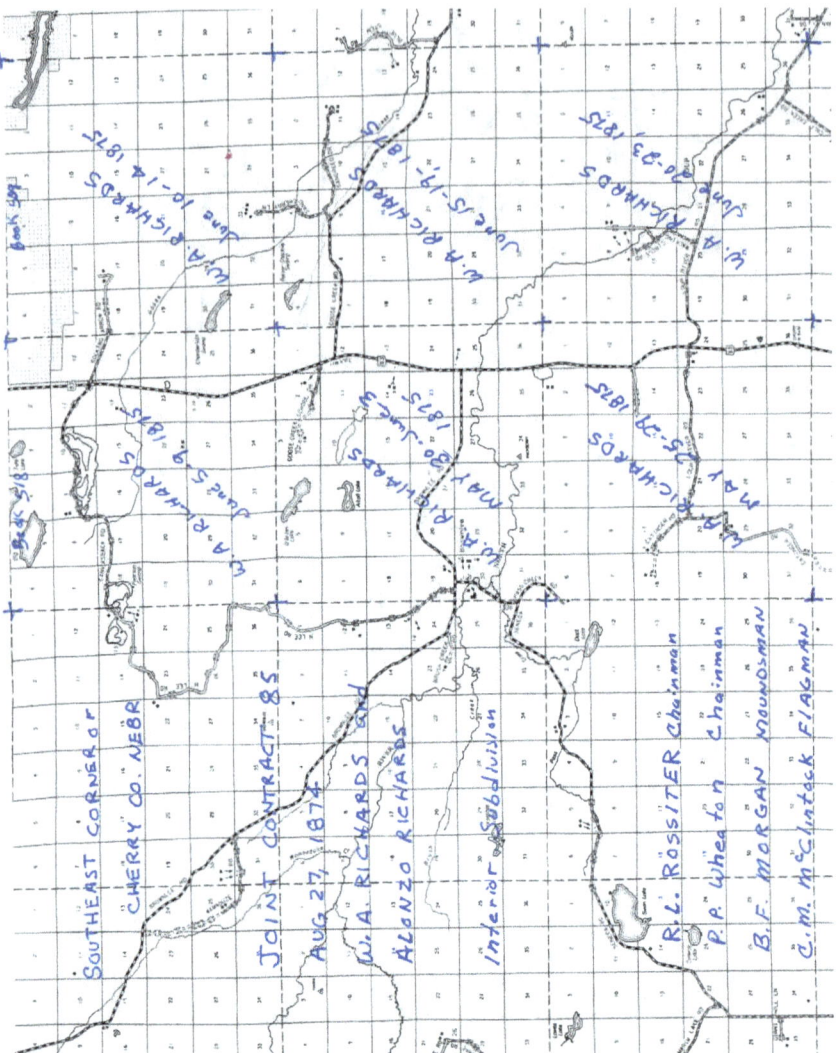

W. A. Richards's joint contract with A. V. Richards for the interior subdivisions (section corners) in the southeast corner of Cherry County, Nebraska, executed in 1875. Townships 25-28 N, Ranges 27-28 W. Contract #85, dated August 27, 1874.[8] Crew: Richard L. Rossiter, P. P. Wheaton, chainmen; B. F. Morgan, moundman; C. M. McClintock; flagman. (Morgan and Rossiter were also on the 1873 and '74 Wyoming boundary surveys: Morgan as chainman and cook in 1873, and cook in '74. Wheaton served as topographer in '74.) Expected pay was $4,800, and a bond of $10,000 was put up by Wallace R. Bartlett and Casper E. Yost. Bartlett was a Republican who served in the Nebraska state legislature in 1872 and '74. Yost was Omaha Postmaster and would have known William and A. C. Richards from their employment there.

Map by Gene Thomsen

248

Instruments Listed in the 1873 Boundary Survey Field Notes[9]

Astronomical Transit 30 inches focal [length] made by Temple of Boston. This transit was purchased of the state of California through Prof. Whitney of Boston, who used it in the Geological Survey of that State.

It was used in the determination of the latitude stations, and at the Evanston Longitude Station.

Astronomical Transit 30 in. focal [length] No. 19 by Würdemann.

This transit is the property of Brigham Young and was used at the Salt Lake observatory in the Longitude observations for determination of Evanston.

Sidereal Box Chronometer [timepiece] No. 1051 (with Break circuit attachment by Bond) Heath of London

> There are two basic systems of time—solar and sidereal. Solar time refers to the civilian time scale which is the elapsed time the earth revolves around the sun in one year (also called Universal Time or mean time). The solar year approximately equals 365.25 solar days. Because of the reference as to when the observer's meridian transits the celestial reference (Sun for solar time and distant fixed stars for sidereal time), the earth appears to have one additional day of rotation when viewing the stars. Then, the sidereal year approximately equals 366.25 days. However, the solar year exactly equals the sidereal year.
>
> All astronomical phenomena/events are referenced to sidereal time. Therefore, if astronomical observations are being made, it is simpler to have the actual "time of the observation/event" be in sidereal time units, thus eliminating the tedious computation of converting solar time to sidereal time.
>
> Bond (of Boston) was the foremost maker of precise time pieces and their accessories in the U.S. during the last half of the nineteenth century.
>
> —Dr. Stoughton

Mean Time Box Chronometer No. 2392 by Dent. Property of Brigham Young and used at Salt Lake only in exchanging signals for longitude.

Sextant by Lorieux of Paris.

Transit Theodolite by Stanley of London.

Two pocket aneroid Barometers by Casella of London.

Washington mean time pocket chronometer No. 333 by Barraud of London

Two 4-pole* brazed steel chains by Gurley of Troy, N.Y.

One standard 4-pole chain tested by U.S. Standard in Surveyor General's office at Plattsmouth, Neb.

---

*A 4-pole chain has 100 links whose total length is the same as four of the 16.5-foot wooden poles once used in surveying. The wording was retained even when the unwieldy poles were replaced with more easily transported chains.

One Telemeter by Lorieux of Paris for testing measurements across streams, cañons, &c.

Two Fahrenheit Thermometers

Sidereal Box Chronometer No. 279 by Bond.

Instruments Listed in the 1874 Boundary Survey Field Notes[10]

The transit itself
A.V. Richards papers

For running the line a fine transit theodolite made to order by Buff & Berger of Boston expressly for this work, was used. Horizontal circle 7 in. dia. graduated to read to 10″ or 5″ by estimation. Vertical finding circle of 5 in. dia. It is also supplied with diagonal eyepiece, and was used for the Azimuth and Time observations along the line. The eyepiece is supplied with a set of stadia lines which were found very useful in testing measurements across canyons rivers &c. All the lines were cut in glass by Prof. W. A. Rogers of Harvard observatory, and are very much superior to the spider web lines generally used, not being affected by changes of temperature, and being very much finer, make errors of "setting" much smaller.

For time on the line Sidereal [star time] Box Chronometer No. 2016 by Frodsham

The approximate elevations and depressions for the profile accompanying the map were measured with a Casella Aneroid Barometer, which was carefully compared with mercurial barometers, and corrections made, whenever opportunity offered.

Flagstaffs were made 3 inches wide by 8 feet long, and the face painted in diamonds 1 foot long—or rather half diamonds, the points coming together in the center of the rod. On the back of the staff was fastened a small spirit level, on a level with the flagman's eyes. This arrangement was found to be much superior to a plumb[-bob] line.

For the Latitude observations a 30 in. [focal length] Astronomical Transit was used. It was made by Temple of Boston, and is the same instrument used in the Southern Boundary of Wyoming in 1873 by me.

Four-pole brazed steel chains were used where the country was smooth enough. They were however provided with snaps for shortening, and were used but very little after the first fifty miles. They were tested according to instructions with standard chains for this purpose.

Memoranda

In making observations for true meridian two Azimuths of Polaris were usually taken reversing the instruments between them to eliminate any pivot errors, or eccentricity of circles, if any existed. After each azimuth a tally pin was set as far from the instrument as practicable and the mean or middle point, if any difference between them taken for true meridian. Observations for true meridian were taken as often as practicable. After reaching the mountains north of Snake river it was often impossible to get near the line with camp so that nocturnal observations were out of the question. Many times too when on the line observations could not be made on account of clouds, which prevailed a great majority of the time among the mountains.

The best timber the country afforded was secured for posts. For the first 60 miles posts were hauled from Evanston.

Flagstaffs, Stadia Rods, and Other Sighting Targets
by Dr. Herbert W. Stoughton, P.E., P.L.S., C.P., Geodetic Engineer*

The flagstaff was employed to place a surveyor's assistant (chainman, axeman, etc.) on the required survey line/boundary or a point on the survey line(s) in order to measure angles, such as the one between a boundary line and the north-south meridian. The flagstaff has been known by numerous names—flagstaff, flagpole, range pole, range rod, etc. Also, there is another type of survey rod known as the "stadia rod" or "stadia board." In the nineteenth century General Land Office (GLO) contract literature the survey assistants using the flagstaff were called flaggers or flagmen. The persons handling the flagstaffs or range poles were untrained surveying assistants, but with some instruction were able to hold the pole vertically over a specific point for measuring angles or indicating location of boundary without difficulty.

Since the area being surveyed in Nebraska and Wyoming was "virgin"

---

*A professional engineer (civil), professional land surveyor, and certified photogrammetrist, Dr. Stoughton has written numerous books, reviews, technical papers, and reports. He taught surveying at the University of Michigan, SUNY Alfred A&T College, and headed the surveying and mapping program at the Metropolitan State College of Denver. He was also a geodesist with the U.S. Defense Mapping Agency, executing survey programs for the Department of Defense weapon systems and NASA.

(unsettled) with respect to the existence of boundaries, the forward flag-gers and the chainmen had to indicate the location of the survey boundary on the ground in order to reach the site of the next GLO corner. The flag-men had two essential roles: (1) to place the flag at a previously estab-lished survey point/corner for the transitman to sight and establish a line of sight and from which to measure/layoff a previously determined angle to produce another survey line; and (2) with the assistance of the transit-man indicate the direction of the line to be surveyed so that chainmen, axemen, and mound builders (monumentation personnel) could clear the survey line of impediments (trees, brush, undergrowth, etc.), and execute their associated tasks. The chainmen were required to chain the distance along the survey line. If either end-point of the surveyors' chain was off-set from the survey line a significant error could be introduced predicated on the linear magnitude of the offset.

Flagstaffs and range poles (or rangepoles) were usually six to ten feet long, and three inches, or less, in diameter. In cross-section these units would be circular, hexagonal, or octagonal. The stadia boards were about four inches wide, seldom exceeded six-inch widths, and usually were about the same length as flagstaffs/rangepoles.* Usually, these boards were painted white (the background) and had numbers or geometrical symbols (triangles, squares, etc.) painted on the board's face. The arrange-ment of these numbers and symbols made it feasible to measure linear distances from the transit to the stadia board. There are several proce-dures including stadia (a method incorporating principles of geometrical optics in the telescope and directly reading the rod scale) and vertical or horizontal subtense (utilizing computational trigonometry). The proce-dures utilize the common surveyor's transit without any specialized acces-sories. Subtense methods were never popular in the United States. Stadia surveying was predominately employed until the advent of electronic tacheometry (c. 1970s). Stadia surveying was discovered in about 1770, by James Watt (inventor of the stationary steam engine in Scotland). The sta-dia-measured distances are not as accurate as measuring distances with a surveyor's chain, but can be used when lower accuracy distances are suit-able. In some surveys an "error" in a distance measurement of 2 to 4 per-

---

*Certain surveying and mapping organizations designed and used stadia boards that were about 16 feet long, but might have been as long as 20 feet. These latter boards were two pieces with a hinge in the middle (folding to one-half the length). The longer stadia boards were usually associated with national mapping and charting organiza-tions (Coast Survey; Lake Survey; Geological Survey; Corps of Engineers; etc.).

cent of the length of the line is acceptable. Reports have been published where surveyors have measured over 600 stadia observations (distances) in an 8-hour survey session. Stadia boards were predominately made of wood, and after 1900, range poles were manufactured from aluminum or steel. After the Korean War plastic or polymer materials have been used to make both range poles and stadia boards.

Although the previous discussion addressed stadia boards, there is a group of these instruments known as stadia rods and level rods. These were two, three, or four pieces of wood which, instead of folding, slid in grooved tracks to be extended to their full length. These rods were about two to two and one-half inches wide and a little thicker because of their design. On the face of each section was a linear scale addressing only the length from a specific graduation on the rod section below when the section was extended. Usually, the smallest graduation thickness was 0.01 foot. Every foot was numbered. The background of the rod face was white, and the graduations were black. On some rods, the 0, 5, and 10 numbers were red. By World War I, these stadia rods had replaced the stadia boards in many engineering and surveying organizations, except for the special boards used by the Federal and specialized organizations, which usually manufactured their own boards. Inspection of the stadia rods literature will find that they were variously named. These names were based upon the geographical location at which they originated and the slight differences between the patterns of the scales. For instance, there have been the Boston rod, Chicago rod, Detroit rod, Frisco (San Francisco) rod, New York rod, and Philadelphia rod, to identify a few. All these units were basically the same, but were regionally used. However, by the 1970s, the Chicago, Frisco, and Philadelphia rods became the predominate rods, and were manufactured through the last quarter of the twentieth century, until the advent of electronic tacheometry.

Mr. Richards was working on the GLO contract surveys in Nebraska. These surveys specifically laid out the townships and subdivided them into sections. Usually, the survey party had two flaggers providing back sights and fore sights for survey alignment and taping/chaining, and the surveys were conducted under the jurisdiction of the local U.S. Surveyor General (Nebraska in this case). The traditional flag poles were usually wood, had a flag attached, and frequently were not painted. For the two Wyoming surveys with which Mr. Richards was associated, the assignment was to lay out and monument the territorial/state boundaries, and were conducted under the direction of the Commissioner of the General

Land Office (Washington, D.C.). State/territorial surveyors general had no jurisdiction over these projects during the contract period (which ended 30 June 1910). Also, the survey equipment, education/training of the survey personnel (including an astronomer), and the survey procedures were vastly different from those procedures employed in the Nebraska surveys. The boundary survey parties sometimes used flagstaffs and stadia boards. On the Wyoming surveys, it appears that flag staffs were not used, and when alignments were needed, the stadia boards were used (which was acceptable). Both types of equipment could adequately complete the assignment.

During the era of these surveys, flagstaffs and stadia boards were commonly "homemade." The previous stated dimensions were common, but some surveyors decorated the units (diamonds, squares, etc.) to facilitate easy sighting/location in the field. Also, a spirit level (vial) was attached to the reverse side of the staff/board. This permitted the flagger/rodman to hold the staff truly vertical while standing behind the unit and watching the instrumentman/transitman. The flagman would point the face of the rod toward the survey instrument, such as a transit. By standing behind the board/staff, the flagman could monitor the level vial's bubble for verticality and watch the instrumentman's directions (by hand signals) to place the flagstaff on the predetermined survey line.

The plumb bob with target card were two other "sighting targets" used. The plumb bob gained popularity on engineering and municipal surveying projects because the surveyors required more accurate angular data and alignment placement. Also, the sight distances were considerably shorter (less than 300–400 feet). Eventually, a target card was attached to the plumb-bob cord containing a checkered board design (four quarters) in red and white. At distances over about 200 feet, the plumb-bob cord is difficult to see (and bisect) with the surveyor's transit. However, with the target attached (the cord was in the same straight line with the vertical graduation division line) the surveyor had little difficulty sighting the cord.

The stadia board mentioned earlier was specifically designed to facilitate the measurement of linear distances optically. To the uninitiated, the stadia board, flagstaff, range pole, are just surveyor's accessories. However, on the face(s) of the stadia boards there are carefully applied numbers and line/block graduations. The board is painted white and the graduations and numerals are either red or black (or both colors). The stadia boards were developed to make it possible to optically measure sight distances between the board and the transit/level. In the arrangement of the lenses inside the telescope, a reticule (system of cross hairs) is placed at the telescope's focal plane. When viewed through the telescope, four black lines—one vertical and three horizontal—appear. The three horizontal lines (also called threads or wires) appear to be evenly spaced. The surveyor would point the telescope at the stadia board. When properly focused on the board, the threads appear to lie on the stadia board's scale (these are called intercepts). Subtract one intercept from either of the two remaining intercepts to compute a "stadia difference." Multiply this difference by the appropriate factor. Today, these factors are usually 100, 200, or 300. The resulting product is called the sight distance between the center of the transit or level and the face of the stadia rod/stadia board. I have made and used a stadia board made from a 1 by 4 inch board between 14 and 16 feet long (folding to one-half that length). Stadia distances are not as accurate as chaining (estimates are up to about five percent uncertainty). Throughout the history of the GLO/BLM, stadia surveying was the very last procedure for linear distance measurement. Only when the most adverse topographic conditions, such as the 1874 Wyoming boundary survey, were encountered the deputy surveyor could petition the surveyor general for permission to employ stadia surveying techniques.

To my knowledge most flagstaffs were "homemade," or locally made. If there were any specific markings/symbols on flagstaffs, they were probably the preference of the surveyor or local custom. In the GLO surveys, flaggers were to indicate where the survey line/boundary should be in the field. It should be noted that the GLO deputy surveyors and assistants were mostly laying out original boundaries in a minimally mapped countryside. Occasionally, deputy surveyors did retrace established surveys, but this effort was minimal, and necessary to start/continue new surveys.

Most land surveyors needed to monument a survey line/boundary on the ground using the compass for the bearing/direction of the boundary. To my knowledge, flagstaffs were not a standard item in instrument manufacturers' (Gurley, Buff & Buff, White, etc.) inventories. They were not described in manufacturers' catalogues or surveying textbooks. When surveyors replaced the compass with the surveyor's transit, and angles between survey lines were observed/measured, the range pole became an important accessory. By the 1880s, range poles were manufactured by principal surveying instrument manufacturers. By 1900 the surveyor's plumb bob and range poles were the primary targets to sight upon for measuring angles.

Classical spherical trigonometry, cont. from p. 77 The enclosed drawings illustrate the principle (Figures 1 and 2). The viewer is above the North Pole looking downward onto the plane of latitude at which the survey is occurring (for our case latitude 41°). In surveyor's language, the field procedure is known as the "tangent-offset" method. The surveyor set the theodolite at point *C* (having a known/specified latitude and longitude), and then points the theodolite's objective (telescope) due north (usually determined by observing Polaris (North Star/pole star) or other stars. Then, turning counter-clockwise or left (to look westward) lay off a right angle (90°). This is a right angle perpendicular to the plane of the meridian (plane of longitude). The line of sight is *CA*, while arc *CO* is the arc of the parallel of latitude through *C*. It is desired to set the survey monument on the parallel of latitude (at *O*). At one mile (arc *OC*), (due to the earth's curvature) point *A* is 0.874 link (0.577 ft. or 6.92 inches) south of the true parallel of latitude. Also, the distance *AC* is 5,280.000 feet. At six miles (arc *OC*), the earth's curvature has point *A* at 31.42 links (20.735 ft. or 20 ft. 8.8 in.) south of the (true) parallel of latitude.

The general survey procedure to lay off one township was to set the theodolite at *A*, turn the counterclockwise angle of 90° from the meridian (True North). Lay off the appropriate (computed) arc distances from *C* to *A* (1), *A* (2), *A* (3), *A* (4), *A* (5), and *A* (6). At each point turn the appropriate counterclockwise angle from the survey line *C A* (*i*) (computed). This angle is to the line *A* (*i*) − *O*(*i*) [*i* = 1, 2, 3, 4, 5, 6, etc.] (the *offset*) is a portion of the meridian (due North) *A* (*i*) − *O* (*i*) − *B*. The points *O* (*i*) are the true

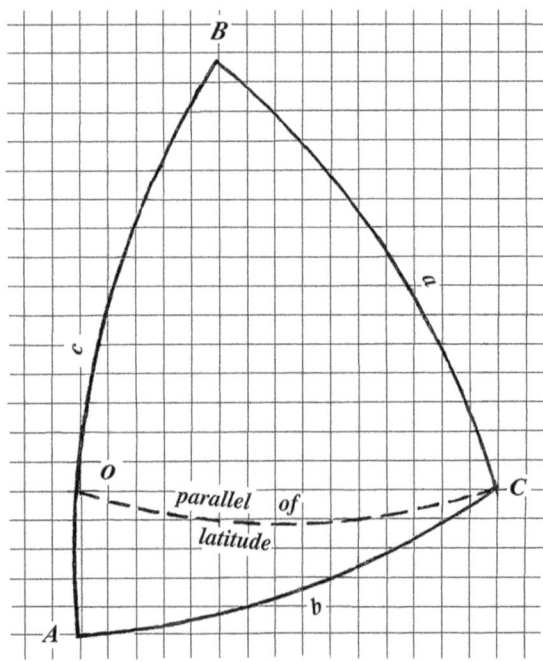

Figure 1. The geometry of the tangent-offset method to lay out a parallel of latitude

points on the parallel of latitude at specific distances from C. Theoretically, the number of points $[A(i)]$ is not limited to 6. However, periodically, the surveyor will set the instrument (theodolite) at either the offset or the corresponding $A(i)$ where the astronomic latitude and longitude are observed/determined to verify that the survey is "on course" [departure in latitude from the true parallel and approximate distance westward along the parallel toward the stipulated meridian].

The instructions for the survey were to start at the southeast corner of Wyoming (set by O. N. Chaffee in 1869), proceed westerly along the parallel of latitude (41°), set a permanent monument at every mile (80 chains). Today (2020), these monuments are called a *mile post* (MP), (usually not a *mile corner* (MC)). I suspect Richards used "M.C." in his diaries (edited to M.P. throughout) because, in his 1869 work, he was setting section corners, which are one mile apart. Without reviewing the actual field notes, it is unclear what caused the line to be so far south. I suspect that early on in surveying this parallel of latitude Richards did not understand that the physically surveyed line $(C-A)$ was not the parallel of latitude (as discussed earlier). The survey party had an eminently qualified astronomer, Augustus MacConnel (from Harvard University). I suspect that Richards may not have been familiar with spherical trigonometry, and did not realize that the actual survey line would depart south from the parallel of latitude (as shown in Figures 1 and 2) until he had witnessed MacConnel's efforts. The party was very fortu-

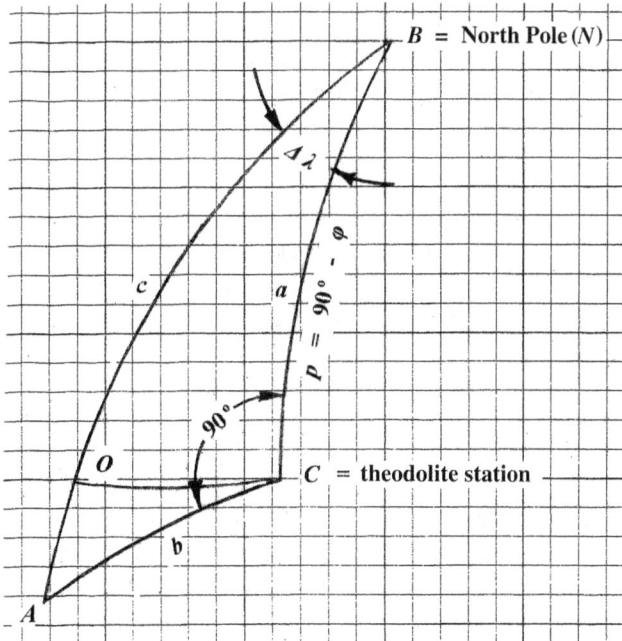

Figure 2. The geometry of the spherical triangle and the tangent-offset method

nate to have a very knowledgeable and experienced astronomer (MacConnel) who was well versed in addressing this problem. MacConnel would execute a similar astronomic survey in 1902 for the General Land Office. —Dr. Stoughton (HWS)

Theodolites: The term "theodolite" (comes from "theodolitus") is the European name for all forms of surveying, mapping, engineering, astronomical transits. Until the early decades of the nineteenth century, the telescope was so long that it could not revolve a full circle in the vertical plane. If the surveyor wanted to observe behind him, to prolong a straight line, there were two procedures which could be employed. On, the telescope was "lifted up" from the wyes (Y's) its trunnion axis was resting and reversed the telescope. The second method was to read the angle of the horizontal circle on the backsight, unclamp the horizontal motion, and rotate the telescope around the horizon to the circle reading exactly 180 degrees from the backsight reading. These two procedures accomplished the procedure of "transiting the instrument/telescope." However, a number of instrumental errors resulted, which degraded the accuracy of the surveying observation. Eventually, instrument makers were able to shorten the length of the telescope without serious degradation of the optical capabilities. Then, with the shortened telescopes, the telescopes could rotate through the entire vertical circle without contacting the instrument's plate. Then, instrument makers and surveyors called these instruments transit theodolite, which indicated the instrument had the ability to transit the telescope. Eventually, the name "theodolite" was dropped. In Europe and elsewhere around the world, "theodolite" is the correct name for all the instruments.

In the United States, the surveying community used the term transit. Until recently, when the term theodolite was used, American surveyors identified it with European-made instruments. When I use the term theodolite, it results from my education and the use of instruments from different countries and organizations.—HWS

Mound building. The concept of creating mounds as memorials probably got its start when the early General Land Office surveys left the forests of the Old Northwest Territory and Alabama, Mississippi, and Louisiana for the open prairie. For the surveys of Minnesota, Nebraska, western Illinois, Missouri, and Arkansas, the *Instructions to Survey the Public Lands* (1855 and later) specified that if no trees were near the site of the survey monument (section corner, one-quarter section corner, meander corner, or witness corner), a mound was to be raised around the survey corner monument. The perimeter of the mound would be a trench (which provided the earth for the mound). As the GLO. surveys progressed into the Rocky Mountains, the deputy surveyor was encouraged to collect local rocks/stones to place at the base of the survey monument. I personally have not seen any evidence of a dirt mound (in the plains of eastern Colorado and eastern Wyoming). In eastern Wyoming (and probably eastern Colorado) these mounds would have been obliterated by "blow sand" from the great dust storms of the 1920s and 1930s. In eastern Wyoming I have found section corners buried under three to four feet of blow sand.—HWS

The Tangent-Offset Method for Surveying a Parallel of Latitude
by Dr. Herbert W. Stoughton

*Figure A-1 depicts a right spherical triangle **ABC** with the right angle situated at **C**.*

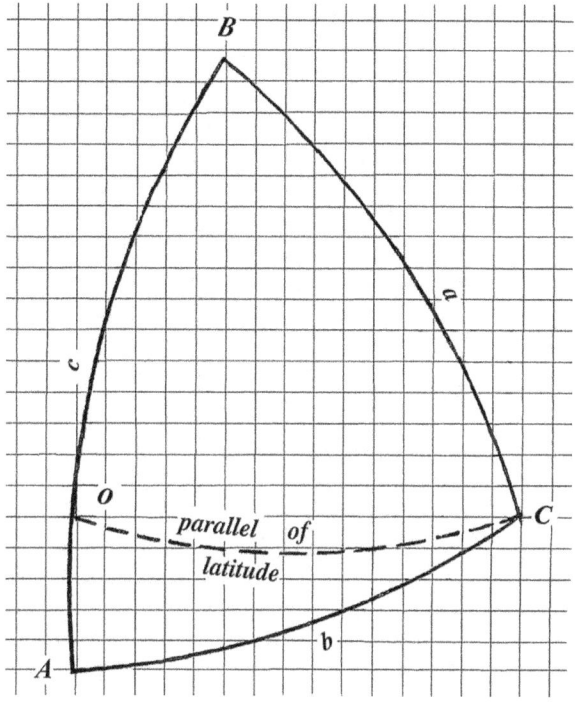

Figure A-1

For a right spherical triangle, the following formulas apply:

$$\sin a = \tan b \cot B = \frac{\tan b}{\tan B} \qquad \text{(A.1.a)}$$

$$\sin a = \sin a \sin c \qquad \text{(A.1.b)}$$

$$\sin b = \tan a \cot A = \frac{\tan a}{\tan A} \qquad \text{(A.1.c)}$$

$$\sin b = \sin B \sin c \qquad \text{(A.1.d)}$$

$$\cos A = \tan b \cot c = \frac{\tan b}{\tan c} \qquad \text{(A.1.e)}$$

$$\cos A = \cos a \sin B \qquad \text{(A.1.f)}$$

$$\cos B = \tan a \cot c = \frac{\tan a}{\tan c} \tag{A.1.g}$$

$$\cos B = \cos b \sin A \tag{A.1.h}$$

$$\cos c = \cot A \cot B = \frac{1}{\tan A \ \tan B} \tag{A.1.i}$$

$$\cos c = \cos a \cos b \tag{A.1.j}$$

If the earth is a *sphere*, the known (given) quantities are: C (90°); a (90° − φ_c); B ($\Delta \lambda$).

In Figure A-1:

    i.   Arcs $A\,B$, $A\,C$, and $B\,C$ are portions of *great circles*.

    ii.   Pass a plane perpendicular to both the plane of the great circle arcs $A\,B$ and $B\,C$. The arc of intersection of this new plane with the surface of the sphere intersects arc $A\,B$ at point O. Unless side a equals 90° (φ_c equals 0°); arc $B\,O$ equals the arc length of side a; and the arc length of side c is greater than a.

    iii. The radius of the sphere is R, (also designated Rφ).

    iv. For "short distances" along arc $O\,C$, the linear arc length of $O\,C$ is:

$$O\,C \text{ (linear)} = R \cos \varphi_c \ (\Delta \lambda)_r \tag{A.2}$$

Note: The subscript "**r**" indicates that the angular quantity is reported in radian measure, where:

$$1 \text{ arc second} = 1" = 4.8481\ 3681\ 1095\ 36 \times 10^{-6} \text{ radian}$$

And:

$$\Delta \lambda = B$$

If arc $O\,C$ is specified as a linear distance (which is the usual case), then:

$$\Delta \lambda" = \frac{O\,C \text{ (linear)}}{R \cos \varphi_c \ \text{arc } 1"} \tag{A.2.a}$$

Recall, and rearrange eq. No. (A.1.a):

$$b = \tan^{-1} \left(\sin a \ \tan B \right) \tag{A.3}$$

$$= \tan^{-1} \left(\cos \varphi_c \ \tan \Delta \lambda \right) \tag{A.3.a}$$

Then, by the law of sines (spherical trigonometry):

$$\frac{\sin a}{\sin A} = \frac{\sin b}{\sin B} = \frac{\sin c}{\sin C} \tag{A.4}$$

Then, since a, b, and B are known:

$$A = \sin^{-1} \left(\frac{\sin a \ \sin B}{\sin A} \right) \tag{A.5}$$

Note: There are *two* numerical values for angle A $[90° - \theta$ or $90° + \theta]$. For this problem, the numerical magnitude of A is always *less than* $90°$.

Since C equals $90°$, $\sin C$ equals $+1$. Then:

$$c = \sin^{-1}\left(\frac{\sin a}{\sin A}\right) \tag{A.6.a}$$

$$c = \sin^{-1}\left(\frac{\sin b}{\sin B}\right) \tag{A.6.b}$$

The arc length (a linear quantity) CA, which must be surveyed is:

$$b = R\,(b_r)$$

Where: b_r equals the angular value of the arc CA converted to *radians*. Then, arc OA (in angular units) is:

$$OA = c - a \tag{A.7}$$

$$OA \text{ (linear)} = R_\varphi\,(c - a)_r \tag{A.8}$$

Geodetic Application

The previous discussion addressed the problem employing an earth being a *pure sphere*. Unfortunately, the mathematical model of the earth used in geodesy and surveying is an *oblate ellipsoid*. The departure from a sphere is very small. There have been over one dozen nationally/internationally recognized/accepted ellipsoids (called reference ellipsoids). If a equals the length of the equatorial radius, and b equals the polar radius, then the ratio $b : a$ for the two reference ellipsoids employed by the General Land Office are:

Bessel:

$$\frac{b}{a} = 0.9966\ 5722\ 6846$$

Clarke 1866:

$$\frac{b}{a} = 0.9966\ 0992\ 4696$$

Note: The quantities a and b related to the reference ellipsoids have no mathematical relationship to the "a" and "b" in the spherical triangle.

The mathematical parameters defining the reference ellipsoid are the semi-major axis (equatorial radius) (a) and the square of the first eccentricity (e^2). The numerical values are:

Table A.1

Ellipsoid	a (in meters)	e^2
Bessel	6,377,397.155	0.0066 7437 2231 8022
Clarke 1866	6,378,206.4	0.0067 6865 7997 6096

From analytical geometry and calculus there are *four* principal radii of the reference ellipsoid at every point. Two of these radii are *primary* and the third and fourth radii are *secondary*. The primary radii are called the *radius of the ellipse in the meridian* (meridional radius) and the *radius of the normal* (to the meridian) (the normal). And:

Radius in the meridian:

$$R_\varphi = \frac{a\,(1 - e^2)}{\sqrt{(1 - e^2 \sin^2 \varphi\,)^3}}$$

(A.9)

The Normal:

$$N = \frac{a}{\sqrt{(1 - e^2 \sin^2 \varphi\,)}}$$

(A.10)

Where:
a = length of the semi-major axis of the reference ellipsoid.
e^2 = square of the first eccentricity of the reference ellipsoid.

The primary radii are employed to calculate the secondary radii, and are employed for the highest accuracy. The secondary radii are employed for less accurate work, but if carefully applied over reasonable areal extent, will produce accurate results.

When the geodetic latitude for the survey of a parallel of latitude is chosen (φ_C), then the there are two spherical radii applied.

The radius of the reference ellipsoid required to compute the radius of the parallel of latitude is:

$$N_C = \frac{a}{\sqrt{(1 - e^2 \sin^2 \varphi_C)}}$$

(A.11)

Then, the radius of the parallel φ_C is:

$$r_C = N_C \cos \varphi_C$$

(A.12)

In the corresponding spherical triangle:

$$C = 90°$$

$$a = 90° - \varphi_C \qquad \text{|side } \boldsymbol{B\,C} \text{ in the spherical triangle|}$$

Then:

$$\varDelta \lambda" = \frac{O\,C \text{ (linear)}}{r_C \text{ arc } 1"}$$

(A.13.a)

$$= \frac{O\,C \text{ (linear)}}{N_C \cos \varphi_C \text{ arc } 1"}$$

(A.13.b)

$$= \frac{O\,C \text{ (linear) } \sqrt{1 - e^2 \sin^2 \varphi_C}}{a \cos \varphi_C \text{ arc } 1"}$$

(A.13.c)

Then, from the previously described spherical trigonometry:

Eqs. No.s (A.3) and (A.3.a):

$$b = \tan^{-1}\left(\sin a \tan B\right) \tag{A.3}$$

$$= \tan^{-1}\left(\cos \varphi_c \tan \varDelta \lambda\right) \tag{A.3.a}$$

Eq. No. (A.4):

$$A = \sin^{-1}\frac{\sin a \sin B}{\sin b} = \sin^{-1}\frac{\sin \varDelta \lambda \cos \varphi_c}{\sin b} \tag{A.14}$$

Recall eqs. No.s (A.6.a) and (A.6.b):

$$c = \sin^{-1}\left(\frac{\cos \varphi_c}{\sin A}\right) \tag{A.15.a}$$

$$= \sin^{-1}\left(\frac{\sin b}{\sin \varDelta \lambda}\right) \tag{A.15.b}$$

Then, the offset $A\,O$ (an angular quantity) is:

$$A\,O = c - a$$

$$= c - 90° + \varphi_c$$

Then, the offset distance at A to set point O on the parallel of latitude through C is $A\,O$ (a linear quantity). Then:

$$A\,O \text{ (linear)} = (A\,O)_r \frac{a(1 - e^2)}{\sqrt{(1 - e^2 \sin^2 \varphi_c)^3}} \tag{A.16}$$

The linear distance $C\,A$ is:

$$C\,A \text{ (linear)} = b_r N_c \tag{A.17}$$

Numerical Example

Until 1986, only two different reference ellipsoids had been employed to compute the tangents and offsets to establish/monument a specific parallel of latitude. Below is a comparison of the numerical results to establish a monument six miles west of the starting corner (point C) at geodetic latitude φ_c equals $41° \ 00' \ 00''$. The two reference ellipsoids were the Bessel and the Clarke 1866.

Bessel	Clarke 1866
$a = 6{,}377{,}397.155$ m.	$a = 6{,}378{,}206.4$ m.
$e^2 = 0.0066\ 7437\ 2231\ 8022$	$e^2 = 0.0067\ 6865\ 7997\ 6096$
eq. No. (A.9):	eq. No. (A.9):
$R\varphi = 6{,}362{,}227.869$ m.	$R\varphi = 6{,}362{,}819.649$ m.

continued on next page   continued on next page

Bessel		Clarke 1866	

eq. No. (A.11):

$$N_C = 6,386,577.239 \text{ m.}$$

eq. No. (A.12):

$$r_C = 4,820,011.027 \text{ m.}$$

$O\,C$ (linear) $= 6$ mi.$(1,609.3472\ 187)$

$$= 9,656.0833 \text{ m.}$$

eq. No. (A.13.a):

$$\Delta \lambda" = 413.2169\ 29"$$
$$\Delta \lambda = 0°\ 06'\ 53.2169\ 29"$$

eq. No. (A.3.a):

$$b = 0°\ 05'\ 11.8589\ 5"$$

eq. No. (A.14):

$$A = 89°\ 55'\ 28.9068\ 1"$$

eqs. No.s (A.15.a) and (A.15.b):

$$c = 49°\ 00'\ 00.2049\ 4"$$
$$c = 49°\ 00'\ 00.2049\ 4"$$

$A\,O$ (angular) $= c - a = 0.2049\ 4"$

$A\,O$ (linear) $= 6.321$ m.

$$= 20.739 \text{ ft.}$$
$$= 248.872 \text{ in.}$$
$$= 31.42 \text{ links}$$

$C\,A$ (linear) $= 9,656.0888$ m.

$$= 31,680.018 \text{ ft.}$$
$$= 6 \text{ mi., } 0.018 \text{ ft.}$$

eq. No. (A.11):

$$N_C = 6,387,517.633 \text{ m.}$$

eq. No. (A.12):

$$r_C = 4,820,720.751 \text{ m.}$$

$O\,C$ (linear) $= 6$ mi.$(1,609.3472\ 187)$

$$= 9,656.0833 \text{ m.}$$

eq. No. (A.13.a):

$$\Delta \lambda" = 413.1560\ 93"$$
$$\Delta \lambda = 0°\ 06'\ 53.1560\ 93"$$

eq. No. (A.3.a):

$$b = 0°\ 05'\ 11.8130\ 4"$$

eq. No. (A.14):

$$A = 89°\ 55'\ 28.9449\ 5"$$

eqs. No.s (A.15.a) and (A.15.b):

$$c = 49°\ 00'\ 00.2048\ 8"$$
$$c = 49°\ 00'\ 00.2048\ 8"$$

$A\,O$ (angular) $= c - a = 0.2048\ 8"$

$A\,O$ (linear) $= 6.320$ m.

$$= 20.735 \text{ ft.}$$
$$= 248.822 \text{ in.}$$
$$= 31.42 \text{ links}$$

$C\,A$ (linear) $= 9,656.0888$ m.

$$= 31,680.018 \text{ ft.}$$
$$= 6 \text{ mi., } 0.018 \text{ ft.}$$

Length of the Parallel of Latitude 41 ° 00' 00' from 104 ° W to 110 ° W

By legal statute, the latitude of the south boundary of Wyoming was 41 ° 00' 00" N., extending westerly from 104 ° 00' 00" W to 110 ° 00' 00" W longitude. The question is: "Is the linear length of the south boundary of Wyoming different numerical values for the two reference ellipsoids?"

Given: $\quad \varphi_C = 41°\ 00'\ 00"$

$\quad\quad\quad r_C$ (Bessel) $= 4,820,011.027$ m.

$\quad\quad\quad r_C$ (Clarke 1866) $= 4,820,720.751$ m.

Computation:

$$\Delta \lambda = 6°\ 00'\ 00"$$
$$= 21,600"$$

$A\,O$ (linear : Bessel) $= \Delta \lambda" \ r_C$ arc 1" $= 504,750.374$ m.

$$= 1,656,001.853 \text{ ft.}$$
$$= 313.6367 \text{ mi.}$$

$A\,O$ (linear : Clarke 1866) $= \Delta \lambda" \ r_C$ arc 1" $= 504,824.696$ m.

$$= 1,656,245.692 \text{ ft.}$$
$$= 313.6829 \text{ mi.}$$

Diff.: 0.0462 mi. $= 243.936$ ft.

Quod erat demonstratum

* * * * * * *

Astronomical Azimuth Observations/Determinations
by Dr. Herbert W. Stoughton

The use of the term "taking an azimuth" is technically incorrect surveying/mapping terminology. By **definition**: "Azimuth is the horizontal direction (angle) reckoned from the meridian plane." [Hugh Chester Mitchell (15 April 1879 – 20 November 1956): *Definitions of Terms Used In Geodetic and Other Surveys*; U.S.C.&G.S. Spec. Publ. No. 242 (Washington: G.P.O. 1948); p. 8]. Mitchell continues: "By definition the meridian is *assumed*; *astronomic*; *geodetic*; *grid*; *magnetic*; *true*; etc." These various azimuths are based upon how the meridian (meridional plane) is itself *defined*. For the General Land Office surveys, the meridian chosen is astronomic. The astronomic azimuth is the clockwise horizontal angle at the point of observation measured from the vertical plane containing the center of the theodolite "point" (hereafter called the theodolite) and the celestial pole clockwise to the vertical plane through the theodolite and the celestial object (star, planet, sun).* The celestial pole is that point on the celestial sphere (the apparent surface upon which the stars are situated) where the extension of the earth's axis of rotation (upward) (the earth's pole) intersects the celestial sphere. When a surveyor observes a star (or the sun), the surveyor is measuring the horizontal angle from the vertical plane through the theodolite and the object (star/sun) to the vertical plane through the theodolite and a specific reference point (target, range pole, etc.) on the earth. At that *instance* when the surveyor bisects the star/sun, the precise time (either civil or sidereal) is recorded. At that moment in time the surveyor also reads the horizontal angle to the star/sun. Immediately, the surveyor measures the angle from the star/sun to the terrestrial target (which is also called the *azimuth mark*) on the earth. By subtracting the horizontal circle reading to the star/sun from the horizontal circle reading to the azimuth mark, the surveyor has the angle between the two objects. This angle is then *added to the azimuth* from the theodolite to the star/sun, to obtain the azimuth from the theodolite to the azimuth mark. Except for the instances of culmination (2) and elongation (2) [to be discussed shortly] the azimuth from the theodolite to the star must be computed. A person cannot "take" an azimuth, but "can transfer" the azimuth of a line (in this case) to a reference line on the surface of the earth (the theodolite station to the azimuth mark).

Before continuing this discussion, an introductory explanation about the star's "behavior" (journey across the heavens) is presented. Because the earth rotates about its polar axis and around the sun, careful monitoring of the geometrical position of the stars, the stars appear to move in concentric circles. The center of these concentric circles is the celestial pole (the extension of the earth's pole). Each star completes one "orbit" in 23 hrs. 56 min. 04.... sec. (the sidereal day). This means that the azimuth of the vertical plane between the theodolite and the star continuously changes. There are

---

*For an explanation of theodolite, see p. 258.

only two instances as the star moves through this "orbit" (astronomically called the *diurnal circle*) will the azimuth be *exactly the same value*. When the surveyor bisects the star (and notes the precise time—either civil or sidereal), the azimuth from the theodolite to the star is *only that numerical value* at **that instance in time**. If the star is observed a few minutes later, a new value of the azimuth from the theodolite to the star results. Figure 1 illustrates a star in the heavens (looking up from the earth). Every star has this geometrical relationship.

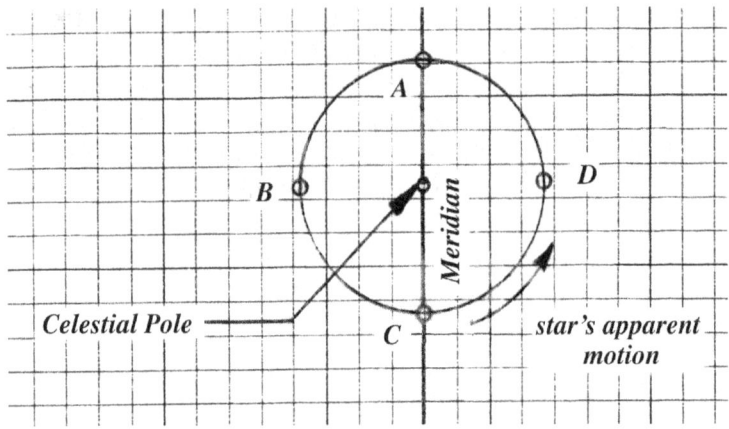

Figure 1. The motion of a star through one sidereal day

In Figure 1, the pole and the complete diurnal circle are visible. For stars south of the latitude (and a belt of stars north) of the theodolite the stars are only visible for a portion of the sidereal day, and are said to rise and set. However, whenever *any* of these stars are visible, they can be used to determine azimuths, latitudes, and longitude. Inspection of the star as it travels in its diurnal circle reveals it crosses the meridian (points *A* and *C*, and is said that the star is at *upper culmination (A)* or *lower culmination (C)*. For that brief *instance in time* the azimuth from the theodolite to the star is North (or azimuth 0° 00′ 00″) or South (or azimuth 180° 00′ 00″). When the star is at upper or lower culmination, it appears to move horizontally. Also, the center of the theodolite, the celestial pole, and the star are on a single straight line. When the star is at points *B* and *D*, the star is said to be a *western elongation (B)* and *eastern elongation (D)*.

A star's geographical location/position in the heavens (celestial sphere) is analogous to latitude and longitude on the earth, and these elements are called *declination* (latitude) and *right ascension* (longitude). The meridional distance from the celestial pole to the star is called the polar distance, which is the difference of 90° minus the star's declination. The arcs used between various points on the celestial sphere are portions of great circles. Thus, spherical trigonometry is the method of computing the various angles and arc lengths between objects and reference points. The North Star is the closest visible star (to the naked eye) to the north celestial pole. The North Star is a portion of the constellation Little Dipper (Little Bear or Ursae Minoris). If a person watches the Little Dipper for several hours, it would appear to rotate in the heaven, but the "tail star" (the North Star) appears to be stationary to our unaided senses, thus appearing to be at the "pole of revolution." In fact, the polar distance is approximately $0° 48' - 0° 49'$ (1983). This means that the azimuth from the theodolite to the North Star at elongation is approximately:

Western Elongation: Azimuth = $359° 12'$

Eastern Elongation: Azimuth = $0° 12'$

Since the star is continuously moving, the measurement of the angle from the star to the azimuth mark is needed to "preserve" the azimuth to the star on the earth, because it cannot be reobserved. We can observe the star at any other time, but we must compute the actual azimuth from the theodolite to the star, and then add the value to the angle observed for that particular observation from the star to the azimuth mark to memorialize the azimuth. This latter procedure is called observing the star's azimuth by the "any-hour-angle method."

For any stellar observation the latitude and longitude of the theodolite (station) and the declination and right ascension of each star are required. The general field procedure is depicted in Figure 2. If upper/lower culmination, or eastern/western elongation are to be employed, the surveyor must pre-compute the local time the event occurs in order for the observer to be afield and tracking/chasing the star "into" the event to set the line of sight from the theodolite to the star "exactly" when the event occurs. If the opportunity is "missed" or a check is desired, the surveyor must wait approximately six hours before the next event would occur. There are only four opportunities each sidereal day to make these four single determinations. For the any-hour-angle method, the surveyor (usually with an associate) must correctly identify the actual time (employing either a civil or a sidereal chronometer) when the star is observed (but the star can be observed at any time the opportunity presents itself). Then, employing spherical trigonometry, the right ascension and declination, the latitude and longitude of the theodolite, astronomical ephemeris data, and the time of observation, the direction to the meridian (azimuth $0° 00' 00''$) is determined by computing the azimuth from the theodolite to the star at the instance of observation. The surveyor makes multiple pointings to the star (time) and measures the horizontal angles from the star to the azimuth mark for each pointing.

The any-hour-angle method is considered more accurate and precise than the methods of culmination or elongation. Any of these procedures indirectly determines the "direction of the meridian through the theodolite." Inspection of the field notes/ observations will identify the procedure employed. If the surveyor prefers to use cul-

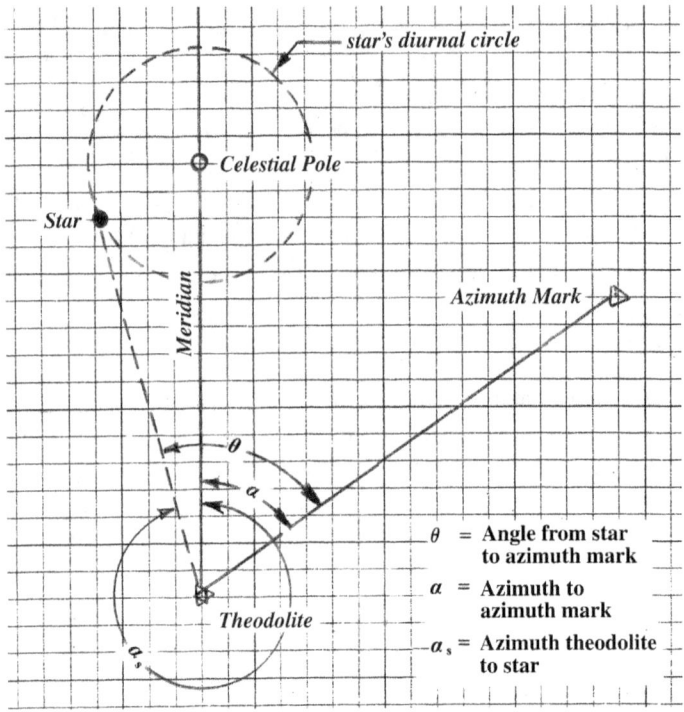

Figure 2. The observing setup for an azimuth determination

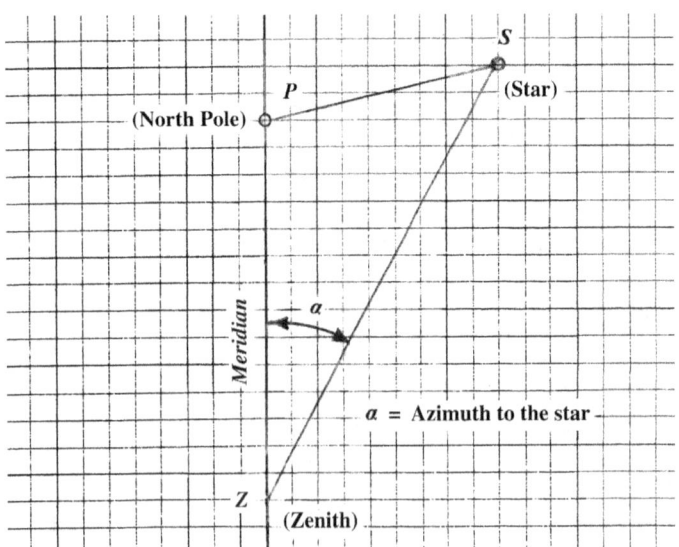

Figure 3. The P-Z-S triangle as seen from the earth

mination, it is possible during a portion of the year that both the upper and lower cul-minations could occur during daylight.

The same is true if elongation is preferred. The memorial of that determination is the azimuth of the line from the theodolite to the azimuth mark. The use of the term to "take an azimuth" is incorrect. All the processes are the "determination of the azimuth." In all the processes, we actually **determine** *three* azimuths: (1) the direction from the theodolite to the celestial pole; (2) the direction from the theodolite to the star; and (3) the direction from the theodolite to the azimuth mark. Only the third line is physically monumented (the theodolite station/point and the azimuth mark).

Figure 3 depicts the spherical triangle employed (called the "PZS" triangle) as viewed from the earth. The vertices are "P" (Pole); "Z" (zenith); and "S" (star or sun). The angle between the meridian and the line of sight from the theodolite to the star is the azimuth (α). The arc PS is the polar distance (90° minus the star's declination) to the star. The arc PZ is the polar distance to the theodolite (90° minus the latitude of the theodolite).

The author identifies the observing processes for either culmination or elongation as analogical (although some pre-observing computations are required) process. When employing these procedures, the latitude, longitude, and local time are required in order to compute the approximate time the event will occur. Then, the surveyor sets up the theodolite, locates the star, and "tracks/chases" the star until the culmina-tion/elongation "event" occurs. It is hoped/desired that the surveyor *instantaneously* "recognizes" the event's occurrence. Once the actual event occurs, we cannot "go back" to recreate the event. The statistical uncertainty of identifying the instance of the event's occurrence is extremely difficult to quantify. Then, the angle from the star to the azimuth mark is observed. Observing either at culmination or elongation is con-sidered less accurate than the any-hour-angle method. Using the North Star, or anoth-er star close to the celestial pole, is preferred, because the apparent "horizontal" or "vertical" motion of the star will start "to bend" very shortly (in time) after the event occurs. Depending upon the surveying equipment used (usually third-order theodo-lites/transits) having circles graduated between twenty arc seconds and one arc minute (usually the latter value), the accuracy of the azimuth between the theodolite and the azimuth mark could be uncertain as much as two times the horizontal circle's small-est graduation. However, employing the any-hour-angle method (even through upper/lower culmination or eastern/western elongation) provides a statistical evaluation for the "goodness" of the observations and subsequent azimuth. Also, the any-hour-angle method provides the opportunity to refine the resulting precision and accuracy of the azimuth from the theodolite to the azimuth mark.

Zenith Telescope

Hugh Chester Mitchell provided very concise definitions and descriptions of the zenith telescope and the zenith telescope method of latitude determination.

Zenith Telescope: A portable instrument adapted for the measurement of small differences of *zenith distance* (the great circle distance from the point on the celestial sphere directly above the theodolite and the star being observed), and used in the determination of *astronomic latitude*.

The instrument consists of a *telescope* equipped with an *ocular micrometer* (defined below) and a *spirit level*, and so mounted on a *vertical axis* that it may be placed in the plane of the *meridian* for observation on a star *culminating* north (or south) of the *zenith*, and then rotated 180° in azimuth and a second star observed as it *culminates* south (or north) of the zenith. The differences of the *zenith distances* of the two stars is measured with *micrometer*; the *spirit level* is used to determine any change that may occur in the direction of the axis of *rotation* of the telescope (also called the trunnion axis) between the two observations. In its present form, this instrument is essentially the invention (in 1834) of Captain Andrew Talcott (U.S. Topographic Engineers). [Mitchell, p. 87]

Ocular Micrometer: A *filar micrometer* so placed that its wire (in the reticule) moves in the principal focal plane of the *telescope*. Also termed an eyepiece micrometer.

The *ocular micrometer* is used in surveying and astronomical work for making accurate and precise measures of small *angles* between lines to objects viewed with the It is mounted in a frame which is perpendicular to the longitudinal axis of the telescope, and can be rotated to measure an *angle* in any plane containing that axis. It may be adjusted to measure *angles* in a plane which contains the longitudinal and horizontal axes of the telescope, as in observing *time* using the *transit micrometer* (which is an ocular micrometer); or it may be adjusted to measure *angles* in a plane containing the longitudinal axis but perpendicular to the *horizontal axis* of the *telescope*, as in observing latitude with the zenith telescope. [Mitchell, p. 58] **Zenith-telescope method - latitude determination:** A *precise* method of determining *astronomic latitude* by measuring the difference of the meridional *zenith distances* of two stars of known *declination*, one north and one south of the *zenith*.

The observations are made with the *zenith telescope* or with an astronomical transit which can be converted to serve as a *zenith telescope*, such as the *meridian telescope* and the *broken-telescope transit*. The two stars have approximately the same meridional *zenith distances*; and their *culminations* occur within a few minutes of the same time. The *astronomical latitude* of the point of observation will be one-half the sum of the *declinations* of the two stars, plus or minus one-half the differences of their *zenith distances*. This method is also known as the Horrebow-Talcott method, latitude determination, and the Talcott method, latitude determination. While Peter Horrebow (1740–1789) (not Harrebow) published an account of his method in 1732, it was buried in obscurity, and there is good reason believe that Captain Andrew Talcott (20 or 27 April 1797 – 22 April 1883) had no knowledge of Horrebow's work when he announced his own discovery of the method in 1834. [Mitchell, p. 87] —HWS

Sources and Notes

INTRODUCTION Pages 1–12

1. Marie Barlett, "Walking the Line," *Oregon Surveyor*, Vol. 40, No. 6 (Tigard, OR: Professional Land Surveyors of Oregon; November/December 2017), 15. http://www. associationpublications.com/flipbooks/plso/2017/NovDec/#zoom=z, accessed March 20, 2021. Information revised June 12, 2021, via email to author from Denny DeMeyer, retired, founder of Northwest Surveying and GPS, Lynden, Washington. At the time of the article's publication he was co-chairman of North American Land Surveyors.

2. All except Roosevelt are from "8 of America's most famous land surveyors," https:// pdhacademy.com/2017/08/31/8-Americas-famous-land-surveyors. Roosevelt: https://www. berntseninternational.com/news-events/three-surveyors-and-the-other-guy; Washington: https://founders.archives.gov/documents/Washington/02-01-02-0004; Jefferson: https:// founders.archives.gov/documents/Jefferson/01-01-02-0074; Mahbub Rashid, "Thomas Jefferson's Plan for the Rectilinear Survey of 1784," 84th Association of Collegiate Schools of Architecture Annual Meeting Regional Papers, 1996, https://www.acsa-arch.org/proceedings/ Annual%20Meeting%20Proceedings/ACSA.AM.84/ACSA.AM.84.125.pdf; Lincoln: http:// www.surveyhistory.org/abraham_lincoln_-_the_surveyor1.htm#:~:text=Abraham%20Lincoln %20-%20The%20Surveyor,a%20job%20as%20his%20assistant. All accessed June 20, 2022.

3. History Nebraska, RG0720.AM; and William A. Richards Collection, H-215/MSS 83, Wyoming State Archives (WSA).

4. Frison Collection, P82-57/36, Subject Negative 5568, WSA.

5. *Surveying and Land Information Systems*, Vol. 51, No. 4 (Bethesda, MD: American Congress on Surveying and Mapping; December 1991), 202-03.

6. "Historic Preservation on the Public Domain," *CRM*, Vol. 22, No. 4 (Washington: U.S. Department of the Interior, National Park Service, Cultural Resources; 1999), 24–26. http://www.nps.gov/CRM/v22n4.pdf, accessed June 6, 2021.

7. From author's extensive research of primary sources for a biography of Richards, particularly the collections at the Wyoming State Archives and American Heritage Center. Secondary sources, newspapers, and latter-day recollections, which tend to be unreliable, have been used sparingly and checked when possible.

8. Papers of A.V. Richards, courtesy of his great-granddaughter Sally Mergener, Germantown, WI.

9. Author's research; 5 boxes of letters in H82-61, William A. Richards Collection, WSA (hereafter cited as WSA H82-61); www.wyomingnewspapers.org, and newspaper clippings in family papers.

10. Silvio A. Bedini, "Along Came a Spider—Spinning Silk For Cross-Hairs," *The American Surveyor*, Vol. 2, Nos. 2 and 3 (Frederick, MD: Cheves Media LLC; March/April and May, 2005).

Steven Turner, "Spiders in the Crosshairs: Cobwebs, Instruments Makers, and the Search for the Perfect Line," *Journal of the Antique Telescope Society*, Vol. 1, 1992, 10. www.adsabs. harvard.edu/full/1992JATSo...1...10T, accessed June 20, 2022.

Dr. Herbert W. Stoughton, Wyoming surveyor, geodetic engineer, and historian, letter to author, June 1, 2020.

11. https://americanhistory.si.edu/collections/search/object/nmah_745877, accessed October 25, 2022.

12. Dr. Stoughton, letter to author, June 1, 2020.

13. https://americanhistory.si.edu/collections/search/object/nmah_1065091, accessed October 25, 2022.

14. Alonzo V. Richards, U.S. Astronomer and Surveyor, *Field Notes of the Survey of the Western Boundary of Wyoming Territory* (Washington: General Land Office, 1874). National Archives at College Park, College Park, MD. Record Group 49, Case F, #118, 243. The page numbers are from the duplicate notes at the state office of the BLM, Cheyenne: FN_226913_Survey_88315.pdf).

15. Barlett, 15.

16. Earl F. Henderson, PLS, "Retracing Colorado's South Line," *Professional Surveyor Magazine*, Vol. 30, No. 7 (Frederick, MD: XYHT. July 2010), http://www.zenithls.com/wp-content/uploads/2014/12/retracing-colorados-south-line.pdf, accessed June 11, 2021. Also https://www.archives.profsurv.com/magazine/article.aspx?i=70768, accessed June 21, 2022.

PART 1 YOUNG MAN GOES WEST Pages 13–72

1. History Nebraska, RG0720.AM.

2. Clarence L. Smith, Miner/Minor family genealogist, email to author, February 7, 2001.

3. http://www.templarhistory.com/independent-order-of-good-templars/, accessed April 18, 2022.

4. Nebraska County Map of 1859. In *Publications of the Nebraska State Historical Society, Vol. XIX*, Albert Watkins, ed. (Lincoln: Nebraska State Historical Society, 1919), 200.

5. Field notes of Contract #16, April 27, 1869, to Wiltse & Lonsdale. History Nebraska RGS 10, U.S. Surveyor General Records: 1850–1904, Surveying District of Kansas and Nebraska territories, and of the District of Nebraska, including Iowa. https://sso.nebraska.gov/pdf/fieldbooks/487.pdf, 4, accessed October 9, 2022.

6. Dr. Stoughton, letter to author, June 1, 2020.

7. http://history.nebraska.gov/collections/eugene-asa-carr-rg2688am, accessed April 18, 2022.

8. Senator Hitchcock served as U.S. Surveyor General for Iowa and Nebraska (a single office for two states/territories) from April 1867 until Livingston assumed the office in April 1869. Dr. Stoughton, letter to author, June 1, 2020, and other sources.
Lon's lobbying effort: A. V. Richards to W. A. Richards, March 7, 1871, WSA H82-61.

9. Frison Collection, P82-57/36, Subject Negative 26762, WSA.

10. Today it's the International Organization of Good Templars. "W.T.C." per *Ritual of the Independent Order of Templars*, 1864, 7. http://www.archive.org/details/ritualofindepend00inteiala, accessed June 24, 2022. Richards is listed as an officer in articles about Nebraska's Grand Lodges in the *Beatrice (Nebraska) Express* provided by the Nebraska State Historical Society, now History Nebraska. He was listed as the G.W.T. of that lodge on January 27, 1872, the G.W. Secretary on January 23, 1873 and on January 22, 1874. The office paid $300 per year. He may have met his future wife in Omaha's Hope of the West Lodge, of which she was a member.

11. "Vinnie Ream," http://www.aoc.gov/explore-capitol-campus/art/vinnie-ream, accessed June 24, 2022.

12. Wikipedia and other general sources.

13. Employment with *Tribune* per letters from A. V. Richards to W. A. Richards in April and May 1871, WSA H82-61. Employment with *Republican* in 1875 per Gov. W. A. Richards's interview in an unidentified Omaha newspaper, quoted in Mrs. Alice McCreery and Tacetta B. Walker, "Wyoming's Fourth Governor—William A. Richards," *Annals of Wyoming*, Vol. 20, No. 2 (Cheyenne: The Wyoming Historical Department; July 1948), 116.

14. A. C. Richards to W. A. Richards, February 21, 1876, WSA H82-61.

15. Richards's letters through 1884 in WSA H82-61 and items in his scrapbook, H63-86, in Alice Richards McCreery Collection, WSA.

16. A. V. Richards to W. A. Richards, March 10, 1871, WSA H82-61.

17. A. V. Richards to W. A. Richards, December 21, 1875, WSA H82-61.

18. A. V. Richards to W. A. Richards, October 13, 1878, WSA H82-61.

Part 2 Wyoming Boundary Surveys Pages 73–151
1873

1. William J. Gribb and Lawrence M. Ostresh, *Databases and Algorithms to Determine the Boundary of Wyoming* (Laramie: University of Wyoming, Department of Geography, n.d.), 1, 3, http://proceedings.esri.com/library/userconf/proc04/docs/pap1718.pdf, accessed June 22, 2022.

2. Bill Hubbard, Jr., *American Boundaries: The Nations, the States, the Rectangular Survey.* (Chicago: University of Chicago Press, 2009), 168. Also Dr. Stoughton, letter to author, June 1, 2020, and email to author, October 13, 2022.

3. Alonzo V. Richards, *Field Notes of the Survey of the South Boundary of Wyoming Territory* (Washington: General Land Office, 1873). National Archives at College Park, College Park, MD. Record Group 49, Case F, #116, 345-49. (Hereafter cited as "1873 field notes.")

4. "The First U.S. Naval Observatory 1844-1893," from Naval History and Heritage Command, http://www.history.navy.mil/browse-by-topic/exploration-and-innovation/first-us-naval-observatory.html, accessed October 28, 2022; other sources as well.

5. http://www.penryfamily.com/surveying/swcorner3.html, accessed November 14, 2020.

6. A. V. Richards to W. A. Richards, March 6, 1873, WSA H82-61.

7. Dr. Stoughton, letter to author, June 1, 2020.

8. 1873 field notes, 186.

9. Ibid., 342.

10. Dr. Stoughton, letter to author, June 1, 2020.

11. Crew was identified from letters (WSA H82-61) and the 1873 field notes. Names in brackets appear in the diary; some cannot be matched up with ones on the list.

12. Herbert W. Stoughton, "Silas Reed: The First Surveyor General of Wyoming," *Lines & Points*, Vol. 22, No. 2 (Cheyenne, WY: Professional Land Surveyors of Wyoming, April 2011), 7–8.

13. *The History of Jo Daviess County Illinois* (Chicago: H. F. Kett & Co., 1878), 4333. http://www.archive.org/details/historyofjodavie00kett, accessed October 28, 2022.

14. A. V. Richards's letter to his wife, August 5, 1873, A.V. Richards papers.

15. William A. Richards Family Papers, ACC 118, American Heritage Center, University of Wyoming (AHC).

16. 1873 field notes, 345.

17. Gene A. Thomsen, "Timing Space: Determining the Western Boundary of Nebraska," *Nebraska History* 80 (1999): 123-28, http://history.nebraska.gov/files/doc/publications/NH1999Boundary.pdf, accessed November 15, 2020.

18. http://wyoshpo.wyo.gov/homestead/pdf/historic_context_study_011311.pdf, accessed March 17, 2022.

19. *Cheyenne Daily Leader*, April 18, 1873.

20. Dr. Stoughton, "Reed."

21. Dr. Stoughton, letter to author, June 1, 2020.

22. Dick Blust, Jr., "The Diamond Hoax: a Bonanza That Never Was," https://wyohistory.org, published March 9, 2020, accessed June 9, 2021.

23. George Richards's brand ad, which mentions Red Creek, in *Sweetwater Gazette* of April 28, 1887, and in other issues on wyomingnewspapers.org. He is George W. Richards in a news item in that issue. The *Rock Springs Miner* of February 1, 1893, reported that his cattle, sheep and horses were in fine condition.

24. Chinese population per Barbara Ellen Bogert, "Evanston, Wyoming," wyohistory.org. The railroad reached Evanston in 1868; its population was 77 in 1870 and 1,277 in 1880, per http://eadiv.state.wy.us/demog_data/cntycity_hist.htm, accessed February 26, 2023.

25. Dr. Stoughton, letter to author, April 30, 2020, and 1873 field notes, 185.

26. Dr. Stoughton, letter to author, June 1, 2020.

27. 1873 field notes, 185.

28. Ibid.

29. Thomsen, "Timing Space."

30. 1873 field notes, 338–39.

31. 1874 field notes, 246–47.

32. A. V. Richards to W. A. Richards, November 8, 1873, WSA H82-61.

33. Ibid.

34. A. V. Richards to W. A. Richards, January 22, 1874, WSA H82-61.

1874 Boundary Survey

1. Unidentified newspaper clipping, A.V. Richards papers.

2. Alonzo V. Richards, U.S. Astronomer and Surveyor, *Field Notes of the Survey of the Western Boundary of Wyoming Territory* (Washington: General Land Office, 1874). National Archives at College Park, College Park, MD. Record Group 49, Case F, #118, 246–47. (Hereafter cited as "1874 field notes." The page numbers are from the duplicate notes at the state office of the BLM, Cheyenne: FN_226913_Survey_88315.pdf).

3. Ibid., 258–59.

4. *Rand, McNally & Co.'s Indexed Atlas of the World* (Chicago & New York, 1895).

5. 1874 field notes, "Plat No. 6, West Boundary of Wyoming, Longitude 34 West, From mile-post No. 142, to mile-post No. 170," Plat_83117_1.pdf, Wyoming office of the BLM, Cheyenne.

6. Gustavus R. Bechler and F. V. Hayden, "Map of the sources of Snake River: with its tributaries together with portions of the headwaters of the Madison and Yellowstone from surveys and observations of the Snake River Expedition," dated "187?," http://www.loc.gov/item/2009579469, call number G4242.S6 187–.B4, accessed February 20, 2020.

7. 1874 field notes, 246.

8. Ibid., 193–96, September 10, 1874.

9. Ibid., 257.

10. Alicia Murphy, park historian for Yellowstone National Park, email to author, February 25, 2019.

11. Dr. Stoughton, letter to author, June 1, 2020, and email, January 24, 2023.

12. John Wesley Powell, *Report of the Lands of the Arid Region of the United States.* (GPO, 1878). Report is discussed in Wallace Stegner, *Beyond the Hundredth Meridian: John Wesley Powell and the Second Opening of the West.* (Lincoln: University of Nebraska Press, 1982), 219–40.

13. *The United States Biographical Dictionary – Portrait Gallery – Eminent and Self-Made Men.* Illinois volume (Chicago and New York: American Biographical Publishing Co., 1883), 661, https://archive.org/details/unitedstatesbiog00amer/page/660/mode/2up?q=Richards, accessed November 25, 2022.

PART 3 SURVEYORS TREK BACK TO THE BOUNDARIES Pages 153–165

1. Howard B. Carpenter, U.S. Surveyor, *Field Notes of the Survey of the Boundary Line Between the States of Idaho and Montana* (Washington: General Land Office, 1907), National Archives at College Park, College Park, MD. Record Group 49, Case F, #30, Vol. 3, original notes, 251, 260.

2. Unidentified clipping in W. A. Richards' scrapbook, H63-86, Alice Richards McCreery Collection, WSA.

3. Carl W. Sumpter and Leslie J. Gross, *Field Notes of the Remonumentation of Certain Corners… in Wyoming*, Department of the Interior, Bureau of Land Management, Cheyenne, approved February 27, 2012, 1–5.

4. Raymond Hill, "Position of the North-South State Boundary Between Montana and Wyoming," *Topographic Division Bulletin*, Vol. 9, No. 1 (Washington, D.C.: U.S. Department of the Interior, Geological Survey, June 1959), 34–37.

5. Dr. Stoughton, June 1, 2020.

6. Murphy, February 25, 2019.

7. http://www.usgs.gov/media/images/sixth-principal-meridian, accessed June 13, 2022.

8. Scott A. Scherbel of Surveyor Scherbel, Ltd., Big Piney, Wyoming, email to author, March 16, 2020.

9. Margaret Matray, "Cmdr. Paul Scherbel, Big Piney," *Lines & Points*, Vol. 23, No. 1.

10. Jerry Penry, one of the surveyors, http://penryfamily.com/surveying/6thpm.html, accessed November 25, 2022. Also *The American Surveyor*, Vol. 4, No. 6.

11. Ronald K. Baugh and Paul N. Scherbel, *Original Field Notes of the Dependent Resurvey of the Boundary Between the States of Utah and Idaho from the Initial Point to Mile Post Number 1 and the West Boundary of the State of Wyoming from Mile Post Number 68 to Mile Post 70 Common to the States of Utah, Idaho and Wyoming.* United States Department of the Interior, Bureau of Land Management, approved August 28, 1992, 4. BLM Wyoming office, Cheyenne.

12. "Remonumentation of the Tri-State Corner for Wyoming–Utah–Idaho and the Initial Point for the 42nd Parallel," *Lines & Points*, Vol. 4, No. 3, October 1992, 9–10.

13. Edward M. Reading, PLS, former Wyoming surveyor and at the time of this writing county surveyor of San Luis Obispo County, California, email to author, July 29, 2022. Reading said he, Scherbel, and Todd Cedarholm set the new monument and that Reading was among the 20 who took part in Scherbel's preliminary reconnaissance of the Northwest Corner.

14. 1992 dependent resurvey field notes, 5.

15. Ibid., 2.

16. 1874 field notes, 194.

17. *Lines & Points,* October 1992, 9.

18. 1992 dependent resurvey field notes, 2.

19. They were still on display as of this writing. Phone call to a museum contact, January 28, 2023.

20. *Lines & Points*, October 1992, 9.

21. Plaque text is transcribed from a photo.

22. Jerry L. Messick, Stephen D. Albright, Ronald W. Allen, and Paul N. Scherbel, *Field Notes of the Remonumentation of the Northwest Corner of Wyoming, on the Montana State Boundary, of the Montana and Sixth Principal Meridians*, United States Department of the Interior, Bureau of Land Management, approved February 9, 1995, 1, 5–7. Thanks to Stanton J. Abell for providing the notes and inspiring the remonumentation story.

Small replicas of the stone under the marker were created for belt buckles. Reading, email to author, July 29, 2022.

23. BLM, "NW Corner of Wyoming Remonumentation" and "Idaho-Montana Corner on West Boundary of Wyoming Revisited," *Line & Points*, October 1994, 7–8. Articles were submitted by members of the cadastal survey office in the Wyoming branch of the BLM.

24. 1994 remonumentation field notes, 2.

25. Ibid., 4.

26. 1874 field notes, 193–96.

27. Glenn Borkenhagen, email to author, October 24, 2019.

28. Cody Schatz, email to author, September 8 and 12, 2019.

29. Transcribed from photo. Acronyms were explained in Schatz's email to author, September 12, 2019.

30. "Idaho-Montana Corner…," *Lines & Points*, October 1994, 7.

31. *The Summit County Bee*, Coalville, UT, October 4, 1996. From Paul Scherbel's scrapbook, scans of which were provided by Scott Scherbel in email to author, August 8, 2022. Also phone interview with, and text messages from, Welby Kim Aagard, August 12–20, 2022.

32. *Summit County Bee*, October 4, 1996.

33. Warranty Deed No. R 77676, dated September 24, 1996, Summit County, UT. Scherbel's scrapbook.

34. Unidentified newspaper clipping in Scherbel's scrapbook.

35. *Bee*, October 4, 1996.

36. Historical Marker Database, https://www.hmdb.org/m.asp, accessed August 21, 2022. Wording and punctuation confirmed by 1873 field notes, 335–36. Periods apparently got shot off. Photos in Scherbel's scrapbook taken at the remonumentation ceremony show the same damage, indicating little or no damage occurred after the remonumentation.

37. J. G. Staack, USGS Bulletin 913, "Triangulation in Utah 1871–1934," GPO, 1940, 19, https://pubs.usgs.gov/bul/0913/report.pdf, accessed August 11, 2022. Also the moderator of https://surveyorconnect.com/community/surveying-geomatics/testing-new-gnss-receiver-yesterday/, accessed June 5, 2022.

PART 4 EXPLORING AND HOMESTEADING IN WYOMING'S BIGHORN BASIN 167–208

1. Her photo is from author's collection. It must have been taken at the same time as the one on their wedding certificate, since her dress and hairdo are the same. His is from the certificate, in the W.A. Richards Collection, H82-61, WSA.

2. *BRAND BOOK* (Cheyenne: Wyoming Stock Growers' Association). C.T. & Co.'s is from the 1884 book and Booth & Crocker's is from 1885. Google books.

3. Certificate of Incorporation #958, filed on July 11, 1885, Johnson Co. Misc. Record "A," 278–79, copies at the Big Horn County offices in Basin, Wyoming, and the Washakie County offices in Worland, Wyoming.

4. http://www.shadedrelief.com/physical/pages/about.html, accessed June 1, 2023. Colorized.

5. "Irrigation Diversion Operation and Description Memoranda," prepared by BRS Engineering and published by Wyoming State Water Plan, Wyoming Water Development Office, Cheyenne, 2003. https://waterplan.state.wy.us/plan/bighorn/techmemos/diversions/bighorn. html, accessed June 15, 2023.
The original size of the Big Horn Ditch tract seems to have exceeded 15,000 acres. All but two of the 26 investors obtained patents, and a few sold out before Hanover came calling. The BLM's General Land Office Records website lists 23 of them: https://glorecords.blm.gov/ search, accessed again on June 15, 2023, and another is listed in the Johnson County land sales abstracts, for a total of 14,335.69 acres. If the other two had originally claimed a section each (and many of the parcels were smaller), the total acreage would have been 15,615.69.

6. Obtained from many primary-source documents such as letters and official records. Secondary sources and latter-day recollections have been used sparingly. Books and articles by Bighorn Basin historian Lawrence M. Woods, with whom author has exchanged information and documents, have been quoted extensively because he is so careful.

7. Letters in WSA H82-61.

8. An 1887 newspaper article said that the station, coal office, and agent's residence were moved in 1881 to facilitate coal shipments. "Carbon, A Victim of Progress," *Annals of Wyoming*, Vol. 19, No. 1, January 1947. The cowboy story is from article by John James Fox, "The Far West," *Annals of Wyoming*, Vol. 21, No. 1, January 1949. Fox was a newly arrived Englishman bedazzled by the Wild West.

9. George Cram, *Cram's Unrivaled Family Atlas of the World* (Chicago, IL: A. C. Shewey & Co., 1883), 76. David Rumsey Map Collection, https://davidrumsey.com, accessed June 5, 2023.

10. From a newspaper, *Wyoming and Its Future, Laramie Territory, 1887 Holiday Edition*. https://www.hannahistory.com/1868---1892-town-of-carbon-aka-old-carbon-and-carbon-city.html, accessed February 19, 2023.

11. Information about the various Quealys is available online. Numerous references to P. J. are contained in the Guide to Wyoming and the West Collections at the AHC.

12. https://topozone.com/wyoming/ Annotations derived from diary entries, current maps, consultation with Terril Mills, and WY Map by US Department of Interior, General Land Office, 1892, File/Item #132, Identifier MCDB_1266500205, WSA.

13. *CATTLE BRANDS, Published by the Wyoming Stock Growers' Association, Second Edition.* (Chicago: The J. M. W. Jones Stationery & Printing Co., 1883).

14. Multiple sources, particularly Lawrence M. Woods's "When Cattle Came to—and then Left—the Nowood Valley," *Annals of Wyoming: The Wyoming History Journal*, Vol. 89, No. 1, 27–28.

15. *BRAND BOOK for 1884, Published by the Wyoming Stock Growers' Association, Third Edition.* (Cheyenne: Northwestern Live Stock Journal). Google books.

16. Woods, "Cattle," 28.

17. Ibid., 9, 27. Also Lawrence M. Woods, *Wyoming's Big Horn Basin to 1901: A Late Frontier.* (Spokane: The Arthur H. Clark Company, 1997), 83. WP brand found in brand ad of Gilchrist, Plunkett & Windsor in 1883 brand book and that of the Union Cattle Company in the 1884 book.

18. Obituary, *Worland Daily News*, June 9, 1944. Thanks to Terril Mills for providing it.

19. Diary of Horace Plunkett has John Booth on Medicine Lodge Creek: Woods, "Cattle," 30. BLM patent records show both.

20. Woods, "Cattle," 28–29, 35–36.

21. Ibid., 25.

22. Ditch claim #2023, filed for Johnson County record August 30, 1886. R.A., A. F. and L. Waln, owners of the Waln Bros. ditch. Ditch claim #2749, filed for record June 7, 1887. Claim to water right. Ashbury F. Waln, Lincoln Waln and John Burke. Johnson County records at county offices in Basin and Worland. His name is given as Asbury elsewhere in the document.

Robert A. Waln entry in *Progressive Men of the State of Wyoming* (Chicago: A. W. Bowen & Co., 1903), 701, https/archive.org/details/progressivemenof00awbo/page/700/mode/2up, accessed June 28, 2022. Born 1856 in Iowa, in 1878 he was a freighter at Ft. Fetterman and in 1884 took up residence in the Bighorn Basin. He farmed and raised cattle and horses.

23. Woods, "Cattle," 27.

24. *Progressive Men*, 704. Information about Abel is from W.A. Richards's letter to David Loban, January 31, 1888. H-215/MSS 83, WSA.

25. Woods, "Cattle," 26.

26. Obituaries and census data from http://www.mcalearfamily.com, accessed August 1, 2020.

27. Woods, "Cattle," 33. Also numerous ads in *Omaha Daily Bee*, https://chroniclingamerica. loc.org.

28. Woods, "Cattle," 27, and Woods, *Big Horn Basin,* 106; also from obituaries of Wells in *Worland Daily News,* June 6 and June 9, 1944, provided by Terril Mills.

29. http://places.wyo.gov/places-calendar/january/january4, accessed June 28, 2022.

30. Multiple sources including letters, cross-checked newspaper articles, and county records.

31. Will Gamble's last name per Richards's letter to his wife, June 15, 1885 (see p. 213).

32. Big Horn Ditch Co. certificate of incorporation.

33. Ibid.

34. Woods, *Big Horn Basin*, 76–77.

35. *CATTLE BRANDS Owned by Members of the Wyoming Stock Growers' Association.* 1882, (Chicago: The J. M. W. Jones Stationery & Printing Co.) First edition.

36. *Big Horn Sentinel*, October 6, 1888, *Buffalo Bulletin,* January 8, 1891; January 11, 1895.

37. Woods, *Big Horn Basin*, 101. Multiple other sources.

38. http://www.kayceewyoming.org/category/history.html, accessed June 28, 2022. Nolen spelling is per http://www.hoofprintsofthepast.org, citing Powder River Heritage Committee's *Our Powder River Heritage*, 4–5. Also per patent records on http://www.glorecords.blm.gov.

39. Woods, *Big Horn Basin*, 104, and *Horace Plunkett in America: An Irish Aristocrat on the Wyoming Range*. (Norman: University of Oklahoma Press, 2010), 22, 25, 69.

40. Woods, "Frank Sykes: A Study in Oral History," *Annals of Wyoming*, Vol. 83, No. 4, 3. Also Woods, *Big Horn Basin*, 110. "[I]rascible" is from Woods, *Plunkett*, 56.

41. Woods, *Big Horn Basin*, 110.

42. The first were the daughters of Andrew B. Wilson, who homesteaded on Meeteetse Creek in 1881, according to Charles Lindsay, *The Big Horn Basin*. (Lincoln: University of Nebraska Press, 1930), 135.

43. Woods, "Sykes," 5.

44. Big Horn Ditch Co. certificate of incorporation.

45. Avent spelling is per the article about him in *Progressive Men* and official records in newspapers. His signature on a letter to George B. McClellan (McClellan family papers, AHC) looks more like Avent than Avant. Leaving LU for the Pitchfork in 1888 is from Bob Edgar and Jack Turnell, *Brand of a Legend.* (Cody, Wyoming: Stockade, 1978), 61. *Progressive Men* is the source of most other information, and many Big Horn County newspaper editions in 1915–17 list him as a Big Horn County commissioner. Avent is listed as a property owner in Big Horn County in 1921, but he may not have been living there. Census record for 1940 is linked on http://www.ancestors.familysearch.org/en/LH6K-GMH/cicero-avant-1860-1942 (*sic* Avant, but census page clearly says "Avent"). This website is the source of death and burial information.

46. H. S. Ridgely, "Historical Facts," *The Basin Republican*, June 30, 1911. The story may have come from Tom Gebhart, who was still alive and talking. "In the spring [*sic*] of '85 Teton Jackson, the famous horse thief and notorious outlaw, camped on the west side of the Big Horn river opposite the ditch camp. He had with him two companions and a bunch of thirty odd head of horses. Jackson visited the ditch camp three or four times during his stay in that vicinity, but his companions remained on their side of the river and closely herded the horses. There was at the ditch camp a new Sharps rifle belonging to...Richards, and Jackson tried his best to trade Mr. Richards out of it. Failing in this he decamped following the river to the north. About a week after his departure a United States marshal and three deputies put in their appearance trailing the Jackson party. From them, for the first time, Gebhart and his party learned the identity of their visitors. Jackson and his companions had stolen the horses they had from the Arapahoe Indians. The United States marshal and his deputies trailed them down the Big Horn to the mouth of the Greybull and up it to where Jackson had crossed the mountains leading in the direction of Jackson's Hole, but they never came up with the wily Teton." Thanks to Terril Mills for this story. Author is wary of Gebhart's latter-day recollections: He may have *thought* he spent the winter of 1885–86 at Red Bank, but Richards's diary and contemporary papers have him in Colorado. If only Richards's diary had more details about this Jackson! His grizzly bear story on p. 220 mentions his Sharps rifle.

47. Dr. A. J. Woodcock, "A Hot Corner on Bears," *Recreation* magazine, Vol. IX, November 1898, 323.

48. Left side is in author's collection, right side in the Washakie Museum and Cultural Center.

49. "Memories of Cheyenne 1889–1894," Alice Richards McCreery collection, H63-86, WSA. "Buttes" is also frequently used.

50. McCreery and Walker, "Wyoming's Fourth Governor—William A. Richards," 104.

51. Richards was "authorized" (apparently as a county commissioner) to offer Coleman the job at $60 per month. W. A. Richards to A. C. Coleman, September 1, 1888, W. A. Richards collection, WSA. *The Rustler*, April 12, 1890, has Coleman returning at the end of school year from Hyattville. (Microfilms, Coe Library, University of Wyoming.)

52. Wikipedia, citing Jim Forte's https:www.postalhistory.com, accessed June 22, 2023.

53. The monument may have been Frison's idea. Funds for the monument and its dedication were raised by the South Flat Women's Club under its president, Opal Agee. *Northern Wyoming Daily News*, July 18, 1969. The area of Richards's ditch and the Lower Hanover Canal came to be known as the Colorado Flats, after the Colorado-based Big Horn Ditch Co.

Part 5 Related Letters and Stories Pages 209–237

1. W. A. Richards to his wife, June 15, 1885, WSA H82-61.

2. W. A. Richards to Col. John W. Clark, letter, December 24, 1896, letterpress vol. 2, page 312, box 1, RG0001.14, Governor William A. Richards Records, Wyoming State Archives.

3. Senate Bill No. 1737, "A bill for the relief of William A. Richards, United States surveyor-general of Wyoming," Report No. 311 by Senator Joseph M. Carey, member of the Committee on Public Lands, March 3, 1892. From *Reports of Committees of the Senate of the United States for the First Session of the Fifty-Second Congress. 1891–'92*, Vol. 2. (Washington: GPO, 1892). The bill was approved by the commissioner of the General Land Office, Thomas. H. Carter. Its related exhibits (affidavits, receipts, etc.) are repeated in Warren's 1900 bill, from the U.S. Congressional Serial Set, Volume 3886, 56th Congress, 1st Session.

4. About $9,770 in 2021, per measuringworth.com purchasing-power calculator.

5. Senate Bill No. 1737, Report No. 311.

6. Ibid.

7. Congressional Record—Senate, March 20, 1900, 3076.

8. W. A. Richards family papers, AHC.

9. A. C. Richards to W. A. Richards, February 5, 14, and 16, 1885, WSA H82-61.

10. Woods, *Plunkett*, 13.

11. This may be the original publication if Richards sent the story to his old friend first. It could not be found in existing online newspaper databases. *The Pioneer* became a daily paper on April 20, 1903, per https://www.mnhs.org/newspapers/hub/bemidji-pioneer, accessed March 29, 2021. The earliest dated story found is "Richards's Wild Ride for Life." in the *Los Angeles Times*, February 20, 1903. It seems unlikely that Richards sent his story to the *Times* first.

The story is not found in the database's *Pioneer,* but the typography is similar to that paper, and no other papers with that name from that time have been identified.

12. Washington: Island Press, 1998, 245.

Part 6 Appendix Pages 239–270

1. Nebraska County Map of 1859, op. cit.

2. Except where indicated, all details of contracts and bonds are from History Nebraska, RG510 U.S. Surveyor General, Records: 1850–1904, Surveying District of Kansas and Nebraska territories, and of the District of Nebraska, including Iowa. Series One, microfilm rolls 3–26, field notebooks of deputy surveyors. Series Seven, contracts and bonds, 1854–1904, Box 14, Folders 18–20 (1871–73); Box 15, Folder 21, 1874; 22, 1875.

Surveying details are superimposed on maps from the Nebraska Department of Transportation except for the one on p. 246, which is in Mr. Thomsen's personal collection.

3. Contract #85, WSA H82-61.

4. Contract #69, WSA H82-61.

5. This stipulation appears on the standard printed form used by the offices of the U.S. surveyors general for contracts at that time. The form was used for contracts #69 and #85.

6. Some information is from Addison E. Sheldon, *Land Systems and Land Policies in Nebraska*. Publications of the Nebraska State Historical Society, Vol. XXII. (Lincoln: Nebraska State Historical Society, 1936), 204–06.

7. NET Learning Services map based on map in 18th annual report of the Bureau of American Ethnology. Plate CXLVIII.

8. Contract #85, WSA H82-61.

9. 1873 field notes, 185.

10. 1874 field notes, 243

INDEX

www.ingramcontent.com/pod-product-compliance
Lightning Source LLC
Chambersburg PA
CBHW060903120626
46553CB00001B/191